# Bar Mitzvah

## A Guide to Spiritual Growth

© Assouline 2005
Assouline Publishing
601 West 26th Street, New York, NY 10001 U.S.A.
Tel: 212 989 6810    Fax: 212 647 0005
 www.assouline.com

Translated from the French by Nicholas Elliott and Molly Stevens, The Art of Translation.
ISBN: 2 84323 718 1

Color separation: Open Grafic Media
Printed and bound by RR Donnelley

Marc-Alain Ouaknin
Françoise-Anne Ménager

# Bar Mitzvah
## A Guide to Spiritual Growth

*Illustrations by Gérard Garouste*
*Photography by Laziz Hamani*

**ASSOULINE**

*To my father Max Assouline who taught me the values of
dignity, responsibility, and fidelity.
To my son Alexandre, so he may never forget them.*
Prosper Assouline


*To my children Gaddiël-Yonathan, Sivane-Mikhal, Shamgar-Maor,
Nin-Gal, who, each in their own way, knew, know, and will
always know how to understand and receive my love...*
Marc-Alain Ouaknin


*To Laurianne and Léo for inventing the life they have given me
and for inspiring another life.*
Françoise-Anne Ménager

# Contents

Preface                                                        9

Introduction                                                  17

Becoming Bar Mitzvah: Looking at a Rite of Passage           38

The Jewish Identity                                          68

The Synagogue                                                92

The Kippah                                                  112

The Tallith                                                 122

Tefillin: Anatomy of a Symbol                              140

Prayer                                                     176

Receiving the Torah                                        200

The Bible                                                  220

The Ascent to the Torah                                    238

The Haftarah                                               260

The Speech                                                 270

Shabbat                                                    284

The Bar Mitzvah Party                                      316

Bar Mitzvahs Throughout the World                          328

Bibliography                                               351

Acknowledgments                                            356

Photography and text credits                               367

*If you can keep your head when all about you*
*Are losing theirs and blaming it on you,*
*If you can trust yourself when all men doubt you.*
*But make allowance for their doubting too;*
*If you can wait and not be tired by waiting.*
*Or being lied about, don't deal in lies,*
*Or being hated, don't give way to hating,*
*And yet don't look too good, nor talk too wise:*

*If you can dream—and not make dreams your master*
*If you can think—and not make thoughts your aim*
*If you can meet Triumph and Disaster*
*And treat those two impostors just the same;*
*If you can bear to hear the truth you've spoken*
*Twisted by knaves to make a trap for fools.*
*Or watch the things you gave your life to broken,*
*And stoop and build'em up with worn-out tools:*

*If you can make one heap of all your winnings*
*And risk it on one turn of pitch-and-toss,*
*And lose, and start again at your beginnings*
*And never breathe a word about your loss;*
*If you can force your heart and nerve and sinew*
*To serve your turn long after they are gone,*
*And so hold on when there is nothing in you*
*Except the Will which says to them: "Hold on!"*

*If you can talk with crowds and keep your virtue,*
*Or walk with Kings—nor lose the common touch,*
*If neither foes nor loving friends can hurt you,*
*If all men count with you, but none too much;*
*If you can fill the unforgiving minute,*
*With sixty seconds' worth of distance run.*
*Yours is the Earth and everything that's in it,*
*And—which is more—you'll be a Man, my son!*

Rudyard Kipling, *If...* (1910)

# Preface

*No matter how we interpret or formulate it, our humanity must be filtered through the constant awareness of our responsibility for others, for all the others.*
Emmanuel Lévinas

This book was originally commissioned by a passionate publisher known for taking risks and following his dreams. This rare specimen also happened to be a father reflecting on his 12-year-old son's upcoming bar mitzvah.

Prosper Assouline's questions regarding the meaning of this essential Jewish rite of passage quickly developed into the idea for a book about bar mitzvahs. The book was to be for Prosper an attempt to answer his questions about transmission, ethics, and the meaning of life. It was also to be a book for his son, a gift that would mark this milestone in the boy's life.

The book was initially intended for Assouline's *Symbols* collection, a series of books that offers readers an informative and visually attractive approach to religions such as Judaism, Catholicism, Islam, and Buddhism through words and pictures (by the great Laziz Hamani). Alexandre, the future bar mitzvah boy, would assiduously follow the development of the project by assisting on Laziz's photo shoots and reading the texts I wrote in response to the pictures.

Yet we quickly realized that the bar mitzvah required a different approach. Despite the fact that the photo shoot the three of us conducted in a synagogue was a great success, and provided several of the photos selected for this volume, we realized the question of "growing" could not be expressed in a pre-existing format.

With the support of the project's editor, Martine Assouline (who also happens to be Alexandre's mother), Prosper Assouline and I followed our instincts and changed the concept of the book. We decided that the text would have greater importance than initially planned, though it would still be devised in response to photos and illustrations. I then asked Françoise-Anne Ménager, a literature and history teacher in Mantes-la-Ville, to share some of the studies we had conducted together on the subject of the culture of the written word and its transmission, beginning when I had first spoken about reading in the Jewish tradition at the "Teaching Literature in the Remote Control Age: Should, Could and Must" conference organized by her students. This initial desire to explore the symbols of the bar mitzvah led to *Bar Mitzvah, A Guide to Spritual Growth*. In this new version, the future bar mitzvah boy's role was no longer as my "on-set assistant," but as the book's first and intended reader. Alexandre's participation in the photo shoot had been dictated by the fun he was having. But with the onset of this edition, he took on the role of virtual reader with devotion and seriousness.

On several occasions after I had finished the manuscript, I met with Alexandre to gain a sense of what he had learned, and to verify the educational pertinence of my work. These encounters were so honest, so dense with information, that I was overwhelmed. I found myself facing a young man who had accepted to enter into a sincere, profound dialogue about theological and psychological questions, and even certain practical ones, such as our choice of couscous in the restaurant in which we had selected to meet. I gave Alexandre a detailed overview of the ethics of the bar mitzvah, or, in other words, of the rigor required to be a good man. Alexandre's "fragility"—common among teenagers—and vivacious intelligence were not his most striking features. What really touched me about Alexandre was his demand for honesty and ethical truth. I have no doubt that what I told Alexandre about uprightness; about the evil of dissimulation and lying; the right to heresy; the power to discover one's potential for confrontation in order to avoid fleeing; the art of saying "thank you";

generosity; and respect for one's parents, teachers, and friends took root not only in his mind, but in the very core of my being, if I may be so bold as to use an expression that may seem excessive. I was no longer writing a book about bar mitzvah, I was actually experiencing the responsibility of passing on, not words, but a power which gives the other the possibility of growing. I understood that the bar mitzvah is crucially important not only to teenagers, but also to parents and educators, who carry the double duty of having to pass on the meaning and value of responsibility to the future adult, and of skillfully yet decisively detaching themselves from a child who, in truth, is no longer a child.

I remembered the powerful experiences I had during the bar mitzvahs of my two sons, Gaddiël and Shamgar, and the bat mitzvahs of my two daughters, Sivane and Nin-Gal.

At the time, I intuitively understood the concepts listed above, but I had probably not internalized them enough to pass them on as powerfully as I now passed them on to Alexandre. Of course, it is always easier to educate your friends' children, or children entrusted to you (let me take this opportunity to salute Rémy Rossin, in tribute to our "Scribes and Tefillin" adventure). Or perhaps those milestones that bring us joy and profound responsibility can only truly be savored with maturity and the passage of time.

May this book also be dedicated to my children, as a way of expressing my love for them (an endless task), and my confidence that they will pursue their paths in a constantly renewed "growing" as righteous as it is true.

I would like to thank Alexandre for giving me the opportunity to pronounce these essential words, and to tell him what a pleasure it was to meet him. I hope that this book allows him to fully appreciate the way his parents chose to pass the teachings of tradition on to him. May these teachings accompany him and give him strength every day of his happy existence. I hope Alexandre will also fully realize that this gift expresses the most beautiful forms of parental responsibility, respect and love.

As Emmanuel Lévinas said, the preface is always written after the book. This preface took me a long time to write, much longer than it had taken to write the prefaces for my previous books. This is probably due to the fact that this volume's subject implies a greater and more truthful commitment. "The words which help us to grow are not always the ones which first come to mind. Those words are often false. There are words which must be waited for and pursued." As Rav Kook said, these righteous words, which take so long to be found and properly employed, are the ones to generate a generous social link consisting of *chesed* (generosity) and *tzedek* (being just); a "*tzedek*" which means "being just" rather than "justice." If we want words to bless us, we must know how to wait for them, like we wait for a seed to sprout."[1]

I would like to add a few remarks on the genesis of this volume, to tell the story of a few other seeds of blessing. The further I advanced on this project, the clearer it became to me that I needed to write differently, from another point of view, drawn directly from a pedagogical experience. Rather than drawing purely from the world of books to write my own book, I needed to have direct contact with teenagers. I knew that I needed to record impressions of a more direct, even universal nature. I could also feel that the question of "growing" did not only concern Judaism, which only provided a partial answer. It seemed important to confront the Jewish approach with approaches taken from outside the Jewish world, in order to touch on the full extent and universality of the human event.

I believe one of the essential triggers that allowed me to penetrate the world of adolescence was the encounter I had some years back with a teacher and a group of students in a vocational high school.[2] Thanks to the vision and encouragement of their literature and history professor, Françoise-Anne Ménager, about twenty young women in their junior and senior years at vocational school (there was only one boy in the class) had pulled off the challenge of organizing a masterful colloquium on "Thinkers in the City" for two years running.

With the guidance of their professor, these young women studied demanding literary and philosophical works, elaborated original and involving study themes, chose and contacted the participants, then managed the logistics and communication required to set up what very few institutions succeed in pulling off so successfully: fascinating, enriching colloquiums, as successful on the intellectual level as on the human level of personal encounters.

At the first colloquium, I gave a philosophical and Talmudic reading of Saint-Exupéry's *Little Prince,* in which I brought together Sartre and Plato, the Boa and the Rose, Rabbi Akiva and Proust, Deleuze and Spinoza, essentialism and existentialism, liberty and determinism to draw my conclusions on the meaning of life and our place in the world based on the beauty of poetic and metaphoric links such as the laughter of the stars, the sonata of a rusted pulley, the color of the wheat fields, the prayer of a rose, and the tears of a fox.

I remember the glimmer of pleasure and surprise I detected in the students' eyes. I could see the pleasure they derived from listening, discovering, and learning. I could see how they enjoyed developing themselves, or, in a word, outdoing themselves. I understood then that at that specific moment and place something more had happened, an "event" beyond words and beyond literature. Or rather, perhaps, the very essence of literature: the experience of an encounter!

At the students' request, this encounter was extended by high school seminars held in an atmosphere of enthusiastic, jubilant study, as if we were outside the bustle of the world, but in complete communication with it. Of course, I was not able to explain everything about Judaism, but the essential aspects of its foundations were touched on, and we were driven by something of the spirit of the Talmud.

I discovered on this occasion that it was possible to share the question of growing and the bar mitzvah with students of all traditions. To allow the reader to fully appreciate this story, I should mention that the class did not include any Jewish students. The girls were essentially practicing or traditional Muslims, Christians, or "non-believers." Furthermore, most of the class was of African background.

Many of the questions raised with these students have been included in this book on bar mitzvahs. This book is my tribute to the students' wonderful hospitality and the rich, fecund dialogue that we began at that point and which has continued into the present.

One question in particular had an especially deep effect on me. One of the students of African background asked:

"There is a question I've been wanting to ask for several years. Back home in Africa, when the white missionaries came to teach Christianity, I always had a lot of trouble praying and accepting this idea of Christianity because I imagined, and I think we were taught, that God was white and Adam, the

13

first man, and Eve, and all the people in the Bible, were all white. I've always been a fervent believer, but how could I address a God Who created human beings who were so different from me, and how could I read a book that kept reminding me I was not created in His image? If the first man was white, and the first woman was white, what does it mean to you, as a rabbi, that I am black?"

Real dialogue is a cataclysmic event. We do not know where it will lead us. Neither the teacher nor the students know what they will say or how they will react. Dialogue confronts us with a state of unknowing, and this unknowing is the very essence of time.

If we knew everything ahead of time, there would be no time. After the fact, I am able to state that this encounter allowed me to truly understand the meaning of the bar mitzvah; that I experienced, felt, and understood that "growing" is not only a word, but a real event. As Henri Maldiney wrote, "the event, the real event—a happening which confronts us with the danger of becoming another—is unpredictable. It is an encounter with otherness, the inexpressible significance of which reveals our own significance. It is the transforming self."

This encounter came to represent the power of new horizons for me, when the conjunction of place, speech and silence allows us both to hear a question and to plumb the depths of our imagination to find the answer.

I answered the question by telling the students that in Genesis, man is named Adam,[3] which comes from *adama,* the ground, the matter of which he was "formed." I also explained that the root of the word *adama* is *adom,* which means "red," for the first ground, the ground of the Garden of Eden, was a red ground.[4]

Therefore, according to the Biblical text, man was born of red earth, and is himself referred to as red! And if, as the Biblical text specifies, man is made in the image of God, to look like God, then, as the students and I jointly concluded: God isn't white, or black, he's red![5]

But in this case, red does not refer to the color of skin, but to the color of blood, which is appropriately called *dam,* a word obviously found in *adam,* and which refers to the questions of interiority and life and death. It also refers to the question of responsibility in the face of life and death. Man is the man of the infinite greatness of this responsibility. As the Scriptures put it: "I have set before you life and death, blessing and cursing: therefore choose life."[6]

My first speech, on *The Little Prince*, is probably the source of the image that most frequently recurs when I think of these students. It is the image of roses. I was able to perceive the students in this way, because the soil of the garden had been prepared for me. Their talented professor had patiently devoted herself to using analysis and commentary to instill a love of words and texts, and of books and literature, in these students. She had made them trust in the difficult but enriching path of a culture which "elevates" life and provides a lighter, more joyous atmosphere, which draws us in to life with greater strength and responsibility.

I hope my account of these various encounters serves to shed light on the tone and orientation of this volume. I would like to thank Françoise-Anne Ménager for sharing this incredible experience with me. I can only wish that this book, a musical partition written for four hands, provides the reader with as much pleasure and happiness as we experienced writing it.

Marc-Alain Ouaknin

---

1. Gilles Bernheim, *Le Souci des autres* (Caring for Others), Calmann-Levy, 2002.
2. The class in question was the senior class of the Camille Claudel vocational high school in Mantes-la-Ville. I would like to start by thanking the principal, Mr. Christian Montet, and his entire team, for the warm welcome that made Françoise-Anne Ménager's project possible. My experiences with the students followed their encounter with the novelist Philip Roth and the eminent intellectuals who accompanied him to the Écritures Croisées festival in Aix-en-Provence. This initial meeting had inspired the students to organize a cultural event that would bring intellectuals from various fields to Mantes-la-Ville.
3. Genesis 1:26-27 and 2:7.
There are two different accounts of the creation of man. I refer to the second.
4. Indeed, according to the indications given by the Bible, the place described as the "Garden of Eden" is in Mesopotamia, between the Tigris and the Euphrates (Genesis 2:13-14), where the ground really is red!
5. It is significant to show how the magic of encounters builds a life, how, through the exchange of ideas, these ideas circulate, transform, transmute, amplify, comment upon each other, are enriched, in an authentic alchemy of words and image. Several months after I met the students in Françoise-Anne Ménager's class, my friend Radu Mihaileanu told me he was making a film about the "Falashas." I told him about the students I had met and the question about God's color. We then met to discuss the Midrashic and Talmudic sources of this question. I told Radu about the students, about their questions and their responses, and how moved we all were by the experience. Radu alluded to this meeting in his film "Va, vie et deviens" (Go, live and become), capturing his impressions of it with extraordinary talent and absolute accuracy. Adam's red became the "red skin" in Radu's film, an authentic masterpiece carried by a truly messianic spirit, in the Kabbalistic sense of the term.
6. *Ubakharta bakhayim*, Deuteronomy 30:19.
This final part of the commentary is by Françoise-Anne Ménager.

# Introduction

*One night, they lost sight of the star.*
*Why did we lose*
*The star? For having looked too long...*
*Being wise men of Chaldee, the two white kings*
*Drew circles on the ground with their sticks.*
*They made calculations, and scratched their chins*
*But the star had vanished like a fleeting thought.*
*And these men whose souls were thirsty*
*to be guided*
*Cried as they pitched their cotton tents.*
*But the poor black king, who was held in contempt*
*by the others,*
*Told himself: 'Think of the thirst which is not yours,*
*I must still give the animals water.'*
*And as he held a bucket of water*
*by the handle,*
*In the humble sliver of sky where the camels*
*drank,*
*He saw the golden star, dancing in silence.*

Edmond Rostand, *The Three Kings*

# Introduction

A Journey to the Land of Unfamiliarity

**"Not a Prince, No, Better, a Man!"**

The Mathematics of Maturing

**One... Two...**

Three...

**The "Three" and "Weaning"**

Self-Confidence and Self-Esteem

**And... four!**

The Horrifying Cry

**Various Approaches**

Entering the Community Through the Book

**"Philip Roth's Bar Mitzvah"**

# A Journey to the Land of Unfamiliarity

*I want this work to be written in a language of my invention, which will allow me to pass back and forth from the bizarre to the common, from fantasy to extreme rigor, from prose to verse, from the most prosaic reality to ideals that are the most ... the most fragile...*
Paul Valéry

In *Chronicles of the Guayaki Indians*, Pierre Clastres relates the following anecdote :

"One day, the father decides that his son's childhood has come to an end... For the first time, the *kybuchu* (children aged 7 or 8 to the age they are recognized as adolescents) begin to sing, however timidly; their untrained mouths struggle to express the men's *prerä* (chant restricted to men). From farther a field, the hunters respond with their own chant, encouraging the chant of the future *beta pou* (new initiates). This singing lasts a long time, in the heart of the silent night and the flickering fires. Then the voices of the women rise up, like a protest, like a sorrowful, regretful complaint. These voices belong to the children's mothers.

They know they are going to lose their children, that soon they will be men, more worthy of respect than their *memby* (little

child). The *chengaruvara* (women's chant) expresses their ultimate effort to hold back time, but it is also the first song of their
separation. It is a celebration of that separation.

The cried-sung refusal of the women to accept the inevitable is
a challenge to the men: their *prerä* becomes twice as powerful,
nearly violent. It becomes aggressive, practically covering over
the humble lament of the mothers as they listen to their sons
singing like men.

The young men know that they are the object of this struggle
between the men and the women. It encourages them to vigo-
rously fulfill their role: tonight, they are no longer part of the
group, they no longer belong to the world of women; but they
aren't men yet, they are from nowhere, and for that reason they
occupy the *enda ayiä* (an initiation hut built by the young
men). It is a different type of place, a transitory space, the
sacred frontier between a before and after for those who will
die and be reborn. The fires die down, the voices drift away, the
singers fall asleep."

This book on the bar mitzvah does not begin with a story about a South
American Indian tribe on a whim.[1] My aim is to introduce the rite of bar
mitzvah, not as a phenomenon particular to the Jewish world, but as a
singular way of looking at questions faced by every human being during
the difficult but crucial adventure of becoming an adult.

Man is the other, man is me; he is me by the understanding I can have of the
other, not to master him, but truly to understand him and understand
myself in return. Beyond the two of us, this relationship allows me to
understand what it is to be human.

Studying other civilizations, whether contemporary or ancient, does not
only consist in finding unknown customs and beliefs. By studying other
civilizations, we go beyond that, putting our own culture in perspective by
confronting its conceptions with those of other eras, other places, other
languages and other traditions.[2] The objective of learning ancient and
foreign languages in school, for instance, is not only to acquire a linguistic
tool which allows us to travel and communicate, but, essentially, to open

Paresi Indian chief (Central Amazonia) holding his hunting bow.
His son stands to his right, dressed for an initiation dance for adolescent males.

ourselves to another culture, to open up by opening to the world through the intellectual method which we could join Lévi-Strauss in calling the "technique of the unfamiliar."[3] Like the Guayaki ceremony related by Pierre Clastres, the bar mitzvah is a "rite of passage" that allows the child to enter adulthood and the age of responsibility. It allows the child to grow up.

Beyond explaining the bar mitzvah and its human component within the specific terms of Judaism, this book should allow followers of other faiths and traditions to put their own cultures in perspective through the "technique of the unfamiliar." This process is not intended to estrange believers from their own cultures, but to help them open up to the world, and better discover themselves via difference and convergence.[4]

For the Jewish reader, this ethnological voyage should be highly unfamiliar. It will allow the Jewish reader to put his own Jewish culture in perspective and return to it in an equally different spirit. The question of Jewish identity, to which I have devoted a chapter, is at the heart of this question of difference.[5]

## "Not a Prince, No, Better, a Man!"

> *Being human means to live as if one is not just*
> *a being among all beings.*
>
> Emmanuel Lévinas

A "religious majority" is often alluded to in reference to the bar mitzvah. Yet how are we to define "religious majority" in the case of those numerous young people who have a bar or bat mitzvah despite the fact that they are not religious in practice or in beliefs?

This may be an opportunity to recall that Judaism is not only a religion in the sense of a religious practice. It is also the singular expression of one of man's primary concerns. Judaism expresses man's confidence in his ability to express his greatness and dignity.

Through the powerful "rite of passage" of the bar mitzvah, Judaism offers a series of texts and actions which are host to these invariants of human nature that allow the child to open himself to life with stronger direction and consciousness. For this reason, it is interesting to understand the specific elements which are the foundation of the Jewish approach to the major human event of this "right to become." It is equally significant to ask what the universal reach of the rite of bar mitzvah is.

Growing up isn't a simple matter. It's a whole life's work. To Kipling's famous "You'll be a Man, my son!" quoted at the beginning of the book, I must add a wonderful line from Mozart's *The Magic Flute*:

*–Er ist ein Prinz?*
*–Nicht ein Prinz, nein, mehr, ein Mensch!*[6]

## The Mathematics of Maturing

> *The words which help us to grow are not always*
> *those which first come to mind;*
> *those first words are often the most false.*
>
> Gilles Bernheim, *Le Souci des autres* (Caring for Others)

The bar mitzvah is a play in three acts and four characters. The three acts are the preparation, the synagogue ceremony, and the family party. The four characters are the child, the mother, the father, and transcendence. The latter "character" has been given various names over the ages: God, the Infinite, exteriority, the Divine, the Heavens, the Being, the Supreme Being, the Eternal, the Name, our Blessed Father, etc.

## One... Two...

> *In Greek, return is* nostos. Algos *means suffering. Nostalgia, therefore,*
> *is suffering caused by the unappeased desire to return.*
>
> Milan Kundera, *Ignorance*

Every human being is born of a woman. Every human being is initially conceived inside a woman and, with a few exceptions, it is inside the woman that the first few months of life take place.[7] At the beginning, we were "one," "two in one." This simple fact opens the way to significant consequences. Birth, the exit into "the air of the world," the first separation, introduces us to the dimension of "two."

Over the course of a life, this separation must continue to be enacted and developed, despite the fact that the natural tendency could be to return to the "one," to the source, to the maternal womb, to the nine-month Eden where we were fed, housed, and carried in weightlessness.

Isn't this the meaning of the "Jonah complex" by which man would rather huddle in the belly of a boat, then of a great fish, than face the voice which orders him to *"Lech lecha!"*, "Go you forth!"?

Isn't this the *"Thalassal* regression," a theory proposed by Sandor Ferenczi, a disciple of Freud, which drives us to return to the amniotic world, a return to the sealife from which man emerged in primeval times?[8]


## Three...

*A loving father is not a moralist, but one who offers moral support.*

Françoise Dolto, *L'Image inconsciente du corps*

The mother and the child pass from "one" to "two." Aside from the biological facts of birth, this passage is only possible because there is a "third," the "father" (or a paternal figure generically referred to as the paternal function). In fact, it is interesting to note that in Hebrew, the word "father," *av*, is spelled 1-2 *(alef-bet)* and its letters have the numeric value of "three."[9]

"The role of the father is to defuse," writes child psychiatrist Marcel Rufo. The father's role is essential, irreplaceable, in that he gives the mother the strength to avoid exclusively focusing on her baby. The baby quickly feels that there is a pole of interest other than him in his mother's life. It is because the father interests the mother, that he also becomes interesting to the baby. From the first days of the baby's life, the father introduces the crucial notion of difference. Because Daddy does not have the same skin texture as Mommy, and he doesn't have the same voice, or the same way of carrying the baby, of giving him the bottle, of playing with him, the child begins to notice that between him and his mother, there is already a third, some difference, some "same" and "not same" which will help him move out of fusion and open himself to the world.[10] Rufo adds that, "though the baby will initially nearly exclusively identify with the person caring for him—the mother—he will gradually find other models to identify with, including the father, who is indispensable to his development."

The father is the one who must distract the mother from her baby, while helping her and supporting her in her maternal mission. He is someone who must be there from the beginning. Each child should be given the impression that starting from before his birth, his father was with his mother, that she was never alone and that consequently the child was never the only object of her love. Women who choose to have children with short-term lovers, as well as those who are abandoned during their pregnancy, should always tell their children that they were conceived out of love, not only because the child needs to believe this, but, especially, because he needs to know his mother has loved other people than him. The child will nonetheless probably conserve the hope that he was the only object of his mother's love, but because this hope always retains an element of doubt, it is far less toxic than the certainty that he is indeed his mother's only love, a certainty induced by the absence of the father. Between knowing and hoping, there is a whiff of uncertainty which may make separation just a little easier.

In any case, the absence of the father should not prevent the presence of a third party between the mother and the child: another partner, a member of the family, a close friend... Someone who is there, not to forbid fusion, but to penetrate it. Without this, fusion becomes a trap."[11]

Françoise Dolto, the legendary French child psychoanalyst, approaches the question in a slightly different, but complementary manner. Of course, the importance of a love object other than the child is important to allow for *defusing* (or what I call "withdrawing"), but the father must also actively speak to his child to somehow explain that, "it is permanently impossible for a son to love his mother the way another man loves her. It isn't because you are young and I am old, but because you are her son, and a son and his mother can never experience the sexual union and have children."[12]

# The "Three" and "Weaning"

*Worse than a perverted soul,*
*a habituated soul!*

Paul Valéry

The father is therefore the "three," the "third party" who allows what the Bible generically refers to as "weaning," or, in other words, "a severance which allows for maturing." Astonishingly, the Hebrew root *gimel, mem, lamed,* means both three and weaning. No weaning without "three," no "three" without weaning!

In Hebrew, the "maturing severances" are called "unions," *berit.* And the act of entering into a marital union is not referred to in terms of the link, but the severance: *likhrot berit,* "severing the union." Each new severance/union is accompanied by a loss: loss of the placenta, loss of the breast, loss of excrement, loss of sperm (the adolescent's nocturnal emissions), loss of blood (menstruation), leaving the parental home (after marriage), etc.

Yet, each of these moments of loss is always socially accompanied by a set of festivities, as if the function of the celebration was not only to reflect a happy event, but also to support people in the difficult period in which they endure a separation. The joy of the celebration compensates for the pain of the loss.

The three family celebrations of the circumcision, the bar or bat mitzvah, and the wedding correspond to those "rites of passage" in which one reaches another stage of life, while relinquishing something or experiencing a separation. (It is important to specify that the body of the mother should not be interpreted simply as the physical body of the mother, but also as all its metaphorical substitutes, and all those potentially maternal groups which include various ideologies, political parties, sports teams, and, in a more dangerous manner, sects.)

Defusing or "withdrawing" requires very powerful wrenching forces. Human beings have an impulse to return to the maternal body and its substitutes, which constantly requires us to reconstruct and recapture our autonomy. Weaning (rupture, loss and separation) is an uninterrupted process which is responsible for life itself.

For the father, the bar mitzvah represents the duty to pass on the strength and energy which will allow the child to realize a "maturing severance." This severance grants the child access to the deepest and truest core of its autonomy and humanity, and turns it into a free, living, and speaking human being. Life and speech can only exist through this severance! Through these many severances! Can a child come into life if we do not first sever the umbilical cord? If he is not weaned from his mother's breast? If he does not learn to be clean? If he cannot tell the difference between masculine and feminine? And, finally, if he does not understand that the mother cannot be the object of his amorous and sexual desire?[13]

All this happens progressively, from birth to the physical and mental autonomy marked by the bar mitzvah period, which is played out not only in the single day of the ceremony, but over the course of several years' preparation before the ceremony, and of several years after the ceremony, to confirm it. It is important to note that, far from closing a process, the bar mitzvah is the gateway and period of commitment to that process. During the preparation, a project is formed to be realized for the bar mitzvah. This is why, in certain communities, the bar mitzvah, which is initiated at 12 or 13, is only considered effective when the child is 16, and some social, community, or other concrete project has been realized to confirm the commitment. This confirmation is celebrated on the Shavuot holiday (the holiday honoring the giving of the Torah) in the presence of family and friends.

Various phases described by psychoanalysis and taking place at specific stages of a child's development are permanently being repeated. The bar mitzvah is something of a synthesis and summing up of the question of the child's development (of severances and balanced maturing).

It is also important, even essential, to underline that these severances are significant not only for the child, but also for the parents and, in particular, the mother. The bar and bat mitzvah show the mother that she has been a good mother, and that now that the child is growing and becoming autonomous and responsible, he considers that whatever was and wasn't done for him was for his good. The mother can therefore pursue her own life without any real or unconscious guilt concerning the way that she raised and fed her child. She fed the child well and no longer has to feed it. The placement of the word "breast" at the heart of the bar mitzvah ceremony evokes this idea.[14]

## Self-Confidence and Self-Esteem

*I don't only see the other's eyes, I also see that he's looking at me.*
Max Scheler

The striking thing about the bar mitzvah ceremony is the confidence placed in the child by his family and friends. The child is at the heart of the event. He is like a performer on a stage. He will read and be listened to. He will make a speech, and his words will have significance. He will receive the encouragement of his family and of the entire audience. And he will receive the blessing of the rabbi and his entire family. The bar mitzvah is the day the child begins to "be counted"[15] as one of the *minyan* (the assembly of ten people which constitutes the required quorum to say the prayer). The child now feels that he counts in the community, and that he can be counted upon. He is becoming responsible, and he can be trusted, and through the trust that he is granted, the child can trust in himself, and accede to righteous maturity.

To be recognized for one's singularity and uniqueness is to have a "face." The unique in each individual means that no one can be locked into any kind of category by which "men would be interchangeable, homogeneous, equivalent, or simply degraded to the rank of being an example, an unlimitedly reproducible sample."[16]

For this reason, each person is called by his own name and the name of his father during the bar mitzvah ceremony and, particularly, the ascent to the Torah, in order to enter him into a filiation, or, in other words, a different, and differentiated, position.

The bar mitzvah is a crucial moment in the life of the child, the moment he feels unconditional trust being placed in him. In this case, "unconditional" means that the ceremony, from its degree of luxury to its various methods, can never be subject to any bargaining. The bar mitzvah cannot be seen as a reward,[17] but rather as an opportunity "to develop the child's self-confidence, including in, and through, failure."[18]

## And... four!

> *The face of my fellow man is an otherness which opens the door to the beyond. One can access God in heaven without diminishing his transcendence, and without negating the believer's freedom.*
>
> Emmanuel Lévinas

The Miró painting on the cover of this book contributes an essential element to our image of the human destiny: "the star." The star represents the necessity for something beyond the family cell (beyond three), something which allows us to open ourselves to a transcendent exteriority. It is a vanishing point beyond the painting, which provides the painting with its opening, and the beyond which allows the presence of the father to open him to another difference, which will in turn lead to the dimension of infinity.

One, two, three, four... and the world opens up to life.

The art of growing according to Joan Miró.

This is probably why the number "four" is preeminent in Kabbalist tradition, which has developed as a quaternary phenomenology.[19]

Transcendence, which in this case is symbolized by the star, participates in a dialogue with the immanence of men and the world.[20] The rite of the bar mitzvah is an opportunity to become conscious of two poles that put forward the idea of an "up/down verticalization," on the one hand, and of circulation between this up and down, on the other.[21] The human consciousness put in place by the bar mitzvah is not only of a Godly transcendence, toward which one should strive. It is also the possibility of having the idea of a code of justice and responsibility descend to man.

It follows that "religious maturity" cannot simply consist of adhering to an unquestioned cultural discipline.

## The Horrifying Cry

*Birth is accompanied by the horrifying cry.*
*Leaving one's mother is the horrifying cry.*
Pierre Legendre, *L'Inestimable objet de la transmission*

The bar mitzvah is an attempt to create freedom by instituting a distance in relation to a whole symbolically represented by the world of the mother, followed by the world of the family.

The bar mitzvah does not only represent the child's separation from the mother, but also the mother's will and ability to allow her child to be. This is a difficult and complex subject. As with birth, "the mother must lose the one she carried," which provokes, however silently, "the horrifying cry," the double cry of the child who has left his mother and of the mother allowing her child to be.[22]

As a rite that involves the child, the mother, and the father, the bar mitzvah is a mutual familial weaning, the stake of which is the exit from childhood.

## Various Approaches

*I do not begin a history by developing my ideas based on the theories of others. That's not how my mind works. In fact, I catch things here and there, I draw from my clinical experience, elaborate my own theories and, at the very end, I try and see what I've borrowed, and from where. Maybe this method is as good as any other...*

D. W. Winnicott

It is of fundamental importance to state from the outset that the various interpretations I provide of the bar mitzvah hardly exhaust the symbolic powers of this rite. My attempt to analyze the bar mitzvah through an anthropological dimension, while referring to psychoanalysis,[23] has no other objective than to make certain aspects of this rite apparent in a formulation that makes sense within the context of the history of thought.[24]

## Entering the Community Through the Book

*I believe in the sun, even when it doesn't shine.*
*I believe in love, even when it doesn't surround me.*
*I believe in God, even when He is silent!*

Graffiti written by an anonymous Jew, cited by Sylvie Germain in *Etty Hillesum*

So what, in particular, does this Jewish approach to the human event of the "right to become" and grow rest on? How does it allow for the necessary "defusing"?
The answer lies in the symbols contained in the rite and the text of the Torah, as an experience of reading and interpretation.
A close analysis of the bar mitzvah reveals that the Book, reading, and interpretation are at the heart of the event.[25]
Our subheading, *A Guide to Spiritual Growth*, underlines this aspect. This is why we have endeavored to explain all the facets necessary to enter the Hebraic world of the book the way a future bar mitzvah boy

would over the course of his preparation. We have insisted upon the way the book is written by presenting the parchments, inks, quills, and the form of the letters of the alphabet. We have also discussed the ritual of synagogue reading and underlined its effects on the young man or young woman who is invited to read.

Though the child sometimes learns the book and the Hebrew letters specifically for this occasion, they become inscribed in his memory, and serve as essential guides throughout his life.

Every aspect of this event pushes the abstract notions of becoming adult and becoming Jewish into a reality that can easily be shared and transmitted. Being adult and being Jewish cannot simply be stated to be accomplished. These concepts are developed... with the book...

"Tell me how you read...and I will have some understanding of who you are" or rather, "Read...and I will see you be."

The child dares to make a commentary before his family, his friends, and sometimes even strangers. By doing so, the child shows that he is becoming able to answer for his reading and that he is worthy of the responsibility to the text to which he has committed.

From that point, the child will of course have to be wisely and perceptively guided in order for the text's significance to be applied to his life.

## "Philip Roth's Bar Mitzvah"

*Imagination is a place where it rains...*

Rabbi Shlomo Eliachov, quoted by Gilles Bernheim

Everything we have just said about the importance of the book, letters, and reading can be found in an admirable passage by Philip Roth, which could easily be called "Philip Roth's Bar Mitzvah," or, more accurately, "Philip Roth's Bar Mitzvah preparation."[26]

"The place reeked of stale cigarette smoke, a smell that carried me back some forty-five years, to the little Talmud Torah, one flight above our local synagogue, where I went unenthusiastically with my friends to study Hebrew for an hour in the late afternoons three days a week in the early 1940s. The rabbi who ran the show there had been a heavy smoker and, as best I could remember it, that second floor of the synagogue back in Newark, aside from smelling exactly the same, hadn't looked too unlike this place either—shabby, dreary, just a little disagreeably slummy.

"They put me in one of the classrooms and closed the door. I was alone again. Nobody had kicked me or slapped me or tied my hands or shackled my legs. On the blackboard I saw something written in Hebrew. Nine words. I couldn't read one of them. Four decades after those three years of afternoon classes at the Hebrew school, I could no longer even identify the letters of the alphabet. There was a nondescript wooden table at the front of the classroom, and in back of it a slatted chair for the teacher. On the table was a TV set. That we did not have in 1943, nor did we sit on these movable molded-plastic student chairs but on long benches nailed to the floor before sloped wooden desks on which we wrote our lessons from right to left. For one hour a day, three days a week, fresh from six and a half hours of public school, we sat there and learned to write backwards, to write as though the sun rose in the west and the leaves fell in the spring, as though Canada lay to the south, Mexico to the north,

33

and we put our shoes on before our socks; then we escaped back into our cozy American world, aligned just the other way around, where all that was plausible, recognizable, predictable, reasonable, intelligible, and useful unfolded its meaning to us from left to right, and the only place we proceeded in reverse, where it was natural, logical, in the very nature of things, the singular and unchallengeable exception, was on the sandlot diamond...

"It had all begun back when I'd first taken my seat in that small, ill-ventilated classroom that was the Newark original of this makeshift Jerusalem replica, during those darkening hours when I could barely bring myself to pay attention after a full day in the school where my heart was somehow always light, the public school from which I understood clearly, every day in a thousand ways, my future was to arise. But how could anything come of going to Hebrew school? The teachers were lonely foreigners, poorly paid refugees, and the students—the best among us along with the worst—were bored, restless American kids, ten, eleven, twelve years old, resentful of being cooped up like this year after year, through the fall, winter, and spring, when everything seasonal was exciting the senses and beckoning us to partake freely of all our American delights. Hebrew school wasn't school at all but part of the deal that our parents had cut with their parents, the sop to pacify the old generation—who wanted the grandchildren to be Jews in a way no one had ever dared to be a Jew in our three-thousand-year history: speaking and thinking American English, only American English, with all the apostasy that was bound to beget. Our put-upon parents were simply middlemen in the classic American squeeze, negotiating between the shtetl-born and the Newark-born and taking blows from either side, telling the old ones, "Listen, it's a new world—the kids have to make their way here," while sternly rebuking the young ones, "You must, you have to, you cannot turn your back on everything!" What a compromise! What could possibly come of those three or four hundred hours of the worst possible atmosphere for learning? Why, everything—what came of it was everything! That cryptography whose signification I could no longer decode had marked me indelibly four decades ago; out of the inscrutable words written on this blackboard had evolved every English word I had ever written. Yes, all and everything had originated here..."

1. I would like to take this opportunity to state my admiration and friendship for Dr. Aldo Naouri, who introduced me to and offered me a copy of Pierre Clastres's book (which he often quotes and comments on in his public appearances). Through the constant dialogue we have maintained over the years, Dr. Naouri has sensitized me to the relationship between parents and children, and allowed me to explore it in great depth.

2. Claude Lévi-Strauss, *Structural Anthropology*, II, Basic Books, 1974, pp. 319-20. I have made a slight change to Lévi-Strauss's statement.

3. *Ibid.*

4. In the following pages of the foreword, I will explain how this introduction to Judaism and the bar mitzvah was originally partially presented in the context of conferences and meetings with female high school students (all of whom were non-Jewish and most of whom were Muslim) at the Camille Claudel vocational high school in Mantes-la-Ville.

5. See below, chapter 2.

6. "Not a prince, no, better, a man!"

7. New techniques of procreation will undoubtedly change human psychology over the course of the coming centuries. See Henri Atlan, *L'utérus artificiel* (The Artificial Uterus), Seuil, 2005.

8. Ferenczi, whom I refer to only as an example, went so far as to suggest a theory of genitality, stating that "the sexual act symbolically represents the desire to return to the maternal womb." See Ferenczi, *Oeuvres Complètes* (Complete Works), 1919–1926, Payot, 1974, p. 250.

This primordial nostalgia can even be found in philosophy. In Plato, for example, where the great texts of Greek literature already contain what could be called a "metaphysics of exile" and/or a "metaphysics of the return." See Lévinas, *Totality and Infinity*, chapter 1, and *Le Temps et l'autre Time and the Other*, Paris, 1947.

9. This method of relating letters and numbers, which is used extensively in Midrashic thought, is known as *Gematria*.

10. Marcel Rufo, *Détache moi, Grandir c'est se séparer* (Untie me, Growing up is separation), Anne Carrière, 2005, p. 51.

11. *Ibid.*

12. Françoise Dolto *L'image inconsciente du corps* (The Unconscious Image of the Body), Seuil, 1984, p. 188.

13. In psychoanalysis, the terms which refer to these various stages vary from one author to the next. I consider the terminology used in Dolto's work to avoid both an excessively sophisticated jargon and ephemeral fashions. She refers to "symbolic or anthropogenic castration" for all those severances necessary to mature. She defines the following types of castration: umbilical (umbilical cord), oral (the breast), anal (hygiene), primary (understanding of sexual difference), secondary (prohibition of incest).

14. The rite of the tefillin (see chapter 6) introduces the God *Shaddai*, which could be translated as, "Enough of the breast!" Weaning is essential for the child, and a mother must be released from the guilt of having badly fed

her child. The breast, when read differently as *"shed,"* means demon. It is extremely interesting to note that the Hebrew sense of the word "demon" concerns any person or situation where there is maternal fusion, or an intensely close immanence between two beings who should be separated. The opposite, angel, the *malakh*, is a word used whenever separation, de-fusion, righteous distancing, just distance, successful weaning, transcendence, and the path to maturity are referred to. (See the remarkable example of Exodus 23:19 and the following verse). And given that angel is also an anagram of the word *maakhal*, food, there is undoubtedly much food for thought here.

15. $1 + 2 + 3 + 4 + 5 + 6 + 7 + 8 + 9 = 45$. It is interesting that the sum of the first nine whole numbers is equal to 45, a figure written in Hebrew as *mah*, the numeric equivalent of the word *adam*, "man." If a single one of these primordial numbers is missing, man cannot be constructed. Every singularity counts.

16. Alain Finkielkraut, *La sagesse de l'amour* (The Wisdom of Love), Gallimard, 1985, p. 165.

17. For having good grades, for example, or for having succeeded at any other endeavor, or for behaving in a particular way.

18. Françoise Dolto, *L'image inconsciente du corps* (The Unconscious Image of the Body), Seuil, 1984, p. 198.

19. It is worth noting that Judaism includes a constant one/four rhythm. I discuss this subject in the chapter on tefillin.

20. The terms "transcendence" and "immanence" have multiple different meanings according to the philosophy in question. In the above paragraph, we refer to transcendence as what is beyond man, such as God, for example, and also as the movement towards transcendence. Immanence is what is on man's side, or moving towards man, towards the finished dimension of man, as opposed to the infinite dimension of the Divine.

21. See "gan-edenization" (a theory developed by Rabbi Nachman of Breslav in *Likute Moharan* I, 286), a tension between the elevated, called "Gan," and the low, "Eden"...

22. See note 18.

23. In its purely Freudian version, or in its later interpretations by Winnicott, Lacan, or Dolto, for instance...

24. I do believe there is a special connection between psychoanalysis and Judaism, and, particularly, the Talmud. I refer, in particular, to the famous 1908 letter, in which Freud writes Karl Abraham that, "it is impossible to think the Talmudic spirit has left us." However, though this special connection can serve to orient us, it should not lock us into a single vision, or limit our explanations to the context of a single interpretation.

25. For a full appreciation of the singularity of this aspect of the bar mitzvah, we notably recommend Tobie Nathan's foreword to Fabrice Hervieu-Wane's *Une boussole pour la vie- les nouveaux rites de passages*, Albin Michel, 2005.

26. *Operation Shylock*, Simon & Schuster, 1993. Thank you to Françoise-Anne Ménager for telling me about this beautiful text, which I reproduce here in reference to these same students' meeting with Philip Roth during a "Master class" in Aix-en-Provence in 1999, following their initiation to his work by their professor.

37

1

# Becoming a Bar Mitzvah

## Looking at the rite of passage

*In and of himself, man is nothing. All he is are infinite possibilities. But he is infinitely responsible for these possibilities.*

Albert Camus

# Chapter One

The Bar Mitzvah: A Rite of Passage

**The Meaning of the Expression "Bar Mitzvah"**

A Special Relationship with the Book

**Intelligence: Thinking with the Other**

Bar Mitzvah and Psychoanalysis

**The Paradigm of the Bond: Cutting Hair and the Hair Cut**

Cutting and Reading

**The Enigma of *The Little Prince* as My First Bar Mitzvah Gift**

Hair, Ties, Tallith, and Tefillin

**Method**

Freedom, The Maternal Body and Leaving Egypt

**God and Jewish Mothers: Unfair Competition!**

The Bar Mitzvah for Boys, the Bat Mitzvah for Girls: A First Look…

**The Three Stages of the Bar Mitzvah**

The Preparation

**The Synagogue Ceremony**

Reading in Bursts

**Reaching Adulthood Through Words and Speech**

The Psychological Significance of the Celebration

**Bar Mitzvah:  Responsibility and Commitment**

The Importance of the Path: Respecting Each Step

## The Bar Mitzvah: A Rite of Passage

*Every word, every flower, every glance is a beginning. Only a language of beginning can respond to the beginnings that constitute reality, to its incomplete articulation. There is no poetry, song, music, art that can escape this fundamental dislocation. There does not exist a complete word, a complete flower, a complete way of looking.*

Roberto Juarroz, *Vertical Poetry*

Every culture has its rites, its "initiation" rites, its "rites of passage," its methods that enable the transition into adulthood. As Philippe Meirieu emphasizes in *Des Enfants et Des Hommes* (ESF, 1999), "Growing up doesn't happen on its own. "And," he adds, "there are so many reasons to remain in childhood's great power, or to settle into the indecision of adolescence, instead of accepting the difficult mission of adulthood. Growing up is not simple, because growing up has always been a tearing apart. Because growing up means renunciation. Because growing up means entering a world one might, at times, want to escape. Because growing up makes us learn through trial and error when we would most likely prefer immediate gratification."

The rites that mark the event of entering adulthood in the Jewish tradition, whether Orthodox, Conservative, or Reform, is the bar mitzvah for boys and the bat mitzvah for girls. This age old ceremony assumes different forms throughout the world, but no matter the specific customs, there is a core that has remained through time and across place. When did this ceremony first come into being? No one can say exactly.

## The Meaning of the Expression "Bar Mitzvah"

> *In each word, a bird with its wings folded awaits the breath of the reader.*
> Emmanuel Lévinas, *New Talmudic Readings*

The word *bar* is an Aramaic word that means "son" (in Hebrew it's *ben*). *Bar* also implies someone who "possesses" something or a quality, someone who is "bound to." The Hebrew dictionary *Even Shoshan* notes that the expression *bar-mazal* means "someone who has luck." *Bar-daat* designates someone who "has knowledge," intelligence. Therefore, a *bar mitzvah* is a person who is bound to the mitzvot.

The word "mitzvah" is rather complex to translate. It comes from the verb *letzavot* which means "to order." *Ani mitzave* means "I am ordered to." The word "order" as in an order given is *tzivuy,* which distinguishes it from the word "mitzvah," which has to be translated and understood as "order received." In everyday language, the mitzvot are commandments detailed in the text of the Torah and elucidated in the Talmud. The mitzvot cover specific instructions on private life—how to act in a marriage, to love one's neighbor. They also direct on the communal—how much charity to give, what prayers to say, how to conduct a business, and even the impalpable—it is a positive commandment to be happy.

The mitzvot are also divided into categories based on those whose rationales are obvious and those that are statutes, or commandments that transcend logic. The rational mitzvot based on social law such as not to kill, steal, or lie are known as *mishpatim.* And the mitzvot that seem irrational and are accepted as divine decrees, are known as *chukim,* such as the dietary restrictions. (A third category known as *eidot* include testimonials or commandments that represent something, and include putting on the tefillin and eating matzoh on Passover.) More precisely, the Torah lists 248 "positive mitzvot" and 365 "negative mitzvot." There are therefore 613 mitzvot altogether, or rather, 613 commandments.

According to the commentaries, the number 248 refers to the number of limbs of the body and 365 to the number of sinews. Therefore, the bar and bat mitzvah also establish an essential relationship between the body and time. Certain commentators think that the expression should therefore have been bar mitzvot, in the plural, which would indicate that upon turning thirteen, a child becomes responsible for carrying out all the commandments.

## A Special Relationship with the Book

*The Human being is not only an in-der-Welt-Sein. But also a* Zum-Buch-Sein *with regard to the inspired Word, an ambiance as important to our existence as streets, houses and clothing.*

Emmanuel Lévinas

43

The word *bar* also has other important meanings. First, *B*, the Hebrew letter *bet*, and *R*, or *resh*, are the first letters of the Torah (The Five Books of Moses), which begins with the word *Bereshit*, which translates as "in the beginning" or "at first." This is key, since it decisively links the status of bar mitzvah to the status of text, and therefore to the question of reading it, and interpreting it—in a word studying. As explained above, each

*Bereshit* is the first word of Genesis. Its first two letters spell the word *bar*; the first and the last spell *bat*.

culture has its own rites of passage, its own ways of approaching the entrance into adulthood. Judaism takes studying the book, or the Torah, as central to this process.

Indeed, this relationship between *bar* and *Bereshit* shows that the book is no coincidence, it is part of the human essence. Man is literally meant for the book. This is why in the bar mitzvah ceremony, the reading of a portion from the book, the parashah, is so central and so important.

## Intelligence: Thinking with the Other

*Existence is rare. We are constantly, but we exist only sometimes, when a genuine event transforms us.*
Henri Maldiney, *Compar(a)ison.*

One might also note that the opposite of *bar* is *rav*, which simultaneously means "a lot" and "master." This is a reminder that in life, both study and intelligence do not come through solitude, but rather through connection and communication: the result of the relationship between master and disciple. One never thinks on one's own. "A thought is always the thought of another," says Georges Bataille, illustrating his words through the extraordinary image of a brick in a wall. The brick, representing a person's thought, could not be supported without the presence of the other bricks that carry it, enclose it, and give it strength. The bar mitzvah is therefore also the relationship of the *bar* to the *rav*, of the son to the master through reading, study, and interpretation. It is the entrance of the young man or young woman into adult life through the pages of a story that is told, transmitted, and interpreted. It is the story of a world in which one has to participate fully, responsibly and in accordance with a code of ethics about the future.

44

## Bar Mitzvah and Psychoanalysis

*I take all the pieces. I barely have to change them. But, I knot them into*
*another language. And the same being will go differently.*
Antoine de Saint-Exupéry, *The Wisdom of the Sands*

Life is but a series of breaks, ruptures, reunions and disappearances. And, as
child psychiatrist Marcel Rufo reminds us in his book *Détache Moi: Se Séparer
Pour Grandir* (Anne Carrière, 2005), "everything begins with a fusion, whereby
the mother and child are one. It's a vital fusion, in which the child draws assu-
rance and strength to set out and conquer the world. However, you have to
grow and, in order to do so, you have to separate and enter new territories of
autonomy and freedom. The psychomotor development of the child, of all
human life, appears like a series of attachments and detachments, of conquests
and separations.... Separation from the maternal womb, separation from the
breast, separation from a piece of oneself during toilet training..."
Living therefore also includes separating, leaving, abandoning, and mour-
ning. But each of these painful stages allows the child to become freer and
more autonomous. Whether it's "separating from a teddy bear," Rufo explains,
"or a teacher, house, toy, pet, friend, or loved one, the child has to separate
every time from one world in order to be able to conquer a new one. All
separation is a challenge from which the child emerges more mature and
more human, a challenge through which he learns that it is impossible to
gain if he does not accept loss, and that the pleasure of conquest soothes the
pain of loss." (Ibid., p.15)
We therefore cannot live without bonds, but once a bond becomes too
exclusive, it threatens to suffocate us. We therefore must learn to loosen
them, to detach, so as to find the right level of closeness between ourselves
and others.
In the Jewish tradition, the bar mitzvah is what enables good bonds, good
fusions, and good de-fusions. The bar mitzvah is, as one beautiful Kabbalistic
expression says, "a science of knots to undo." It is interesting to note that
on the one hand this ceremony marks the entrance into Law, where the
child gains the capacity to fulfill the commandments, the mitzvot. On
the other hand, "permitted" (*mutar*) and "forbidden" (*asur*) in Hebrew
specifically mean "detached" or loose, and "attached" or bound up. The bar
mitzvah distances the child from his parents or family and also amplifies
the child's feeling of belonging to a larger system. It includes several phases,

numerous symbols and a whole series of rituals, which, in an original manner, but also with great impact, make this confrontation with loss and detachment possible. It also gives the child the possibility of growing and discovering new worlds, new relationships and new ways of feeling and thinking.

For the young man or woman, having a bar or bat mitzvah also marks the beginning of sexual maturity, for it is during adolescence that a person discovers his or her body and desires in a new way. The bar mitzvah also represents the trauma of losing a part of oneself through the body. Boys lose sperm (wet dreams and first masturbation). Girls bleed with menstruation (which can be improperly interpreted as punishment for having sexual feelings, whether through masturbation or not). In fact, the Jewish texts have determined that boys reach maturity at 13 years and 1 day, and that girls reach maturity at 12 years and 1 day. These ages correspond closely to the time that the losses described above are first sustained.

## The Paradigm of the Bond: Cutting Hair and the Hair Cut:
### An anthropological approach

> *I like to remember minute facts. They don't prove anything,*
> *but they're life.*
> Maurice Merleau-Ponty

In this first chapter, we would like to show how the ritual of the bar mitzvah can be both a means of becoming conscious of the trauma of loss and a way to confront it and heal.

In the chapter on bar mitzvahs throughout the world, we'll see that there is one ritual in particular in almost every community that illustrates the idea of rupture and separation. It is the ritual of haircutting. In some communities, on the eve of the bar mitzvah, the father and son (sometimes even friends) get their hair cut. This is done to music and is often followed by dance and a light meal. To understand this bar mitzvah haircutting ritual, we're going to take a look at the significance of a haircutting ritual practiced in some Jewish communities that takes place when boys turn three, when the child goes to school for the first time and is about to learn how to read, known in Hebrew as *chalakah* or in Yiddush as *upsherin*.

This haircut, accompanied by songs and dance, and performed in front of guests and key figures, is an act of desistance. It marks a phase of withdrawal from the mother's body. The child is launching into society and what we might call his cultural autonomy.

A three-year-old boy has his hair cut during the *Lag BaOmer* holiday in Merom (Israel), one of the capitals of the mystical tradition.

47

## Cutting and Reading

*Read to live.*

Gustave Flaubert, Letter to Mademoiselle de Chantepie, June 1857

It would also seem that the function of this haircut is to show—both to the child and his family—that he is a boy, because in the first years of childhood, it's sometimes difficult to distinguish between a little girl and a little boy solely by looking at their clothes or hair.

The loss represented by this haircut is immediately soothed by the child's entrance into the world of words and books. In some communities, honey cakes or other sweets shaped like letters are given to the child, who joyfully discovers a new world of shapes and sounds that he can use to communicate with his family and those around him. He goes from the maternal language, which is oral, to the paternal language, which is written. Hebrew also links writing to the paternal language in an extraordinary way. The word "alphabet"—*aleph-bet* in Hebrew —is pronounced *av* and means "father."

## The Enigma of *The Little Prince* as My First Bar Mitzvah Gift

*It is forbidden to be old.*

Rabbi Nachman of Breslav

With regard to first books, first letters, first words, and first childhood games, I can't help but think of *The Little Prince* by Antoine de Saint-Exupéry. It's a book that I read and reread, discovering new meanings every time. Imagine, the book has been translated into as many languages as the Bible!

Why such success? Might it have something to do with the fact that it says something about this "growing up," about this frontier between childhood and adolescence and the adult world? The book challenges the adult conception of the adult world. For sometimes grown-ups are sick of being locked into a strict, limited image of their being. Alexander Jardin named this "pathology" adultism.

*The Little Prince* begins with the narrator remembering his childhood and especially the crucial moment he learned to read (a moment that's even more important for a future writer). *The Little Prince* is a book filled with adults talking about children's books. It's the story about the memory of childhood, about one's first book, and it even has some pictures.

"Once when I was 6, I saw a magnificent picture in a book about the jungle that was called *True Stories*. It showed a boa constrictor swallowing a wild beast. Here is a copy of the picture...

My drawing Number One looked like this:

Adults see a hat! But a child knows it's a boa eating an animal!

On several occasions, Saint-Exupéry reminds us that the child is 6, the age when he would first go to school and learn how to read. The transition is from image to word, from concrete and visual to abstract sounds and words. In fact, one could even uncover a beautiful *A* in the boa and, according to a pun by Hélène Cixous, an *aleph* hidden in an "alephant."

## Hair, Ties, Tallith, and Tefillin

*A Jewish mother has a particularly stormy relationship with her son.*
*They fight and argue constantly. One day she brings him to a*
*psychoanalyst. After two sessions, the doctor talks to the mother.*
*"Madam, your son is suffering from an Oedipal complex."*
*"Oedipal, Shmoedipal," the mother answers, "it's all the same to me.*
*What matters is that he loves his mother!"*

The bar mitzvah, the "science of knots to undo," plays on tying and untying, on loosening and tightening, on all bonds, including familial, communal, emotional, pedagogical, philosophical, ideological, and others. We therefore can understand the role the tallith, the prayer shawl plays at the heart of the bar mitzvah ritual.

The tzitzit ties of the tallith, or prayer shawl are braids or fringes that you wear on your body or over your head, and that you wrap yourself in and remove. And which you cut symbolically.[1]

It should be noted that in the haircutting ceremony, the 3-year-old child receives his first *tallit katan*, or small tallith—the tzitzit, which he will wear regularly, either under his clothes or over them, depending on the tradition. He'll continue to do so when he becomes an adult, including during prayer, when he'll also wear the large tallith.

The idea of the tie is also found in the phylactery ritual, tefillin, in which long strips of leather are worn on the arm and head. They also symbolize hair and they're worn especially so that they can be removed at the end of the prayer. The ties placed around the arm represent the link to the prayer. More on this later on.

50

## Method

Although *chalakah,* the custom of haircutting, is not part of the actual law, it is nevertheless essential. It is a discreet but regular part of the bar mitzvah, acting as a pedagogical example, one that is concrete, easy to remember and easily repeated.

We stress this ritual because it is a good example of how Hebrew thought is symbolic. Rather than being philosophical, speculative, or abstract, it always begins with a fact or concrete object that can be analyzed and referred to as a benchmark. This is true even when more mature thought develops into great, solid intellectual concepts. With this method, which Emmanuel Lévinas calls "paradigmatic," the meaning of a ritual or a symbol is not singular, it's not defined once and for all. The symbol can be interpreted endlessly. "Never does the meaning of these symbols dismiss the materiality of the symbols that suggest the meaning and that always retain some unsuspected power to renew this meaning."[2]

## Freedom, The Maternal Body, and Leaving Egypt

The above discussion leads us to the psychology of the bar mitzvah. We have understood that the ceremony is a rite of passage that includes a separation, then the possibility of building new, broader ties. The break is with the family unit, the "home," the symbol of which is the maternal. The "home" is woman, says the Talmud. The bar mitzvah therefore marks the ultimate rupture and there is no return to the maternal "body." One might even say that the Bible's story is the narration of this break that enables a people to become mature, and an individual to surmount the trial of separation, bringing that individual also to maturity and responsibility. What is characteristic of the Bible is the staging of the geography of the psyche, whereby the mother is represented by the country of Egypt and the woman, the promised one, becomes the sought after "promised land."

In this regard, the bar mitzvah also implies and first requires the recognition of the parents. The father and mother must be the father and mother, so that others don't take on their roles, which would certainly be harmful. A successful bar mitzvah is one that acts as the first step toward the possibility of a possible encounter with a woman. The ritual of the tefillin confirms this idea. Indeed, when the ties are wrapped around the left index finger, one pronounces the two verses from the book of Hosea, the first of the twelve prophets, who suffers anguish from the infidelity of his wife. He eventually forgives her and takes her back. Similarly, God renews his relationship with a repentant people. Hosea expresses God's devotion to the Jewish people this moving declaration:

"And I will betroth you to myself forever; and I will betroth you to myself in righteousness and in justice, in kindness, and in mercy; and I will betroth you to myself in faithfulness, and you will know God."

In this one relationship, therefore, there is a clear link between the tefillin, the woman, and the function of the divine. One can say that, in this context, one of the key functions of the existence of the transcendence of the divine is this possibility of maternal detachment.

## God and Jewish Mothers: Unfair Competition!

> *Rachel, a young wife in despair, goes to the doctor.*
> *"Oh, doctor, I can't take it anymore. No matter what I do, my husband won't look at me. He's always talking about his mother, his mother, his mother! I don't exist to him!"*
> *"Did you try cooking him nice meals?"*
> *"I've tried everything, doctor, believe me. Nothing works. There's nothing left to do."*
> *"Listen, I have an idea. There's an area where your mother-in-law can't rival you, and that's in bed. Tonight, you're going to put on very exciting black lingerie, with a black garter belt. You're going to put on makeup, dark eye shadow, long, never-ending false eyelashes, and black lipstick. You're going to change your sheets and put on black ones. Put on his favorite perfume and put black roses in a vase. In this ambiance, he'll find you irresistible."*
> *Rachel carefully followed all the directions. The makeup, the setting, the decor. She didn't forget a thing. She had never been so voluptuous and arousing.*
> *Her husband came home and with all the unexpected surprises, he became increasingly amazed. In the end, he couldn't contain himself any longer and cried:*
> *"Rachel, all this black! Did something happen to my mother?"*

God is introduced as the one who helps the Jews escape Egypt, which proves how fundamental this departure is. It's key. The rituals that give shape to Jewish life all, without exception, refer to this exit from Egypt, the pillar of memory. This idea of Egypt as the "motherland" of the Hebrew people led to the promulgation of a law forbidding the return to Egypt. Not because it was the country in which the Jews were slaves, but because it was the place of birth, the maternal body. And doesn't slavery represent the return to the mother, an impossible separation? The bar mitzvah is the walk through the desert that separates the two lands, the original land and the promise land. It is the transmutation of nostalgia into desire.

This hypothesis is clearly confirmed by the tefillin ritual, the phylacteries, which will be analyzed in detail in a chapter devoted to the subject. But, in summary, this ritual specifically stages the question of the mother, motherland, and the departure from Egypt. The parchment scrolls inserted into and imprisoned in these small boxes discuss God's redemption of the

54

A pair of folded tefillin and their protective cases.

Jewish people from Egypt, referring to the son asking his father about the meaning of the customs associated with this liberation. The first of the four parchment scrolls speaks of he who opens the womb, the first born, and the consecration to God. The death of the first born in the Bible can be understood in this way. It implies symbolically killing the child who remains in the womb, giving him the opportunity to be released from the bond that enchains him and takes away his freedom. This is a fundamental idea that sheds light on the psychological and philosophical dimension of the divine as transcendence and exteriority, which makes detachment and independence between the mother and child possible. We discover a pattern that psychoanalysis adopts in full. The word of the father, who answers the child and explains the departure from Egypt, makes the separation from the mother possible.

Let us say quickly in conclusion that humor is absolutely central to the question of detachment. It is the intellectual version of de-fusion, of breaking away from the serious mindset in which all thought becomes ideology. Man must constantly try to untangle himself from ideology so as not to fall into the trap of its mothering comfort. Telling jokes, and not only about Jewish mothers, is a way of breaking from fusion and confusion. This question of the Jewish mother is key because it is the humorous version of what all rites of passage and the bar mitzvah in particular share. Joking about Jewish mothers implies that both the person telling the joke and the person hearing the joke are open to growing up. It shows that the question of entering adulthood is movement, a never-ending path, a constant dis-identification.[3]

# The Bar Mitzvah for Boys, the Bat Mitzvah for Girls: A First Look

*The only way to appreciate a creation, is to create it again and perhaps to recreate oneself with it.*

Roberto Juarroz, *Vertical Poetry*

Over time and as women's roles have evolved in modern society, what was once a ceremony for boys only has become a ceremony for girls, aptly called the bat mitzvah. It was Jacob Ettlinger, the great neo-orthodox rabbi of Altona, Germany, who, in the middle of the nineteenth century, suggested there be a ceremony for girls as well that marked the passage into adulthood and into an active Jewish community. This ritual was private at first, but became public in time, first in liberal communities, then among the orthodox. It coincided with the liberation of Jewish women in society. The bat mitzvah was even approved, in 1898, by one of the greatest Rabbinical authorities of all time, Rabbi Yossef Hayyim from Baghdad, known as the Ben Ish Chai.

Obviously, girls face detachment issues, but they involve both the mother and the father. However, considering everything that has already been discussed, it seems impossible that the ceremonies for girls and boys could be identical, since fusion and de-fusion are different for each sex. The debate is still open and the bat mitzvah rituals are still in an experimental stage. In this book, because of space considerations, we will not distinguish between the bar mitzvah and the bat mitzvah, but will consider the above remark. In cases where a ritual is performed solely in a bar mitzvah, we will note it and offer an alternative.

## The Three Stages of the Bar Mitzvah

*Parents dream of the child they would like to conceive, mothers dream about the baby they carry within, children dream about the day they will see the light, and if they all didn't dream together, life wouldn't come into the world.*

Leonardo da Vinci

The bar mitzvah is a ritual that takes place in the home and in the synagogue and includes three parts:

–the preparation
–the synagogue ceremony
–the family celebration

These three stages resemble the three-part structure of various rites of passage described by anthropologists. There is the separation, the reclusion or marginalization, and the reintegration. "Rites of passage," writes ethnologist Hélène Wolf, "have three main functions. They protect against anxiety, they mediate with the divine, and they reinforce the social bond, that is, they integrate adolescents into the social realm as best they can in order to situate them in terms of the sexes and generations. These three functions touch upon three principle elements, faith, the sacred, and the body, and are often realized in three phases. There is a phase of separation, a phase of reclusion, and a phase of return."[4]

## The Preparation

*To grow is to notice that ones parents are not indispensible.*
Neil Bissondath

The bar mitzvah is a doorway into adult life. It is the beginning of a long path. It is a way of gathering strength and making provisions for the greatest success on the journey of life. Gathering strength. Gathering, learning. The bar mitzvah begins with an apprenticeship, that is, with study. Studying! Not only learning, but keeping your mind awake, keeping it moving, in a word, keeping it alive. The bar mitzvah is a symbolic birth. And in the same way that the Talmud says that the child in the womb of his mother is a book turned in on itself, and that he studies the whole Torah and all the world's wisdom in order to be born a second time symbolically, so one should become book again and study all the Torah and all the world's wisdom. For this reason, a few years before the bar mitzvah, young boys and girls immerse themselves in the Talmud Torah, studying on Sundays and Wednesdays (or other days depending on the country), where they learn to read and write Biblical and modern Hebrew and to understand and speak, at least its basics. Learning Hebrew has become even more important since the state of Israel was founded in 1948, and even more so since the end of the Six Day War in 1967. Biblical, Talmudic, and contemporary history are also taught. Students are introduced to the traditional texts of the Bible and the Talmud, and sometimes to Jewish philosophy. Learning prayer, both its structure and practice, is stressed.

But above all, the students learn about the significance of the holidays that dot the Jewish calendar, including the all important Shabbat. These holidays include Rosh Hashanah and Yom Kippur, the three pilgrimage holidays—Sukkot, Passover, and Shavuot—and the two holidays especially loved by children—Chanukah, the festival of lights in winter, and Purim, the carnival in early spring. A year before the bar or bat mitzvah ceremony, young boys and girls begin an intensive special course in which they learn to read from Torah, including all or part of

Children of the North American Ethiopian Jewish community studying.
The first black Jewish community in North America was started in 1921.

the weekly portion, the parashah, and the haftarah, the additional segment from the Prophets corresponding to the Torah portion. They are required to read the text of the Torah (without the Hebrew vowels) on the day of the ceremony. The course of study and the regularity with which it is approached is as important as the ceremony itself. It is during this time that the child discovers Judaism for the first time and that he comes into contact with the Jewish world and its community, the rabbi and the synagogue, and also with friends with whom he will forever be bound because of the experience they share.

This first part or phase of the bar mitzvah begins the process of detachment from the father, the mother and the home. As Hélène Wolf explains, during this transition to independence, equality, and responsibility, "the rabbi plays the role of a temporary intermediary.

The silver reading pointer, or *yad,* makes it possible to read the Torah without touching the parchment. Strangely, touching the parchment is considered "impure" (see Talmud, *Megillah*).

When the boy accepts him as a superior substitute for the father, his guilt is lessened." Separation from the mother is not as brutal as in archaic societies, but a child who is learning his parashah will go to the rabbi's to study every week. He therefore symbolically leaves the parental home for a period of time so as to be introduced to the Torah by a rabbi. It is therefore important that it be the student who goes to the teacher or to the Talmud Torah, and not the teacher who comes to the home of the student to give private lessons.

## The Synagogue Ceremony

> *If everything that a child has put in his toy chest—which,*
> *for personal reasons, are precious to him—has been respected,*
> *the child will naturally respect the personal belongings of others.*

Françoise Dolto, *L'Image inconsciente du corps*

In the spirit of this ethnological approach, the second phase, reclusion, essentially occurs in synagogue when the child is separated from other children and spectators and performs a ritual. He is the physical and symbolic focus—or solitary focus. Slightly outsized on the synagogue platform, he participates in the prayer and reads the Torah. This is how detachment takes shape, how the child "takes off on his own," even if his mother is watching him with worried eyes, either from the women's balcony or from a seat below the platform.

This transition from family to community mostly happens through the learning of a new language—Hebrew—and through a story, one that doesn't belong to the family, but rather to the community and an entire people. The public reading of the parashah, which is the same whether you're in Paris, Jerusalem, New York, or Casablanca, is therefore the passage from family identity to community identity, one might even say national identity. This meta-identity allows the teenager to feel the world opening before him, a world that lies beyond the boundaries of his family.

It is extraordinary to see a whole assembly of people remain silent, sitting respectfully and in wonder, and allowing the child to read and enter the adult

61

community by experiencing the fact that his voice has weight, that it counts, that he can be heard, both in actuality and symbolically.

To be heard! What joy for a child who finds that he has been immediately given the responsibility to speak, who finds that he has suddenly grown and is respected as a new young adult.

The child has encountered this silence before, long ago. It was the day he stopped being nursed by his mother. In Exodus, it says, "You shall not boil a kid in its mother's milk." (Exodus 23:19) The Bible therefore says that the animal should not mature in its mother's milk. We must take leave of the breast to be exposed to silence, to detachment.

Silence is *aleph*. The child's quiet *aleph* when the nipple comes out of his mouth, either for the time being or forever. And, if no words interrupt this silence, the child will naturally fill this void. Psychoanalysts tell us that this is when a child begins to suck his thumb as a tactile substitute for the nipple.

The bar mitzvah is therefore a symbolic way of offering a word to the open mouth, whether it has been satisfied or not. It doesn't stuff it with objects as if it were plugging up a "need," but rather continues to transcend "desire" by seizing the new and joyous opportunity provided by the reading and the singing.

Is this not the very meaning of the *yad*, the silver hand used to read from the Bible? Does it not suggest that the hand goes from a mouth that nurses, to a mouth that reads?

## Reading in Bursts

> *What is natural is to play and...the very sophisticated phenomenon of the twentieth century is psychoanalysis. If the therapist cannot play, it means that he is not suitable for this work.*
>
> D.W. Winnicott

Reading the Torah isn't only about reading words and phrases that tell a story. It's also about delivering the words using the method described by the Talmud. Words literally burst out into letters or into groups of letters, making other words and coming together into a new order. It is this method that the child exhibits when reading out loud.

I've named this game "reading in bursts," a method that also seems to have a special relationship to the break, to separation, detachment and to loss, which make new meanings and new words possible.[4]

The bar mitzvah is therefore a special time when one learns to read. It challenges the linear structure of storytelling. Through it, you discover the creative combinations and recombinations of letters and words. Man is put into play and experiences movement and becoming, change and deep personal modifications. This playful dimension draws him out of mental rigidity, which could otherwise hinder the possibility of growth.

## Reaching Adulthood Through Words and Speech

> *The ideal reader is the writer, right before the words come together on the page.*
>
> Alberto Manguel, *Pour une éthique de la lecture.*

Reading the Torah and reading it out loud, which is the heart of the synagogue ceremony, refers to two different relationships to words and language, and to text and reading.

Let us first note that the Torah is a text without vowels. This means that to learn it, one has to accept being part of a tradition. One cannot learn this vowel-less text on one's own, even if one reads and speaks Hebrew fluently. The reading of the parashah therefore is partly about communication and necessary control, since it reinforces the social and trans-generational bond by allowing the child to be integrated into the community.

Reading seems to be part of every separation and break that leads to growth. And if it's not in the form of a text, there's always language and words.

During circumcision, the child is given a name. But it's also interesting to note that the word "circumcision" itself means "word." When the hair is cut at age three, the child begins to learn the alphabet. At the time of the bar mitzvah, it's the reading of the Torah that is at the very heart of the ceremonies marking the will to and joy of becoming an adult. Text and reading out loud are necessary in order to enter this moment of growth, to gain access to autonomy and responsibility.

## The Psychological Significance of the Celebration

*Adolescence is a unique period in which we break with our past, our childhood and our parents. But the vulnerability of this age exacerbates preexisting and reactive weaknesses resulting from all previous separations. Yet, the adolescent must absolutely detach from his parents in order to conquer and find his own desires. Attachment to the first love object transforms, leaving room for new emotional relationships and love.*

Marcel Rufo, *Détache-moi. Se séparer pour grandir.*

The third phase of the "rite of passage," the return to the community, is experienced though the celebration (and gifts). The child, while still the focus, reintegrates his family and friends. The return is marked by a celebratory meal accompanied by music and dance.

The moments of loss, which we have described above, are always accompanied by festivities. The function of the celebration is not only to rejoice in the happy event, but to lend support to the person going through the difficult transition, one in which he is separating from a source, from his family, in order to create new bonds and relationships. The festivities give emphasis to the initiation, which involve both detachment and the creation of new bonds. For anthropologists, the celebration is the moment of return into society after a period of separation and reclusion, but the idea remains the same. That is, it offers strength to surmount the loss and encourages the individual to enter the new world.

The idea of a celebration accompanying moments of "anthropogenic castrations"—to use Françoise Dolto's expression—is even explored in the Bible. "And the child grew, and was weaned. And Abraham made a great feast on the day that Isaac was weaned"[5] (Genesis 21:8).

## Bar Mitzvah: Responsibility and Commitment

> *If the person I loved most on earth came to ask me what choice to make, and what the deepest, most impregnable and gentlest refuge was, I would tell her to shelter her fate in a soul that is improving itself.*

Maurice Maeterlinck

We have seen that the bar mitzvah plays a fundamental role in the adolescent's psychological, even psychomotor evolution, leading him to autonomy and independence, giving him access to his subjectivity, his self, and his freedom. It is necessary to see, however, that this maturity is not purely individualistic.

In the words bar mitzvah, there is, as we have emphasized above, the word mitzvah, which certain scholars relate to its root *tzevet*, meaning "pinch." It takes two to understand life! The idea is again found in the word *tsevet*, which means "team," and *tzavta* meaning "couple" or "meeting." The bar mitzvah therefore marks the moment when the person can no longer envision life or the world in solitude and in narcissistic confinement. He is called to watch others and must be able to answer their demands, their questions, their needs and desires. This ability to respond is exactly what constitutes the very essence of responsibility.

Responsibility brings man into the world of duties, but it also gives him rights. As an example, a child having a bar mitzvah becomes an integral part of the community and joins the minyan, the group of ten people needed to form an assembly for prayer.

The bar mitzvah is not only a door leading to the self, but also to the self-for-others. The bar mitzvah is indeed modern, it is like a man at the center of his world and universe who is propelled by an ethical code toward responsibility for the other. It is the entrance to a kind of humanism, a "humanism of the other," to use Emmanuel Lévinas's great expression.

65

## The Importance of the Path: Respecting Each Step

*The work is the path.*
Paul Klee

We have considered the bar mitzvah from an anthropological and psycho-analytical perspective to, above all, show how contemporary it is, how modern, and to underline how this event is part of a universal human question. That is, how to help the child separate from various attachments that prevent him from growing.

We henceforth understand the importance of the three phases outlined above: preparation, ceremony, and celebration. For this reason, if the bar mitzvah is reduced to a single phase, as sometimes happens today, the wholeness of the rite of passage is betrayed, and the real event of growing is lessened. It is therefore important for educators and teachers to ensure that the bar mitzvah is not reduced to celebration only. Some humorists —I'm thinking especially of Gad Elmaleh in France—have even used this phenomenon in sketches and comedy acts.

The bar mitzvah is a path, and the whole course is important. As the popular proverb says, "do not seek the path to happiness, for happiness is the path!"

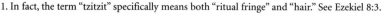

1. In fact, the term "tzitzit" specifically means both "ritual fringe" and "hair." See Ezekiel 8:3.

2. See Emmanuel Lévinas, introduction to *New Talmudic Readings,* (Duquesne University Press, 1999). The Talmud, for example, refers to the laws that guide the creation of the world by talking about an "egg laid one Sunday" and of the law of damages by talking about an "ox that has gored another ox." "Egg" and "ox" are paradigms, but they clearly aren't literal. They represent rich, profound, and complex thoughts that spring from the object, and yet always return to it.

3. Should the reader wish to delve further into this meditation on humor, we recommend Milan Kundera's essays in *The Art of the Novel, Testaments Betrayed,* and *The Curtain.*

4. These sociological models are certainly schematic, but they are effective. The compound dimension is an epistemological choice that will surely have to be considered. Note: some acts belong to many phases at once. In a certain way, but differently, this is reminiscent of the bobbin reel game, which Freud uses to formulate his famous *Fort-Da* game.

5. The Mendelkern dictionary even translates "wean" as "educate."

# 2

# The Jewish Identity

*Yes, I am proud to be a Jew.*
*I am proud because it is a difficult art,*
*There truly is an art to being Jewish.*
*I think that being Jewish means:*
*to be a fighter, to constantly be swimming*
*against the violent tide of humanity.*

Zvi Kolitz

# Chapter Two

Who is Jewish?

**What is a Jew?**

A Story

**Judaism Is Not a Biological Fact**

It's a Jew!

**Jewish Humor and Anti-Semitic Humor**

Jewish Identity According to Hebraic Law: The Classical Approach

**Filiation in the Biblical Era**

Filiation in the Talmudic Era

**Filiation Today**

Conversion to Judaism

**The Conversion Ceremony**

An Important Parental Decision

**Preparation for Bar Mitzvah and Conversion**

Thinking Within the Perspective of Judaism

**Hebraism, Israelites, and Jewishness**

## Who is Jewish?

*Some try to explain the existence of the word "Odradek" by saying it is of Slavonic origin... Others claim it came from the German and was simply influenced by a Slavonic dialect. Yet the uncertainty of these interpretations can justly lead one to believe that both theories are wrong, particularly since neither theory can offer a satisfactory definition of the word...*

Franz Kafka, *The Cares of a Family Man*

The bar mitzvah is a ritual initiation, a chosen path and a ceremony. Beyond the pedagogical aspect discussed in the first chapter, it is also the expression of a desire for a link with the Jewish community, and a de facto reflection on Jewish existence. Evoking this type of reflection leads us directly to a question as complex and difficult as it is delicate: "What is a Jew?" This question is a natural corollary of another, equally complex question: "Who is a Jew?"

When it comes to the bar mitzvah, these questions are of primary importance. Frequently, when the parents of a young man or woman come to the synagogue to meet with the rabbi and initiate the preparative courses for the bar mitzvah or the bat mitzvah, they are greeted with the stunning news that *their child is not Jewish, or only half-Jewish,* with the rabbi quickly going on to assure them that *it's no problem, we'll find a solution,* etc. This situation most frequently arises in the case of mixed marriages between Jews and non-Jews. It is important to consider the Hebraic law's different approaches to the question.

## What is a Jew?

*Judaism: A religion developed among the ancient Hebrews and characterized by belief in one transcendent God who has revealed himself to Abraham, Moses and the prophets and by a religious life in accordance with Scriptures and rabbinic traditions; conformity to Jewish rites, ceremonies, and practices.*

*Merriam-Webster Dictionary*

Ah, the old Jewish question!

Jews have tirelessly attempted to unravel it through sociology, philosophy, and, most notably, literature. Their literary and philosophical questioning seems endless.

Though there are many Jews, each Jew seems to be different from the last. There are Orthodox Jews, ultra-Orthodox Jews, Modern Orthodox Jews, liberal Jews, liberated Jews, Reform Jews, Conservative Jews, and secular Jews. There are practicing Jews, practicing Jewish believers, practicing Jewish non-believers (they do exist), non-practicing Jewish believers, non-practicing atheists, indifferent non-practicing Jews, and scholarly non-practicing Jews.

There are capitalist Jews and communist Jews, French, American, Israeli, Arab Jews, rich Jews, poor Jews, intelligent Jews and not-so-intelligent Jews, Jewish do-gooders and Jewish thugs, and even, as will be seen in the story that follows, religious Jewish atheists, communist Jewish capitalists, do-gooder Jewish thugs, and Jews displaying all potential combinations of the qualities listed above. There are the suffering Jews, the Jews of Memory and even the culinary Jews, whose transcendence is attained through stuffed carp or matzoh brie. One should also note the existence of numerous "Jews by default"; Jews by negative connotation; "the inauthentic Jews" who are only Jews because, as Sartre explains in his "Reflections on the Jewish Question," the other, the anti-Semite, says they are; singled-out Jews; ostracized Jews.

## A Story

*The Jew's lack of self-definition is a precious gift. It shows that historical, sociological, philosophical, ethnic, political, class, and national categories are relative, and that the very idea of the category should perhaps be called into question. It demonstrates the Jewish people's inability to conceive of the world as a whole. The Jewish people do not know who they are, they only know they exist, and that this disconcerting existence blurs the line created by reason between the political and the private.*

Alain Finkielkraut, *The Imaginary Jew*

This story takes place in Poland:

A young Jew leaves his shtetl to spend a few months in the big city, Warsaw. After three months, he returns to his village and gathers all his friends to tell them about his experience:

–You know, Warsaw is truly an extraordinary city! What richness, what diversity! I met an Orthodox Jew who only talks about the Talmud! He meditates over the traditional texts all day, and whenever you speak to him, he starts off every statement with a Biblical citation. When he isn't studying, he's praying! I also met a Jew who is a complete atheist. He doesn't want to hear a word about God or all those old wives' tales that only suckers and kids go for. I met a Jewish industrialist. He heads factories that employ hundreds of workers, and he drives magnificent luxury cars. Now that guy really knows how to live the life! And I met a passionate communist Jew who only talks about equality between men and of struggle and the suppression of the class system. Marx is his God and *Das Kapital* is his Bible!

The young man's friends looked at him with surprise:

–What's so extraordinary, asked one of his friends, Warsaw is the capital, it's a very big city populated with several hundreds of thousands of Jews. It's entirely natural that you met such a wide variety of Jews!

–You don't get it, smiled the young man, it was the same Jew!

## Judaism Is Not a Biological Fact

*This story takes place in a subway.*
*A woman reading a magazine turns to the young man sitting next to her: "You wouldn't happen to be Jewish, would you?"*
*Surprised, the young man politely responds: "No, ma'am, I'm not Jewish." A few minutes later, the woman tries again: "Excuse me, young man, you wouldn't happen to be Jewish, would you?"*
*Ever polite, the young man calmly responds: "No, ma'am, I'm not Jewish." The woman goes back to reading her magazine for a while, then turns to her neighbor again: "Sorry to bother you again, young man, but you wouldn't happen to be Jewish, would you?" Finally, the young man loses his cool. Wanting to put an end to the woman's foolish questions, he answers: "OK! I am Jewish! So what?" And the stunned woman responds: "That's strange! You really don't look Jewish!"*

Attributed to Elie Kakou

The transmission of Judaism is the transmission of values, not of genes or of some hereditary biological traits, as was erroneously formulated by "the Jewish question" raised by the German Nazis. In this case, we were no longer dealing with the *question*, but the *answer*, or perhaps even the *solution,* to a problem, and it is understood that this *solution* was so radical that it could be considered *final.*

The clearest proof is that according to the greatest commentators on Hebraic Law anybody can become Jewish from one day to the next. How could one *become* Jewish if being Jewish depended on genetic, biological or racial criteria?

Additionally, if this genealogic or biological criterion had proven satisfactory, despite its tremendous complexity, wouldn't the question of Judaism and Jewish identity have been laid to rest a long time ago? To the contrary, the question has always been a burning point of debate among Jews themselves, and not only in 1930s Poland, as in the joke I have recounted, but in contemporary life. And it remains, of course, a major question for non-Jews.


## It's a Jew!

> Israelite, *noun (1583; from Israel). A descendant of the Hebrew patriarch Jacob; a native or inhabitant of the ancient northern kingdom of Israel.*
> Merriam-Webster Dictionary

Jewish identity is a question neither of essence nor of exterior signs. Jewishness is not visible.

Evidently, if Jews were so outwardly recognizable or remarkable, it would not have been necessary to attempt to mark Jews with distinctive signs to establish them as different from the rest of the population for so many centuries. We must indeed recall that over several periods in history, in a wide variety of countries, Jews were made to bear distinctive symbols. In the Middle Ages, in France, Spain, and Italy, Jews were legally required to wear a yellow badge in the form of a wheel on their chests (along with a yellow hat). The Catholic Church and, particularly, the Pope wanted Jews to be easily identifiable, especially so unions between Jews and Christians could be avoided. On the occasion of the Fourth Lateran Council in 1215, Pope Innocent III published a decree ordering Jews to wear different clothes than Christians. The specific goal of this decree was to prevent marriages between Jews and Christians. The 1267 Council of Vienna ordered Jews to wear a specific hat, the *Judenhut*.

In 1269, the French King Louis IX, or Saint Louis, ordered Jews to wear two yellow symbols, one on their backs and one on their chests, starting from the age of 14.[1] Women were also required to wear a special hat. (In the following century, the yellow badge was replaced by a large circle divided into a red section and a white one). Yet all this singling out of Jews through their clothing was progressively abandoned in Europe. By the sixteenth century, all these special garments, hats, and symbols had disappeared throughout the continent, except for Venice, where it remained obligatory to wear the hat until the end of the eighteenth century.

In the countries of the Maghreb, Jews were ordered to make themselves recognizable by wearing a special black tunic occasionally accompanied by a black hat. This arrangement lasted until the colonial period and, in some areas, into the colonial period. It is probably superfluous to mention the notorious yellow star used in Hitler's Nazi Germany.

Of course, one frequently hears phrases such as Jews are like this, Jews are like that, he's a real Jew! All these forms of speech about Jews are caricatures. Not only are they slanderous and malicious, but they are indicative of anti-Semitism and racism. I say this in the most serious, thought-out terms.

These caricatures can be found in humorous form, such as in anti-Semitic propaganda (as used by the Nazis, for instance), which displays supposed Jewish traits by accentuating them. In the case of jokes, this frequently leads to laughter at the Jewish people's expense, which unconsciously reinforces anti-Semitic hatred.

A Jew wearing a pointy hat brings the Pascal Lamb into the synagogue.
Illustration by Nicolas of Verdun (1150–1205).

## Jewish Humor and Anti-Semitic Humor

> *Hell is not a place of pain.* It is a place where we are made to suffer.
> Edmond Jabès, *Building Daily, The Book of Margins III*

Clear distinctions can be made between a Jewish joke, a joke about Jews, and an anti-Semitic joke. In a Jewish joke, the description of the Jew does not attempt to lock him into stereotypical criteria: money, appearance. The Jewish joke uses stereotypes to blow them apart, allowing laughter to call things into question. On the other hand, the anti-Semitic or racist joke fixes the identity of a given group, whether it be Jewish, Corsican, Belgian, or Swiss, and uses "humor" to circulate formulas and rumors which lock the group in question further into reductive, slanderous images. *"Why do Jews have big noses? Because air is free!"* A typical example of an anti-Semitic joke. This type of caricature represents a linguistic and ideological cul-de-sac.

78

## Jewish Identity According to Hebraic Law: The Classical Approach

> *Secrets are always in the shape of an ear.*
> Jean Cocteau

Hebraic Law is drawn directly from the Biblical texts, as commented upon in the Talmud (between the second century and the sixth century) and by masters of the Talmudic tradition stretching to the present day. Talmudic commentaries range from those of Rashi (eleventh century) to Maimonides's *Mishnah Torah* code of laws, from Rabbi Joseph Caro's *Shulchan Arukh* (sixteenth century) to the jurisprudence laid down by Gaon of Vilna's *Responsa* (eighteenth century) and by Rav Jehiel Jacob Weinberg (twentieth century). Hebraic Law states that Judaism is transmitted by the mother. According to this ruling, there are therefore two cases in which children are Jewish:
–when both parents are Jewish.
–when the mother is Jewish, even if the father is not.

If the father is Jewish, and the mother is not, the child is not Jewish. This can of course lead to complex questions regarding one's identity, questions which have developed into classic psychoanalysis cases. The problem is a genuine one, particularly because it is often through its name that a child identifies itself and is identified by others, and that name is, of course, the family name passed on by the father. One can easily imagine that a young man or young woman whose mother is not Jewish but whose name is Cohen or Levy (or any other name identifiable as Jewish) could feel Jewish, either because that is its family's chosen lifestyle, or because that is the social image the child's name projects. And yet according to classical Hebraic jurisdiction these children are not Jewish.

First of all, I believe it is important to explain the reason for this law of filiation, in order to allow children and parents to clearly understand the texts of Jewish law which, in a way, they are asking to subscribe to by undergoing a bar mitzvah or a bat mitzvah.

## Filiation in the Biblical Era

> *One day,*
> *One day soon, perhaps,*
> *One day I'll tear out the anchor that keeps my*
> *ship far from the seas ...*
>
> Henri Michaux, *Paintings*

It appears that this filiation "via the mother" is sometimes due to a mistaken understanding of the meaning of the Talmudic texts. In Biblical times, filiation was paternal. A single example among the many available would be the wedding of Moses and an Ethiopian woman, the daughter of a Madian priest. The Bible makes no mention of her conversion. At the time, the principle of a "patrilocal" union was in force. The bride was "sought out" and "chosen" in her father's home and was then taken away from her father's clan to join her husband's. It is true, however, that in general the choice of a bride was made within the groom's clan, whether she was a close relative or a distant one.

Batik on silk representing the seven-pronged candelabra which symbolized the light of the Divine Infinity in Temple. Today it is the symbol of the state of Israel.

## Filiation in the Talmudic Era

*As the poet well knows,*
*there is an inconsolable eternity*
*between the one who gives and the one who receives,*
*between the one who talks and the one who listens.*

Roberto Juarroz, *Vertical Poetry*

In *Kiddushin*, the Mishna seems to teach that in Hebraic Law religious filiation is through the father. Thus, in the case of a Jewish marriage (in which both spouses are Jewish), religious filiation is through the father, since the marriage is within the bounds of "Hebraic Law." In the case of an exogamic marriage, a marriage outside the community, whether it is the father or the mother who is Jewish, the situation is no longer within the bounds of Hebraic Law and filiation through the father is therefore no longer applicable. The child thus inherits its religious identity by default, from its mother. If the mother is Jewish, so is the child, by default. In the opposite case, the child follows the mother's religious tradition, also by default, and can therefore not follow the paternal filiation and be considered a Jew.

We now have three types of standard cases:

–Both parents are Jewish, the child is Jewish.
–The mother is Jewish and the father is not, the child is Jewish.
–The father is Jewish and the mother is not, the child is not Jewish.

An interesting fourth type of case is worth mentioning:

–Neither parent is Jewish, neither is the child, but he or she decides to become Jewish...

81

## Filiation Today

*"Who is Jewish?" In my opinion, the question is not only purely a philosophical one, but also a historical question, or, if you'd rather, a histori-sophical question. I speak as a Jew who is convinced that Judaism is a spiritual phenomenon, a living organism. For most of us, Judaism has become an open, living organism that is not clearly defined. It is a changing phenomenon, one that transforms itself over the course of its own history. Our generation's scholarly research has allowed for the discovery of deep new dimensions, full of life in motion, in what we call Judaism.*

Gershom Scholem, "The Price of Israel," *Political Writings*

Though today most communities follow the consensual filiation through the mother, certain liberal and secular communities have proposed a redefinition of the Jewish identity. For instance, secular Jews have declared: "In the name of the historical experience of the Jewish people, we declare that a Jew is any individual of Jewish ancestry or any person who declares himself or herself a Jew and identifies with the history, the ethical values, the culture, the civilization, the community, and the destiny of the Jewish people."[3]

*The Swarm Guides the Children of Israel,* Marc Chagall (1887–1985).

# Conversion to Judaism

*Whether you write a novel, a poem, or a critical essay, you're always doing the same thing. To write is to ask a question. There are men whose job is to answer questions, to solve problems. It is the job of the politician and the mathematician, the engineer and the surveyor to have an answer for every question. On the other hand, it is the job of the novelist, the poet and the critic to question everything, to question themselves and everything that surrounds them, to call into question what no one would have thought to call into question. They are the world's great askers of questions.*

Claude Roy

Nonetheless, generally speaking, the law of religious and cultural filiation has not changed and continues to stipulate, as I have just mentioned, that filiation takes place through the father in the case of a marriage under Hebraic Law (both spouses are Jewish) and through the mother in the case of a marriage outside of Hebraic Law (one of the spouses is not Jewish).

The only difference between the different currents of Judaism concerning this question is the degree of ease offered to convert, generally before marriage. Orthodox Judaism, which dictates that conversion involve a genuine commitment not only to the values of Judaism but also to its practices, requires that those wishing to convert follow a long course of study and that they learn the religious practices. Additionally, the Orthodox rabbinate only considers conversions made out of love for Judaism as genuine, and frequently refuses those conversions made for conjugal reasons. Therefore, conversion is not offered in a majority of cases when a man or woman requests to be converted in order to marry a Jewish spouse. For this current of Orthodox Judaism, since preparation for conversion can last several years, the persistence of the potential convert is in and of itself a sign of genuine commitment.

83

## The Conversion Ceremony

*—Rabbi, Rabbi, asks the child, why are all men different?*
*—Because they are all in God's image.*

After the convert's long, arduous preparation, the conversion ceremonial takes place in two phases: the boy or the grown man is circumcised, a procedure which consists of the cutting of the foreskin, the skin which covers the glans, and not, as circulated by many prejudiced opinions, of the removal of part of the sexual organ. Once the cut has healed over, the convert bathes in the mikvah, or ritual bath, a natural pool filled with spring water, rainwater, or river water, "living water" which symbolizes life. (Christianity has retained certain of these practices in the baptism ritual.) Given that sexual circumcision does not apply to women, the only ritual ceremony for female conversion is immersion in the mikvah.

Judaic Law is exactly the same in the Conservative and Reform movements, with the exception that the requirements for conversion are more relaxed. Individuals wishing to convert by religious conviction or in order to get married in a Judaic context are quite readily accepted. These movements' preparations for conversion are far more concerned with history, and with learning Hebrew and Judaic philosophy, than with religious practice, though that subject is included in the initial preparatory courses.

Conversion follows the same ceremonial steps of circumcision and the mikvah in Reform, Conservative, and Orthodox practice. However, in the Reform and Conservative movements, circumcision often takes place in a medical setting and the ritual bath (which must always take place before witnesses) can be officiated over by female rabbis.

85

The mikvah in France's oldest synagogue, in Carpentras.

## An Important Parental Decision

> *It is good to love: for love is difficult. The love of one human being*
> *for another may be the most difficult challenge presented to each and*
> *every one of us, it may be the highest testimonial to ourselves; that*
> *supreme achievement for which all other achievements are mere*
> *training... Love is not only to give oneself over to another,*
> *to unite with another. Love is a unique opportunity to mature,*
> *to take shape, to become a world for the love of the beloved.*
> *Love is the most rigorous demand, the most limitless ambition,*
> *a force which turns the one who loves into a member of the elect*
> *who hear the call of the wild.*

Rainer-Maria Rilke

What is the significance of converting for a Jewish marriage? It is not purely a case of following social conventions in order to please one of the spouses' families. It is primarily a question of wanting to provide the couple's future children with a clear identity. A couple chooses to commit to specific values, which can be passed on to young people and provide them with a solid foundation on which to mature. Experience shows that when a child grows into adulthood at the heart of tensions between strongly contradictory religious traditions, no matter how beautiful and intelligent the traditions in question, a whole variety of inexorably complex existential questions always arise.

# Preparation for Bar Mitzvah and Conversion

*A highly progressive, completely atheistic American Jew decided to provide a first-class education for his son. He sent him to one of the best schools in New York called Trinity, which had previously been a religious school but was now secular. After a few days, Danny came home and proudly told his father:*
*—Dad, now I know what the Trinity is: it's the Father, the Son, and the Holy Ghost!*
*The father, seeing his deepest secular convictions under assault, flew into a terrible rage:*
*—Danny, get this straight: we only have one God, and we don't believe in him!*

Children must follow preparatory classes for the bar and bat mitzvahs. By doing so, they commit to leading a Jewish life in practice and to adopting Jewish values. But what of the children who aren't considered Jews according to the ruling Hebraic Law? In their case, the preparation for bar mitzvah can be considered a preparation for conversion. In cases where the father is Jewish, the preparation can be seen as a regularization of the child's identity, if that is his or her choice and/or the choice of both parents. If the rituals have not yet been followed, by the day of the bar mitzvah, boys must have been circumcised and both boys and girls must have bathed in the mikvah.

## Thinking within the Perspective of Judaism

> *To consider Judaism as a science, to analyze Judaism, is to turn its texts into teaching texts again. To date, the Talmudic texts have never been taken seriously in the Occident. Their truth is recognized when they coincide with the most common common sense; the still unfinished dialogue they establish with the world they put into question remains unperceived. Pure philology, which is not sufficient to understand Goethe, is not sufficient to analyze the intellects of Rabbi Akiba or Rabbi Tarphon. If we want to be Jewish, the time has finally come to allow Rabbi Akiba and Rabbi Tarphon to speak, that is to say, to claim them as our own.*
>
> Emmanuel Lévinas, *Difficult Freedom*

There is no Jewish nature, no Jewish soul, no Jewish spirit, no Jewish genes, no Jewish blood, etc. At the risk of shocking my readers, I will also recall that there is no Jewish God! There is no Jewish being, but a Jewish way of being. There is a Jewish existence, a Jewish people, a Jewish fact, a Jewish culture, Jewish languages, Jewish texts, a Jewish message, a Jewish ideal... Thinking within the perspective of Judaism is to choose openness and dialogue, and to reject idols, fixed concepts, prejudices, and certain fixed ways of thinking...

Thinking within the perspective of Judaism is a continued defeat of the human folly which persists in locking people into stereotypes in order to single them out and exclude them. It is a way out of the lure of definitions, of categorizing people and things, of stamping and locking them into little boxes of concepts, little boxes of inflexible, rote thinking.

Thinking within the perspective of Judaism is, according to a beautiful phrase of Bergson's, "to enter into History, which is the constant renewal of unpredictable novelty." It is to demand a flexible, vigilant way of thinking which sticks closely to reality, and is ready if necessary to follow and channel reality. Thought must be risked, and that risk is the unpredictable.

*Jacob's Struggle with the Angel,* Rembrandt (1606–1669).
Though Christian iconography refers to an "angel," Genesis (32:14)
refers to a struggle between Jacob and "Man."

## Hebraism, Israelites, and Jewishness

> *Each generation must maintain the strength to question the world
> in new ways. It is not a question of automatically rejecting what
> was said in the past as if the past should automatically be passed
> over. To understand Aristotle, Maimonides, Hegel, or Rabbi Akiva
> is to rediscover the questions they asked themselves and to measure
> to what extent they are still our questions; it is to think them anew,
> by fully accepting them; it is to open a dialogue with them, and
> therefore to have a dialogue through them, with ourselves and our
> contemporaries, in full conscience of the differences in historical
> situations, but also of the trans-historical dimension which connects
> these various discourses and allows them to communicate, without
> projecting a unification of meaning.*
>
> Eric Weil

To close this chapter, I would like to add some final remarks concerning the various appellations at the heart of this question of identity. Indeed, people seem unable to clearly distinguish the terms Jew, Israelite, Hebrew, and Israeli. What does "Hebrew" mean? The word, which has its root in *laavor*, "to cross," means that to live is to cross, to get to the other side of the river. It is to resist ideology, along with collective and social watchwords. This is the significance of Abraham's monotheism. The "mono" of monotheism is justified by that solitary way of thinking in which a man has found his path and has gathered the strength to say it aloud and share it, without doing violence.

Monotheism is the opposite of being locked into an ideology: it is the ability to get out of all ideologies. "Go for yourself, leave the house of your father, your fatherland, your motherland, and go to the land that I will show you" (Genesis 12:1). The significance of the divine, and of its transcendence, is in this exit and movement towards. Isn't it interesting to note that the word God, *El*, means "in the direction," "towards"?

One of the commentaries says that the word Israel can be read *li rosh*, "I have a head." That head represents the pride of the man standing up straight, dignified and vertical. It is the pride of the subject who holds himself upright and openly announces the way he has chosen to think and to feel,[4] without going against the principles of intelligence and complexity. It is the pride of the man who advances unmasked, face to face.[5]

To be upright and face the truth requires a continuous dialogue with one's self, with others, and with the world. These qualities necessitate great caution in order to avoid making mistakes or locking one's self into one's blindness. They also require a language that says what it must without causing harm.

"Jewishness" is the result of this entire adventure into honesty, to which the essential feeling of recognition of the Other must also be added. The latter feeling allows us to grow and discover the beauty and power of what is alive. "Jewish" is actually an adjective. The Hebrew *yehudi* comes from Yehuda, the name of one of Jacob's twelve sons. It comes from the same root as *lehodot*, to thank, or to be thankful, as does the word *todah*, or thank you. Man is "Jewish" when he knows how to express his gratitude, when he knows how to say "thank you."

1. Why yellow? For Christians, yellow also symbolized betrayal: like the Jews, Judas was represented in a yellow robe. Toward the end of the Middle Ages, yellow was associated with physical disorders and insanity: jesters and dwarves were dressed in yellow (the yellow dwarf). Yellow was associated with Lucifer, with sulfur and with traitors.
2. See, for instance, Father R. Dan, *Histoire de la Barbarie* (History of Barbarity), Paris, 1637, p.98: "They can be discerned by the black hats which they are obliged to wear, and by the rest of their clothing."
3. Resolution adopted by the second international conference of the International Federation of Humanist Secular Jews (Brussels, Belgium, September 30th–October 1st, 1988).
4. This is the significance of the wearing and visibility of the tefillin on the forehead and between the eyes.
5. In *Patrimony: A True Story*, Vintage, 1996, Philip Roth mentions that under the Third Reich, all Jewish men were forced to enter the middle name "Israel" in their passports.

3

# The Synagogue

*"Where does God live?"*
*The Rabbi of Kotzk's unexpected question surprised*
*the group of scholarly characters he had invited to join*
*him for dinner.*
*The wise men mocked him:*
*"What kind of question is that? Isn't the world full of*
*His magnificence?"*
*But the Rabbi answered his own question:*
*"God lives where He is invited in."*

Martin Buber

# Chapter Three

The Word "Synagogue"

**When Were the First Synagogues Built?**

The Minyan or the Assembly of Ten

**The Synagogue as Place of Life and Gathering**

Synagogue Architecture

**Synagogues and Jewish Humor**

Synagogue and Study House

## The Word "Synagogue"

*The awareness of thresholds could shift our attention from one object to another (from one situation to another) in an entirely new way, then from this second object to yet another object, and so on and so forth until the moment arrives when the staircase of peace appears on earth.*
Peter Handke

The word "synagogue" comes from the low Latin *synagoga*, itself derived from the Greek *sunagogê*, or "gathering." This term was originally used by Greek Jews to refer to the gathering of the Jewish community and to the community itself. It was therefore initially used to refer to the Diaspora, particularly in Greek-speaking and Greek-cultured countries. In Hebrew, the synagogue is known as a *Beit Haknesset*, or "place of gathering." The Hebrew expression can also be accurately translated as "meeting room" or "community center," terms which closely describe the synagogue's prime contemporary function. Yet we must not overlook the fact that the synagogue is also a place for prayer.

# When Were the First Synagogues Built?

*In the future, the dew will wake the dead, as was written by the prophet Isaiah: For the dew that descends upon you is a dew of light.*
*Zohar III, 128 a and b*

In fact, historians do not agree on the date when the first synagogues began to appear. It is likely that the institution of the synagogue dates back to a time when the Jews, in exile from their native land and far from the rites of the Temple, searched for an alternative way of expressing themselves through prayer and of creating a gathering place for social exchanges. Following this theory, the exile in Babylon after 586 B.C.E. has been suggested as the period in which synagogues first appeared. This hypothesis tends to be confirmed by certain contemporaneous verses of the Prophet (see Ezekiel 8:1, 14:1, 20:1, and 11:16).

Other historians believe that the first synagogues either appeared earlier, around the time of the first Temple (before 586 B.C.E.), or more recently, during the Hellenistic or Hasmonean eras (second century B.C.E.).

However, a majority of estimates seem to suggest the first century C.E. as the most likely period. According to these estimates, synagogues would therefore have developed in Babylon, in Israel, and in other Diasporas while the Second Temple was still active. The Talmud, Philo of Alexandria, and the Gospel all mention the existence of synagogues in Jerusalem, Damascus, Rome, Cyprus, and Alexandria. However, the destruction of the Second Temple had a decisive impact on the spatial and liturgical structuring of synagogues. With the arrival of the synagogue, the sacrificial ritual was transformed into a liturgy of prayers, with the morning sacrifice becoming the morning prayer, the afternoon sacrifice the afternoon prayer, and so on.

View of the entrance to the synagogue of Bar'am (Israel), 3rd–4th century.

## The Minyan or the Assembly of Ten

*Pity the isolated, they grow foolish.*
Jeremiah 50:36

Following the destruction of the Temple, synagogues ushered in a great change in the Jewish faith by allowing it to evolve from a form of worship limited to priests to a liturgy accessible to all. While prayer had previously depended on the Temple to exist, it now allowed for the existence of the place of worship. Since that time, the only requirement to have a prayer assembly has been to gather a quorum of ten people. These ten people form the minyan or "quorum" necessary to consider that there is enough holiness or sense in the gathering to feel the expression of divine transcendence. In general, the minyan has always been exclusively composed of men, except in contemporary Reform and Conservative circles. It should be noted that the number ten can be found in numerous aspects of Jewish life and culture.

There are Ten Commandments, ten declarations of the Creation, and ten plagues of Egypt. This passing of religious legitimacy from the priesthood to the minyan is considered a democratization of the religion; a democratization which went untouched for many years, until the concept of the rabbi or the religious specialist was introduced. For many centuries, prayer and ritual were shared by all.

## The Synagogue as Place of Life and Gathering

*Man's sins against God are forgiven on the Day of Forgiveness; man's sins against his fellow man are not forgiven on the Day of Forgiveness, unless man has previously appeased his fellow man.*
Babylon Talmud, *Yoma* 85a–85b

As previously stated, the function of a synagogue is closest to that of a community center. It is first and foremost a social place. It is a place to pray, to meet people, to throw parties, to eat, to dance, and to study. Synagogues therefore include large rooms where these activities can take place, along with classrooms, a library, and, traditionally, an annex for the "ritual bath" or mikvah, and sometimes even a kitchen in which to prepare meals. In fact, the synagogue was long used as an inn for travelers passing through. Courts ruled (and continue to rule) in the synagogue, deciding on cases involving marriage, divorce, and commercial litigation. The synagogue has also become a place for young people and youth organizations to gather. Even recreational activities such as bridge and chess clubs may have their place in the synagogue. In short, it is a haven for people from the community to come together. The synagogue is organized like any other association, with its committees, its chairmen, its clerks, and its treasurers, and its active members and its honorary members.

## Synagogue Architecture

*The Temple was in the Book before the Book was in the Temple.*
Edmond Jabès

The first synagogues, which were uncovered in Galilee where Jews gathered after the destruction of the Second Temple in 70 C.E., share a single architectural style: a long central nave facing Jerusalem and two lateral aisles separated from the nave by pillars, which probably supported a gallery. Benches were set along the walls. Despite the distinctly sober interior architecture of these churches, numerous frescos and mosaics representing geometric shapes, men and animals, Israeli fruits, utensils used in the Temple, and symbols of the Zodiac have been uncovered.

No archeological discovery from this era has given any hint that women were allowed a place in the synagogue. Notable synagogues from the era include those in Baram, Kefar Nahum (Capernaum), and Bet Alpha in Israel, and those in Sardis (Turkey), Doura Europos (Syria), and Hammam-Lif (Tunisia).

In the Middle Ages, the synagogue continued to play the same role but assumed a more discrete presence in the Christian world. In an effort to make them blend in with the world surrounding them, synagogues were built in the Gothic and Roman styles and, in Spain, even in the Moorish style. The buildings' facades were passed over in favor of the Holy Ark, which was always placed at the front of the nave, facing Jerusalem, and lavished with artistic touches. As of this period, the central reading table, or bimah, took on a more important role, by being constructed on a platform accessed by steps or ramps. It was also during this period that the first spaces for women began to appear.

A few centuries later, Poland and Oriental Europe witnessed the birth of two new types of synagogues. As of the middle of the seventeenth century, synagogues began being constructed entirely of wood, with interior

Drawing depicting the synagogue-fortress in Luboml, Poland (18th century).

A watercolor depicting a wood synagogue in Wolpa, Poland (c. 1700).

decorations completely covering the walls and the ceilings. Fortified synagogues also became common. These synagogues had battlements behind
which the community could gather and protect itself in the case of an
attack. This type of architecture can still be found in certain synagogues
built by Eastern European communities in Israel. Aside from these "imposing" edifices, every village and, eventually, every city had small synagogues,
frequently limited to a single room, where people could gather in like-
minded groups to pray, recite Psalms, study, talk, and debate. These small
synagogues, or *shteeblach* (from the Yiddish *shteeb*, a room or home), were
the hubs of an entire popular culture based on folkloric tales, songs,
and the discovery of a spirituality spread through Eastern Europe by
Hasidism between the end of the eighteenth century and the beginning
of the twentieth century. Unfortunately, the vast majority of the small
synagogues disappeared during the Holocaust.

As of the nineteenth century, a greater public recognition of Jews, notably
through Napoleon's creation of Jewish institutions (particularly the
Consistory) and the birth of religious reform, led to modifications in
synagogue architecture. Everything became more ostentatious and

imposing. Vast synagogues were built. Some, such as the synagogue on rue des Tournelles, in Paris, had galleries on three levels. These grandiosely designed, beautiful new synagogues began to be referred to as "Temples." Sadly, many of these great European synagogues were also burned and destroyed by the Nazis.

Today, both in the United States and in Europe, the synagogue has returned to its original function as a community center. The social dimension has a greater significance than the religious dimension, except in Israeli synagogues, where the synagogue has remained a place of prayer and worship, with community and social activities being spread over other locations. In the large modern American synagogues frequently associated with the Reform and Conservative movements, there is no longer any separation between men and women.

Over the years, organs and other musical instruments have been introduced in many of these synagogues, largely in imitation of churches and in an effort to heighten the enjoyment and beauty of worship. Interior decoration remains sober, even when great artists are called upon to execute it. Chagall, for instance, designed the stained glass windows for the small synagogue in the Hadassah hospital in Jerusalem. Some elements of synagogue architecture have remained constant: the Holy Ark facing Jerusalem at the front of the space, and the reading table in the center. One also frequently finds a small niche accessed by a discrete staircase, from which the rabbi, the bar mitzvah or the bat mitzvah make their speeches. Ornamentation is frequently limited to large seven-or nine-branched candelabra reminiscent of the Menorah in the Temple of Jerusalem and of the miracle of Chanukah.

Holy ark on the east-facing wall of a synagogue.

## Synagogues and Jewish Humor

> *The practice of Talmudic exegesis of the Biblical texts has taught us that we become so attached to the letter of the fundamental texts to better make them say something that comes from somewhere else.*
>
> Henri Atlan, *Between Crystal and Smoke*

The most surprising thing about synagogues is that they have been at the heart of the development of a whole realm of humor. Jewish jokes thrive in synagogues, including jokes about the synagogues themselves. The following jokes provide a few examples, to be told during a bar mitzvah...in the synagogue, of course!

On Rosh Hashanah, a man rushed into the synagogue, knocking into the *shamash* (the verger) as he entered. "Hey! What about your ticket," the *shamash* called after him. (On holidays, synagogues attempt to deal with the crowds by selling tickets which serve as reservations. Those who have not reserved are unlikely to find a place to sit in the main sanctuary. Adjunct services accommodate the overflow crowds.) "Oh, I don't have a ticket, but I must absolutely see Moshe Cohen. I'll be right out."
"You can't go in without a ticket," the *shamash* answered categorically. "I'm telling you it's an emergency! I'll be right out!" "OK, fine, go ahead," said the *shamash* with a sigh. "But don't let me catch you praying!"[1]

The captain of a ship found a castaway who had been surviving on a tiny island deep in the middle of the Pacific Ocean for over five years. Robinson Crusoe a.k.a. Jeremy Horowitz honored the captain with a guided tour of the island: he had built himself a house and two synagogues, one at the bottom of a hill and one at the top. The captain was surprised: "Why on earth did you build two synagogues?" he asked.
"It's very simple!" Horowitz replied. "The one at the bottom of the

hill is the one I go to, and the one at the top is the one I wouldn't be caught dead in!"

⊙

The synagogue *shamash* couldn't take it anymore: the wedding had been over for two hours and still the guests lingered on in the reception hall, chatting away, with no intention of leaving anytime soon. Facing total despair, he called the rabbi. "What should I do, they won't leave!" he said. "Yell out: 'fire!'" replied the rabbi. "I tried that, but they wouldn't leave!" "Yell out: 'thief!' "I tried that too, but it didn't work." "All right, I have a better idea: ask for donations."

⊙

During a crucially important meeting between Yitzhak Rabin and Bill Clinton, Clinton suddenly leaned over to his Israeli counterpart and discretely asked him: "Tell me, Mr. Rabin, you Jewish people always have the upper hand in business, because you always know everything before everyone else. How is that?" Rabin thought a little, then answered: "Let me tell you why: when the Jews go to synagogue, on the Sabbath, it's to pray, but it's also to meet and do business. It all happens at the synagogue, believe me." Clinton immediately resolved to secretly go to synagogue on the next Sabbath. When the day came, he donned a fake beard, a white shirt, a suit, a yarmulke, and a hat to disguise himself as a Jew and went to one of the many synagogues in the big city. Though he was surprised to find a sense of religious silence hanging over the synagogue, Clinton waited to see what would happen. By the middle of the service, the faithful did not seem any more animated than they had at the beginning. The President leaned over to his neighbor and whispered in his ear. "What's the latest news?" The neighbor answered: "Shhhh! Bill Clinton is coming!"

## Synagogue and Study House

*If there is a world where the search for truth and rules for living leads us not to a world but to a book, to the mystery and command of a book, that world is clearly the world of Judaism. Judaism is the world where at the beginning of everything one finds the power of the Word and the Exegesis, where everything starts from a text and returns to it, a single book into which a prodigious series of books is wrapped up, a library beyond the universal, which replaces the universe with a vaster, deeper and more enigmatic entity.*

Maurice Blanchot, *From Kafka to Kafka*

In Orthodox Communities, the study house, or *beit hamidrash,* frequently doubles as a synagogue. These study rooms or study houses have not changed much over the centuries. The atmosphere found in the Polish, Russian, and Moroccan Yeshivas (Talmudic academies) of bygone centuries reigns more or less unchanged over today's study houses.[2] Stories and testimonials confirm this impression of timelessness and sometimes give us the impression of being drawn closer to some dimension known to the poets as eternity.

Disorder, chaos, vigorous gesticulating, incessant comings and goings: these are the telltale signs of the *beit hamidrash,* the study house which serves as a synagogue and, also, on numerous occasions, as a gathering room. Talmudic students do not share the monk's reserve. Silence is far from the golden rule.

On tables set in disarray across the room, stacks of volumes from the Torah, the *Shulchan Arukh,* and the works of Maimonides tower alongside copies of the *Gemarot.* Students sit, stand, or lean over their texts, side by side or, more frequently, face to face, and read aloud, swaying to and fro, side to side, to demonstrate their enthusiasm, punctuating the most difficult passages of the religious reasoning with aggressive thumbs-up and thumbs-down gestures, slapping the table or the books or even their colleagues' shoulders, feverishly leafing through the pages of the commentaries they grab from the shelves of the vast collection of books surrounding the room and shove back onto the shelf as quickly as they have found what they were looking for.

The protagonists of this "war of interpretation" are attempting to understand, to analyze, and to explain. As time passes, the noise gets

A section of the *Merkaz Harav beit hamidrash,* a yeshiva founded in Jerusalem by Rav Kook (1864-1935). Students work in teams of two as they pore over the Talmud.

louder and the room begins to throb with the sound of creaking chairs and student chatter. Several young people stand near the door, speaking at full volume and making eloquent hand gestures. In fact, the first-time visitor could easily mistake the study room for the heart of an amusement park, complete with the jittery, yapping crowd, and the yelling and gesticulating merchants and trinket sellers. The students, or *bachurim,* rarely agree on the meaning of the passage being studied. Thankfully, they often turn to an older or wiser student, who explains the passage and takes a position on the hypotheses being proposed, momentarily bringing a semblance of calm to the frantic battle of the consultants.

In those Talmudic academies based on the model of the famous Volozhin Yeshiva founded by Rabbi Chaim of Volozhin, studying is not only a science or an art, but the cosmic force that preserves the world. The study houses are therefore provided with guard towers, for even a momentary interruption of study could mean the end of the world. Everything always is moving! The *beit hamidrash* is the site of uninterrupted agitation. The voices and bustle of study ring out all day and all night.

Suddenly the noise is interrupted. There has been no signal, no request for silence: the noise comes to an end on its own, as if it had simply been cut off, as if a door had suddenly slammed shut on a room full of noisy children. The silence which follows all this noise has a strange quality: it is made of expectation, of fervor, of love, of respectful fear. A man slowly walks along the narrow central alley. He is wearing a black caftan and a black hat. As he passes each row of seats, the students rise, bow slightly, and return to their seats. The successive rising of the rows of students looks like the rising and falling of waves on a rough sea. The students have risen and returned to their seats as if guided by an invisible force! The master has passed by.

The Rabbi heads to the back of the *beit hamidrash* and takes a seat. A long, thick silence comes over the room. Nobody moves. The tremulous turning of pages is heard as the students open their books. The Master will soon speak. The lesson has begun.

*Yentl*, starring Barbra Streisand, adapted from the book of the same title by Isaac Bashevis Singer. Singer's *Yentl* argued for women's right to have access to the study of the Talmud in Poland at the beginning of the 20th century; today, study of the Talmud is increasingly open to women.

A synagogue in Carpentras, France.

1. I devoted a chapter to this subject in my book *Tout l'humour Juif* (Jewish Humor from A to Z), written with Dory Rotnemer (Assouline, 2001). Interested readers can refer to it for most of the jokes included in this volume.

2. To experience the atmosphere of the *beit hamidrash*, the reader would be well advised to reread Chaim Potok's famous book *The Chosen* (1967), which helped to inspire the following passage.

Barbra Streisand's beautiful film Yentl, drawn from the eponymous story by Isaac Bashevis Singer, also powerfully evokes the world of the *beit hamidrash*.

# 4

# The Kippah

*For or against God, but not without God.*
Elie Wiesel

# Chapter Four

A Portable Dome

**Priests' Kippot**

A Sign of Segregation

**Kippot For Everybody?**

Kippah Fashions

**Kippah and Bar Mitzvah**

# A Portable Dome

> *Tradition can be the noblest of freedoms for the generation that accepts it with a clear understanding of its meaning, but it can also be the most miserable enslavement for the man who takes up its heritage out of mere intellectual laziness.*
>
> Martin Buber

The kippah is a small hat worn by men and, in liberal circles, certain women, during worship, whether at home or in public. The word kippah comes from a word which means "to cover" and which, in architectural terms, refers to a dome. *Yarmulke* or *yarmulka*, the word for kippah in Yiddish, is quite close to the Hebraic or Aramaic *yirae malkah,* which means "fear of the king." To wear a kippah is a sign of humility, of recognition of one's limits, but also of respect for one's masters and parents, and, in a general sense, for one's elders and for scholars.

## Priests' Kippot

*Once the reader learns that the text is telling him about himself and his own history, he will immediately discover its multiple potential meanings. The reader will learn that the text offers him the nocturnal hush of his most distant, buried, unspeakable life, in coded terms that only he can decipher.*

Serge Viderman

Though it is now the emblematic, undisputed symbol of the Jewish world, the kippah was long controversial. The debate regarding the obligation to keep one's head covered, especially during prayer and study, divided rabbis for many centuries.[1] Indeed, aside from the fact that priests and the high priest used to wear ceremonial headgear, no Biblical source supports the custom of the kippah.[2] According to the Talmud, headgear was primarily worn by masters, as constant reminders of the divine presence above them, or, in other words, to demonstrate their submission, their respect, and their recognition of transcendence. A great part of domestic and synagogue worship is a transposition of Temple worship. It is therefore clear why the custom of wearing a kippah is interpreted by some authorities as applicable only to those moments of worship that take place inside the synagogue, during ceremonial study, and during meals.

## A Sign of Segregation

*It is forbidden to despair!*
Rabbi Nachman of Breslav

Another theory is that like many other Jewish customs, the kippah may have originated outside of Judaism. The kippah has been interpreted as a "residue" of regulations enforced by non-Jews.[3] It is interesting to note that these regulations imposed from outside the Jewish faith have become particularly honored customs, thoroughly integrated and accepted, as if they had originated from within the faith.

## Kippot For Everybody?

*Due to the body's projection into space, the act of walking includes a tremendous risk of falling for humans, a risk which is absent in animal locomotion. This risk alone suffices to qualify the initial appearance of man,* Homo itinerans *before* homo faber...

Antonietta and Gérard Haddad, *Freud en Italie, Psychanalyse du voyage* (Freud in Italy, Psychoanalysis of Travel)

In fact, nowadays the custom of the kippah is so profoundly rooted in Judaism that it is practically written in stone. Orthodox circles go so far as to believe that it must be worn at all times. Some even believe that the kippah is not sufficient for prayer, and that a hat must be worn over it. On the other end of the spectrum, among liberals, the rabbi is frequently the only one to wear a kippah. In fact, it is interesting to note that in these liberal circles, women are frequently those most attached to wearing the kippah, for they consider it a sign of equality between the genders, on the same level as the lack of segregation in seating between men and women in the synagogue.

As for wearing kippot (plural of kippah) in the work place or in public spaces, that depends on sociological habit. In the United States, particularly in New York, as well as in Antwerp, Belgium, the wearing of kippot is a habitual sight, whether on the trading floor, in the subway, or in public parks, and is therefore not subject to surprise or criticism.

In France, however, the question is more delicate, for the affirmation of one's religion is sometimes perceived as an aggressive assertion, particularly in the context of the law on veils and ostentatious religious symbols at school. Moreover, certain French Orthodox rabbis now believe that the kippah should be removed in situations where one wants to recognize someone else's authority or their professional competence, such as in a doctor's office. However, a rabbi should keep his kippah on when meeting with religious or political figures in a professional context.

117

Hand-embroidered modern kippah.
Often, the style of the kippah indicates the specific current of Judaism its wearer belongs to.

## Kippah Fashions

*Philosophers aspire to explain*
*the world in such a manner that everything becomes*
*clear and transparent and that life dissimulates*
*nothing (or as close to nothing as possible)*
*that is problematic or mysterious.*
*On the contrary, shouldn't*
*they strive to show that*
*what man conceives of as clear and*
*comprehensible is strangely*
*enigmatic and mysterious?*
*Shouldn't they attempt to deliver themselves*
*and others from the power*
*of concepts so clear they kill all mystery?*
*Indeed, man's sources are*
*in what is hidden,*
*not in what is discovered.*

Léon Chestov, *Athènes et Jérusalem* (Athens and Jerusalem)

As with all other garments, there are various kippah "fashions." The choice of a kippah style frequently reveals the wearer's affiliation with a specific religious or political group, particularly in Israel. The large black velvet or cloth kippah is the norm in ultra-Orthodox circles, while smaller black-knitted, or even leather or suede kippot, are common among Modern Orthodox Jews. Due to its discrete appearance, the latter kippah can often be mistaken for black hair. Kippot crocheted with various colors (often blue and white) and geometric shapes are often worn by religious Zionists, as is the large multi-color knit kippah, which is also worn by the Breslavs.[4] There are also large embroidered kippot made in the south of the ancient Soviet republics which have no specific political or religious connotations and merely represent an aesthetic variation. In fact, these kippot are worn indeterminately by men and by women.

## Kippah and Bar Mitzvah

*To lose hope is to lose a little of one's freedom,*
*a little of what one is.*

Rabbi Nachman of Breslav

On the day of the bar/bat mitzvah, all the men must have their heads covered during the ceremony. In Orthodox and traditional circles, women have their heads covered as well. In fact, the entrances of synagogues are frequently stocked with a box of kippot and head coverings for the forgetful. Moreover, a new kippah is traditionally purchased for bar mitzvah boys, (and for bat mitzvah girls, in certain liberal circles). It is also common for parents to have the name of the bar/bat mitzvah boy or girl, the date of the ceremony, and even the name of the parashah printed or embroidered on kippot which are offered to all their guests as souvenirs of the milestone in their children's lives.

1. See, for instance, *Beur Hagra, Orah Hayyim* 8:2.
2. Exodus, chapters 28 and 29, and Leviticus, chapter 8.
3. Such as the circular badge and the numerous other distinctive signs that Jews were made to wear so they could not integrate and mix with non-Jewish society.
4. Popular mystical movement made up of followers of Rabbi Nachman of Breslav.

5

# The Tallith

*A philosopher's footsteps always led him*
*to where children were playing.*
*He was constantly on the lookout for young boys*
*playing with spinning tops.*
*As soon as the top began to spin,*
*the philosopher would run to catch it,*
*totally disregarding the cries*
*of the children trying to keep him*
*away from their toy.*
*So long as he could catch the top*
*while it was spinning, he was happy.*
*But his joy only lasted an instant,*
*after which he threw the top back on the ground*
*and went on his way.*
*This philosopher believed*
*that knowledge of something*
*as minor as the rotation of a spinning top*
*was sufficient to have all-encompassing knowledge.*
*This was why he never turned his attention*
*to greater problems.*
*He believed his method was more economical.*
*If one could truly understand the smallest object,*
*one could understand everything.*
*This was why he only occupied himself*
*with the rotation of the top."*

Franz Kafka

# Chapter Five

From Birth to "Beyond Death"

**Tzitzit or Ritual Fringes**

In the Freshness of the Morning Dew

**The Benediction of the Tallith**

Etymology of the Word Tallith

**The Tallith and the Flag of the State of Israel**

Like Desert Nomads

**The Four Corners of the Earth**

The Tallith and Peace

**The Tallith as Reparation of Slander**

The Birds of the Tallith

## From Birth to "Beyond Death"

> *Speak unto the children of Israel, and bid them that they make them throughout their generations fringes on the corners of their garments, and that they put with the fringe of each corner a thread of blue.*
> Numbers 15:38

On the day of their bar or bat mitzvah, young men and women wear the tallith for the first time. From that day on, they will be required to wear the tallith for *Shacharit*, or the Morning Prayer, every day for the rest of their

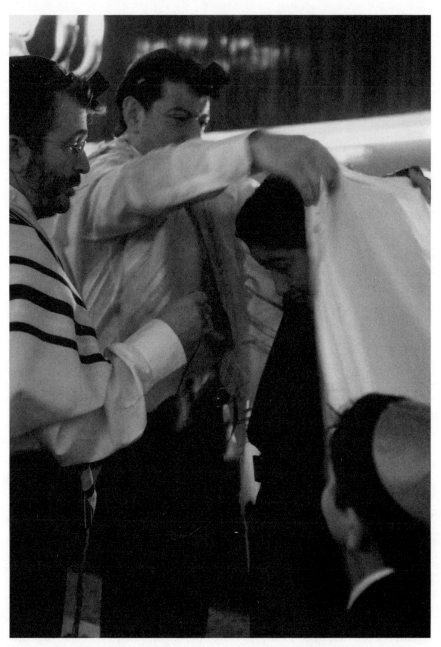

The rabbi and the bar mitzvah boy's father wrap him in the tallith for the first time.

lives. They will also wear the tallith once a year on the evening of Yom Kippur. The tallith accompanies Jewish worshippers throughout their lives, and even beyond, as Jews are buried with their talliths.

The tallith is a prayer shawl. There are two types of talliths: the small tallith, or *tallit katan,* which is worn all day, under one's clothes, and the large tallith, or *tallit gadol,* which is only worn for morning prayer and a few other important events.

The first chapter offered a brief anthropological and psychoanalytic interpretation of the tallith by exploring attachment and detachment, the meaning of the hair, and its mutation into the "symbolic hair" of the tallith's fringes. We will now approach the tallith in a more phenomenological manner, with a detailed description of this aspect of Judaic worship, interspersed with commentaries intended to complete our overview.

## Tzitzit or Ritual Fringes

> *Raba said: As a reward for our Father Abraham having said: "be it a thread, be it the strap of a sandal" (Genesis 14:23), Abraham obtained two commandments: the "sky blue thread" (the Tzitzit) commandment and the "strap of the tefillin" (phylacteries) commandment.*
> Babylonian Talmud, *Hulin,* 88b–89a

The tallith is a cloth square or rectangle made of white wool or silk. It frequently features black or blue stripes. Its corners are lined with ritual wool fringes known as tzitzit.

Each fringe consists of four threads. In ancient times, the longest of the threads was colored sky blue, or *tekhelet.*

The "blue" of the *tekhelet* thread was obtained from sea animals that spit ink out to momentarily blind their attackers and allow themselves a window to escape danger.

The Masters of the Talmud say that the thread's blue evokes the sea, which evokes the sky. The sky evokes the color of the Divine Throne, which in turn evokes the Divine Presence, and thereby opens the doors of infinity to us.

## In the Freshness of the Morning Dew

*Each person born to this world represents something new, something which didn't exist before, something original and unique.*
*Each individual man is a new creature in this world, and he is called upon to fulfill his particular role in this world. This was the idea that Rabbi Zusya expressed shortly before his death: "In the otherworld, I will not be asked: Why weren't you Moses, but why weren't you Zusya?"*

Martin Buber

The Torah refers to "fringes" or tzitzit (Numbers 15:38), to "cords," or *gedilim* (Deuteronomy 22:12), and to "threads" or *petil.*
Fringes (the tzitzit) are twisted, knotted, wound, and woven through an intricate pattern of folds to create a mass of fabric at each corner of the shawl. The fringes are a symbolic way of writing God's name through the Hebrew relationship between numbers and letters. In Hebrew, the Tetragrammaton (the four-letter name of God considered too holy to pronounce) is written YHVH. The letters correspond to the following numbers:

128

$Y = 10$; $H = 5$; $V = 6$; $H = 5$; which add up to a total of $26$.

Therefore, to make the tzitzit, four long threads are passed through holes at each corner of the shawl. There are then four threads on each side, eight threads in all. Two knots are made, after which the longest thread is wrapped around the other seven threads. It is wrapped around 10 times, then another two knots are made. Then the thread is wrapped around another 5 times, and another two knots are made. The thread is wrapped around 6 more times, and two knots are made. Finally, it is wrapped around another 5 times and the last two knots are made. The tallith is now a garment on which God's name has been written in each corner.
In the Ashkenazi tradition, the number of times the thread is wrapped around the other threads is different. The same principle of knots and repeated wrappings is followed, but the thread is wrapped around the shorter threads 7 times, then 8, 11, and 13 times, which corresponds to the expression "God is one," YHVH EHAD, the numeric equivalent of

During the Shema prayer, the tzitzit are held in the right hand and respectfully kissed each time the word "tzitzit" is pronounced.

which is 39 (7 + 8 + 11 + 13). The number 39 is written *tal* (*Tet* = 9 and the letter *Lamed* = 30). This numeric symbolism is behind the prayer shawl's name, tallith, the bearer of the number 39 *(tal)*. And since the word *tal* means "the dew," the tallith, a garment of dew, opens the door to a poetics of morning freshness, a leitmotif which appears throughout the Bible and, particularly, in the Prophets. The Prophet Hosea's famous statement resonates profoundly in this particular case: "I will be like the dew to Israel," *Eheyeh ketal leyisrael.* (Hosea 14:6. Also see Isaiah 26:19).

The word "dew" became a synonym for "God is one" and also for God in motion, for 39 is also the numeric value of the divine name *Kuzu*, which can be obtained by moving the name YHVH, i.e. by transferring letters within the alphabet. Y becomes K, H becomes V (u), V becomes Z and H becomes V (u). The name *Kuzu* is found throughout the Kabbalah as a reminder of the perpetual dynamics of the living and the transcendent.[1]

Therefore, wearing and wrapping oneself in the tallith is a way of entering into the dynamics of life and language, of life through language in motion!

## The Benediction of the Tallith

Before wrapping one's self in the Tallith, one pronounces the following benediction:

בָּרוּךְ אַתָּה, יְהוָה, אֱלֹהֵינוּ מֶלֶךְ הָעוֹלָם אֲשֶׁר קִדְּשָׁנוּ בְּמִצְוֹתָיו וְצִוָּנוּ לְהִתְעַטֵּף בְּצִיצִית.

Transliteration:
*Barukh ata, Adonai, Elohenou melekh ha'olam, asher kideshanu bemitsvotav vetsivanu lehitatef betzitzit.*

Translation:
Blessed are you Adonai, our God, King of the universe who sanctifies us with his commandments and commanded us to wrap ourselves with the tzitzit.

## Etymology of the Word Tallith

*My fabric of reference was not a veil or a canvas, but a shawl. It's a prayer shawl I prefer to touch than to look at. I like to caress it every day, to kiss it without even opening my eyes, or even while it remains in a paper bag into which I plunge my hand in the middle of the night, with my eyes closed.*

Jacques Derrida and Hélène Cixous, *Veils*

The word tallith is not strictly speaking a Biblical word. It entered the Hebraic language sometime later. Its root is *tal,* derived from the hebrew letters *tet* and *lamed,* which means "the dew," a word we discovered in the previous passage.

The roots of the word tallith can also be found in the word *tlai,* which means a small piece of fabric or leather sewn onto a torn garment or over a hole in a shoe. This yellow patch was the forebear of the yellow badge worn by Jews in the Middle Ages, and of the yellow star forced upon them in the twentieth century.

We also find the verb *tileh,* which means "to patch up, to mend, to fix, to repair, etc." *Talu* means to be "spotted," the way a horse or any other animal might be, and, by extension, the way an outfit might have different colored patches. *Taleh, Talia* means the "little lamb." The *tal* root with a double *lamed* makes *tillel,* "to cover," "to make shade," "to make a roof," etc. It is what covers. Therefore, a tablecloth is called *teli,* which also means "to make the dew come down."

The double *tal* root in the word *tiltel* means "to carry," "to move an object from one place to another," an idea also found in the words *tiyel* and *tayal,* "to take a walk," "a walker." "Movable objects" and "movable property" are referred to as *metaltalin.*

131

## The Tallith and the Flag of the State of Israel

*Anti-Semitism, hatred towards the Jewish people,*
*has been and remains a blot on the soul of mankind.*
*So know also this: anti-Zionist is inherently anti-Semitic,*
*and will ever be so.*

Martin Luther King, 1967

The relationship between the tallith and the "yellow star" can be found, with a subtle but saving difference, in the contemporary Israeli flag, which was intentionally conceived as a tallith, with the sky blue of transcendence replacing the yellow of humiliation, thereby sweeping away anti-Semitism, that ever-present ontological form of slander.

Therefore, to reflect on the tallith "today" is to take responsibility for reflecting on human history, a responsibility at the core of history.

The bar mitzvah boy or bat mitzvah girl automatically faces this question, for this "Star of David" is one of the primary symbols of a Jewish adolescent's entry into the community of adults and responsibility. It can be found carved into stone or wood walls, embroidered on the curtains of the Holy Ark, and on the "jackets" of the books of the Torah, or printed on the pages of prayer books and of the Torah.

## Like Desert Nomads

*Blue does not make a sound...Blue indefinitely slips away.*
*It is not, strictly speaking, a color. It is rather a tonality, a climate, a*
*special resonance of the air. It is an accumulation of clarity, a tint born*
*of the void added to the void, as amorphous and transparent in the*
*mind as in the sky.*

Jean-Michel Maulpoix

The tallith is worn throughout prayer. Before placing it on one's shoulders, one covers one's head with it like desert nomads drape their heads to protect

*Magen David* or Star of David.
The most famous symbol of Judaism, the Star of David first appeared in the 14th century
as a protection against the devil and the forces of evil. Though it became an infamous symbol of
humiliation during the Second World War, today the *Magen David* represents redemption.

themselves from the wind, the sand, and the sun. Wrapped in his tallith, man can meditate as if he was in the arid solitude of the desert. As Théodore Monod wrote in *La grâce de la solitude* (The Grace of Solitude, Éditions Dervy, 1998): "In the desert, the biggest thing is the silence. It's perfect there... there isn't any noise! In that kind of silence, you quickly realize that you aren't the center of the world! Life in the desert is very beneficial for learning humility. You discover how tiny you are in the context of the area, and that you are here to obey, not to command." This remark will probably remind the reader that the words bar mitzvah expresses this idea of "being here to obey," of "being ordered," rather than commanding. By placing himself under the tallith, man hears the call of responsibility. In the solitude brought by wrapping the tallith around his head at the beginning of the prayer, at the beginning of the day, man hears his own name resounding ...Moses, Moses ...and Moses answers: "Here am I" (Exodus 3:4). In the solitude of the tallith, man masters his silence. Then, he learns to listen.

## The Four Corners of the Earth

*I study ancient Hebrew because the books of the Mikra are marvelous.*
*I have been able to tentatively approach a language that is the mother*
*of the sacred. I don't feel like I belong to any community or people, but*
*I do belong to this book.*

Erri De Luca

While reading the Shema, the prayer which includes the Biblical passage featuring the law of the tallith (Numbers 15:37–41), the worshipper gathers the tallith's four corners and its ritual fringes in a single hand. As the Vilna Gaon[2] pointed out, this is a way of showing that man brings the four corners of the earth, the whole of humanity, together in his prayer, and that it is only through words that he can find the keys that open the doors to the heavens.

The tallith reminds man of his origins: he is "born of the earth." On this subject, Rashi of Troyes (1040–1105) said something which I consider highly significant:

"What does *dust of the earth* mean? It means that God has taken and assembled dust from the four corners of the earth so that no matter where he dies, the earth will welcome him and offer him a sepulture."

Here Rashi states that man is not made of dust or earth from a particular place, but that he finds his origins in "the four corners of the earth." That is to say that no place of birth has any privilege over any other. No point of origin is better than or superior to any other! No death is superior, and neither is any dead man!

## The Tallith and Peace

> *In and of himself, man is nothing. He is merely an infinite chance. But he is infinitely responsible for that chance.*
> Albert Camus

Earth does not belong to man. Man belongs to the earth, and no earth, no color of earth or color of man born from the earth justifies violence against another man. This is exactly what Rashi makes clear by continuing his commentary with another quote from the Midrash. The word "earth," *adamah,* refers to verse 21, chapter 20, of Exodus, which states that if you want to pay tribute to God through an act of worship, you shall build an altar of earth (*adamah*) and not an altar of hewn stone, for to carve it you will have used your sword and will therefore have polluted the sanctity of the divine. The use of *adama,* in these commentaries very clearly opposes the violence of the sword.

A man of the earth is a man of peace!

And Rashi adds: "May this dust of peace always offer forgiveness to man so that he may continue to hold himself upright, as a human." The "dust of *adamah*" clearly signals a non-violent ethic in place from the birth of man.

## The Tallith as Reparation of Slander

*I can still see this father, though by definition, by the situation we were in, I did not see him then. He blesses his sons who are now bigger than he is, raising his tallith over their heads with both his arms. Bigger than he is and bigger than one another, the sons nearly stifle under the solemn protection, under the roof of that nearby temple, during the interminable prayer in what was called the "great temple," an old mosque in the heart of the Arab quarter that was once Judeo-Arab, a Spanish-style mosque that has since been turned back into a mosque.*

Jacques Derrida and Hélène Cixous, *Veils*

The Talmud states that the tallith is a *tikkun*, a "reparation" of slander. Indeed, whenever slander is mentioned in the Bible, a certain number of elements worthy of analysis always appear. These elements touch on sexuality, in particular the question of virginity, and on thresholds and borders. The issue of clothing, and particularly of the prayer shawl or tallith,[3] systematically recurs in this context.

The fringes of the tallith compose a text made by the knotting of the threads, by a process of weaving and twisting which cannot fail to evoke a form of intelligence not satisfied simply to perceive, understand, and analyze things, but which must connect, weave and twist them together, to offer a complex texture of thought. To quote Roland Barthes, "each thread, each code is a voice; these woven—or weaving—voices form the text: alone, the voice does not work, it does not transform anything: it expresses, but as soon as the hand intervenes to assemble and intertwine the inert threads, there is work, there is transformation."[4]

Therefore, through this science of knots, there is a reparation of slander. Slander is a reduction of the world's complexity! It is a way of thinking that one can grasp the world through ideas and words, when in fact the world can only ever be approached, perhaps caressed. Something always escapes.

# The Birds of the Tallith

*I practically never wear the tallith...I just touch it with my fingers or my lips, nearly every night, except when I'm traveling to the other end of the world, while the tallith waits for me, like an animal, hiding in its hiding place, at home. It never travels. I touch it without knowing what I'm doing or what I'm asking for, without knowing, especially, whom I am placing my faith in, without knowing whom I am honoring.*

Jacques Derrida and Hélène Cixous, *Veils*

I frequently think that the tallith a worshipper wraps himself in is like a cocoon in which man transforms himself into a butterfly through the power of the words of the prayer. In fact, this conception of taking flight is not absent from the rite of the tallith, for each of its corners is known as a *kanaf,* or "wing." Knowing that, one begins to think of the crow and the dove that Noah sent to find out whether the waters from the flood had started to recede and the world could begin to exist again. One thinks of those birds as being somewhat like black ink on a white page, the two colors found on the stripes of the tallith.

So everything happens as if the prayer was indeed that moment of meditation which allows man to take flight, to find one's elevation and transcendence.

If you want to do it, you will be able to...
Son of man, look!
Contemplate the light of the Presence that resides in all that exists
Contemplate the joyous force of life in the worlds above!
See how it descends and fills every parcel of life that you
perceive with the eyes of your flesh and the eyes of your spirit.
Contemplate the marvels of Creation
and the Source of all that lives, which sets the rhythm of every
creature.
Learn to know yourself.
Learn to know the world, your world.
Discover the logic of your heart and the feelings of your mind!
Feel the vibrations of the Source of Life which
is in your depths
and above you

and all around you.
Feel the vibrations,
The glory of the generations of life,
In which you take your place.
Let the love that burns within you rise up,
Let it rise towards its powerful root,
Towards the subtle enjoyment of its splendor.
Spread to the soul of every world.
Look at the lights
Look inside the lights...
Do not let the names, the buds and the words swallow your soul
They are transmitted to you but you do not belong to them.
Rise and rise,
For you possess a powerful force,
You have wings of wind
Noble eagle wings...
Do not renounce them, for fear that they will renounce you.
Search for them and immediately they will find you ...

Rav Kook, *Orot Hakodesh*, I, 64

1. See my book *Mysteries of the Kabbalah,* Abbeville Press, 2000, p. 399.
2. A leader of the Talmudic and Kabbalistic Lithuanian current of which Emmanuel Lévinas was an important proponent.
3. See, for instance, Genesis 37:1; Numbers chapters 12 to 16; and Deuteronomy 22:12. It should also be noted that the slandering of Joseph is followed by the episode of the many-colored tunic, that the slandering of Miriam and the explorers is followed by the mitzvah of the tallith and precedes the slandering of the Torah, and that the slandering of the disappointed husband is preceded by the mitzvah of the tzitzit.
4. Barthes, *S/Z,* in a paragraph entitled "The Weave," pp. 165 and 166, quoted by Zagdanski in *L'impureté de Dieu* (The Impurity of God), pp. 52 and 53.

6

# The Tefillin

## Anatomy of a Symbol

*If Judaism is destined
to have any meaning for us,
it is to show us
that we must always be ready
to pick up and leave,
because leaving (going outside of)
is the inescapable requirement
if we wish to maintain the possibility
of a relationship of justice.
Requirement of uprooting,
affirmation of nomad truth.*

Maurice Blanchot, *L'Entretien infini* (The Infinite
Conversation)

# Chapter Six

Boxes, Straps, and Parchment

**The Verticalization of Man**

The Four Texts Written Inside the Tefillin

**Two Types of Parchment**

The Phenomenology of the Divine: A Dialectic of the "One" and the "Four"

**The Mystery of the Letter *Shin***

"The Day of the Tefillin"

**The Benedictions**

"Phylacteries"

**The Meaning of the Word Tefillin in Hebrew**

The Meaning of the Rite of the Tefillin

*Vehigadetah levinekha*

*Veamarta*

***Veshinantam Levanekha, Vedibarta Bam***

*Velimadeta*

**The Tefillin of Rashi and Rabenu Tam**

History and Memory

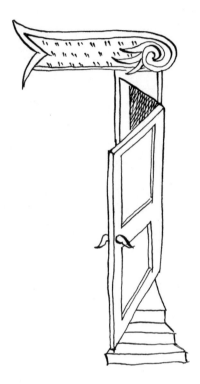

## Boxes, Straps, and Parchment

*The face of man is the proof of God's existence.*
Max Picard

Tefillin are small black leather boxes, through which black leather straps are passed. The box is composed of three parts: the top cube, known as the *bayit*; the base, known as the *titura*; and the small opening through which the straps are threaded, known as the *mahabarta*.
One of the boxes is worn on the arm, on the bicep, (on the left arm for right-handed worshippers, and on the right arm for the left-handed). The other box is worn on the forehead, between the eyes. Both boxes are held in place

The *titura, bayit,* and *mahabarta* of the tefillin.

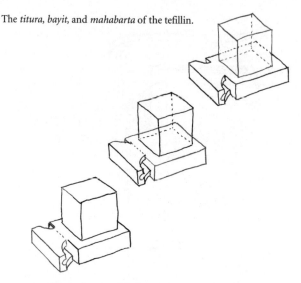

by leather straps, the *retzuot,* which are wrapped onto the head or arm following a specific ritual.

144

## The Verticalization of Man

*What differentiates man from animal*
*is that man is capable of risk, and therefore of falling.*
*If one does not take the risk to risk,*
*one remains in the certainty of the assured gait, the animal's gait.*
*One remains in the 'programmed' and the 'predictable.'*
*Yet the essence of man's intelligence is the ability to escape the*
*programmed,*
*that is to say, to take risks.*

Michel Serres, *En amour sommes-nous des bêtes?* (In Love, Are We Animals?)

The arm-tefillin (*tefillin shel yad*) and the head-tefillin (*tefillin shel rosh*) articulate action and thought, which is essential to the idea of responsibility: do not engage in any action unworthy of the vigilance of your thoughts and the greatness of your intelligence! Tefillin also implement two poles, a high and a low, which offer a means of reflecting on and experiencing verticality. To wear tefillin is to move from a horizontal vision of the world to a vertical way of thinking. The tefillin straps link the two poles and give the wearer a sense of flow, of circulation, and of energy moving, rising, and filling with meaning, giving man strength and freedom. In fact, the concept of freedom is one of the principal themes of the four passages of the tefillin.

In Hebrew, "vertical" is *anakh,* and "I" or "I am" is *anokhi,* which specifically means "I am standing upright in my verticality." The verticality provided by the tefillin allows man to say "I." Through the tefillin, man reaches the dimension of being himself, and becomes a true "subject."

## The Four Texts Written Inside the Tefillin

> *And a river went out of Eden to water the garden; and from thence it was parted, and became into four heads.*
> Genesis 2:10

145

And these boxes are not empty! They contain four passages from the Torah, handwritten in ink on parchment paper. Each passage evokes the mitzvah, or obligation, to wear tefillin. These four passages are:

Exodus 13:1–10;
Exodus 13:11–16;
Deuteronomy 6:4–9;
Deuteronomy 11:13–21.

פרשת "שמע"

(דברים, ואתחנן, פרק ו, פסוקים ד-ט)

שְׁמַע יִשְׂרָאֵל. יְיָ אֱלֹהֵינוּ, יְיָ אֶחָד: וְאָהַבְתָּ אֵת יְיָ אֱלֹהֶיךָ, בְּכָל לְבָבְךָ וּבְכָל נַפְשְׁךָ וּבְכָל מְאֹדֶךָ: וְהָיוּ הַדְּבָרִים הָאֵלֶּה, אֲשֶׁר אָנֹכִי מְצַוְּךָ הַיּוֹם, עַל לְבָבֶךָ: וְשִׁנַּנְתָּם לְבָנֶיךָ וְדִבַּרְתָּ בָּם, בְּשִׁבְתְּךָ בְּבֵיתֶךָ, וּבְלֶכְתְּךָ בַדֶּרֶךְ, וּבְשָׁכְבְּךָ וּבְקוּמֶךָ: וּקְשַׁרְתָּם לְאוֹת עַל יָדֶךָ, וְהָיוּ לְטֹטָפֹת בֵּין עֵינֶיךָ: וּכְתַבְתָּם עַל מְזֻזוֹת בֵּיתֶךָ וּבִשְׁעָרֶיךָ:

פרשת "והיה אם שמע"

(דברים, עקב, פרק יא, פסוקים יג-כא)

וְהָיָה, אִם שָׁמֹעַ תִּשְׁמְעוּ אֶל מִצְוֹתַי, אֲשֶׁר אָנֹכִי מְצַוֶּה אֶתְכֶם הַיּוֹם, לְאַהֲבָה אֶת יְיָ אֱלֹהֵיכֶם וּלְעָבְדוֹ בְּכָל לְבַבְכֶם וּבְכָל נַפְשְׁכֶם: וְנָתַתִּי מְטַר אַרְצְכֶם בְּעִתּוֹ, יוֹרֶה וּמַלְקוֹשׁ, וְאָסַפְתָּ דְגָנֶךָ וְתִירֹשְׁךָ וְיִצְהָרֶךָ: וְנָתַתִּי עֵשֶׂב בְּשָׂדְךָ לִבְהֶמְתֶּךָ, וְאָכַלְתָּ וְשָׂבָעְתָּ: הִשָּׁמְרוּ לָכֶם פֶּן יִפְתֶּה לְבַבְכֶם, וְסַרְתֶּם וַעֲבַדְתֶּם אֱלֹהִים אֲחֵרִים וְהִשְׁתַּחֲוִיתֶם לָהֶם: וְחָרָה אַף יְיָ בָּכֶם, וְעָצַר אֶת הַשָּׁמַיִם וְלֹא יִהְיֶה מָטָר, וְהָאֲדָמָה לֹא תִתֵּן אֶת יְבוּלָהּ, וַאֲבַדְתֶּם מְהֵרָה מֵעַל הָאָרֶץ הַטֹּבָה, אֲשֶׁר יְיָ נֹתֵן לָכֶם: וְשַׂמְתֶּם אֶת דְּבָרַי אֵלֶּה עַל לְבַבְכֶם וְעַל נַפְשְׁכֶם, וּקְשַׁרְתֶּם אֹתָם לְאוֹת עַל יֶדְכֶם, וְהָיוּ לְטוֹטָפֹת בֵּין עֵינֵיכֶם: וְלִמַּדְתֶּם אֹתָם אֶת בְּנֵיכֶם לְדַבֵּר בָּם, בְּשִׁבְתְּךָ בְּבֵיתֶךָ, וּבְלֶכְתְּךָ בַדֶּרֶךְ, וּבְשָׁכְבְּךָ וּבְקוּמֶךָ: וּכְתַבְתָּם עַל מְזֻזוֹת בֵּיתֶךָ וּבִשְׁעָרֶיךָ: לְמַעַן יִרְבּוּ יְמֵיכֶם וִימֵי בְנֵיכֶם עַל הָאֲדָמָה אֲשֶׁר נִשְׁבַּע יְיָ לַאֲבֹתֵיכֶם לָתֵת לָהֶם, כִּימֵי הַשָּׁמַיִם עַל הָאָרֶץ:

Right to left :
Deuteronomy 6: 4–9; Deuteronomy 6:13–21.

פרשת "והיה כי יביאך"
(שמות, בא, פרק יג, פסוקים יא-טז)

פרשת "קדש לי"
(שמות, בא, פרק יג, פסוקים א-י)

וְהָיָה כִּי יְבִאֲךָ יְיָ אֶל אֶרֶץ הַכְּנַעֲנִי
כַּאֲשֶׁר נִשְׁבַּע לְךָ וְלַאֲבֹתֶיךָ, וּנְתָנָהּ לָךְ:
וְהַעֲבַרְתָּ כָל פֶּטֶר רֶחֶם לַיְיָ, וְכָל פֶּטֶר
שֶׁגֶר בְּהֵמָה אֲשֶׁר יִהְיֶה לְךָ הַזְּכָרִים
לַיְיָ: וְכָל פֶּטֶר חֲמֹר תִּפְדֶּה בְשֶׂה, וְאִם
לֹא תִפְדֶּה וַעֲרַפְתּוֹ, וְכֹל בְּכוֹר אָדָם
בְּבָנֶיךָ תִּפְדֶּה: וְהָיָה כִּי יִשְׁאָלְךָ בִנְךָ
מָחָר לֵאמֹר מַה-זֹּאת, וְאָמַרְתָּ אֵלָיו,
בְּחֹזֶק יָד הוֹצִיאָנוּ יְיָ מִמִּצְרַיִם מִבֵּית
עֲבָדִים: וַיְהִי כִּי הִקְשָׁה פַרְעֹה לְשַׁלְּחֵנוּ,
וַיַּהֲרֹג יְיָ כָּל בְּכוֹר בְּאֶרֶץ מִצְרַיִם,
מִבְּכֹר אָדָם וְעַד בְּכוֹר בְּהֵמָה, עַל כֵּן
אֲנִי זֹבֵחַ לַיְיָ כָּל פֶּטֶר רֶחֶם הַזְּכָרִים
וְכָל בְּכוֹר בָּנַי אֶפְדֶּה: וְהָיָה לְאוֹת עַל
יָדְכָה וּלְטוֹטָפֹת בֵּין עֵינֶיךָ, כִּי בְּחֹזֶק יָד
הוֹצִיאָנוּ יְיָ מִמִּצְרָיִם:

וַיְדַבֵּר יְיָ אֶל מֹשֶׁה לֵּאמֹר: קַדֶּשׁ-לִי
כָל בְּכוֹר פֶּטֶר כָּל רֶחֶם בִּבְנֵי יִשְׂרָאֵל
בָּאָדָם וּבַבְּהֵמָה לִי הוּא: וַיֹּאמֶר מֹשֶׁה
אֶל הָעָם זָכוֹר אֶת הַיּוֹם הַזֶּה אֲשֶׁר
יְצָאתֶם מִמִּצְרַיִם מִבֵּית עֲבָדִים, כִּי
בְּחֹזֶק יָד הוֹצִיא יְיָ אֶתְכֶם מִזֶּה, וְלֹא
יֵאָכֵל חָמֵץ: הַיּוֹם אַתֶּם יֹצְאִים, בְּחֹדֶשׁ
הָאָבִיב: וְהָיָה כִי יְבִיאֲךָ יְיָ אֶל אֶרֶץ
הַכְּנַעֲנִי וְהַחִתִּי וְהָאֱמֹרִי וְהַחִוִּי וְהַיְבוּסִי,
אֲשֶׁר נִשְׁבַּע לַאֲבֹתֶיךָ לָתֶת לָךְ, אֶרֶץ זָבַת
חָלָב וּדְבָשׁ, וְעָבַדְתָּ אֶת הָעֲבֹדָה הַזֹּאת
בַּחֹדֶשׁ הַזֶּה: שִׁבְעַת יָמִים תֹּאכַל מַצֹּת,
וּבַיּוֹם הַשְּׁבִיעִי חַג לַיְיָ: מַצּוֹת יֵאָכֵל אֵת
שִׁבְעַת הַיָּמִים, וְלֹא יֵרָאֶה לְךָ חָמֵץ וְלֹא
יֵרָאֶה לְךָ שְׂאֹר בְּכָל גְּבֻלֶךָ: וְהִגַּדְתָּ לְבִנְךָ
בַּיּוֹם הַהוּא לֵאמֹר, בַּעֲבוּר זֶה עָשָׂה יְיָ
לִי בְּצֵאתִי מִמִּצְרָיִם: וְהָיָה לְךָ לְאוֹת
עַל יָדְךָ וּלְזִכָּרוֹן בֵּין עֵינֶיךָ, לְמַעַן תִּהְיֶה
תּוֹרַת יְיָ בְּפִיךָ, כִּי בְּיָד חֲזָקָה הוֹצִאֲךָ
יְיָ מִמִּצְרָיִם: וְשָׁמַרְתָּ אֶת הַחֻקָּה הַזֹּאת
לְמוֹעֲדָהּ, מִיָּמִים יָמִימָה:

Translation of the first text:

*Parashat Kadesh*

(Exodus, *Bo* 13:1–10)

1. And the LORD spoke unto Moses, saying:

2. Sanctify unto Me all the first-born, whatsoever openeth the womb among the children of Israel, both of man and of beast, it is Mine.

3. And Moses said unto the people: Remember this day, in which ye came out from Egypt, out of the house of bondage; for by strength of hand the LORD brought you out from this place; there shall no leavened bread be eaten.

4. This day ye go forth in the month Aviv.

5 And it shall be when the LORD shall bring thee into the land of the Canaanite, and the Hittite, and the Amorite, and the Hivite, and the Jebusite, which He swore unto thy fathers to give thee, a land flowing with milk and honey, that thou shalt keep this service in this month.

6. Seven days thou shalt eat unleavened bread, and in the seventh day shall be a feast to the LORD.

7. Unleavened bread shall be eaten throughout the seven days; and there shall no leavened bread be seen with thee, neither shall there be leaven seen with thee, in all thy borders.

8. And thou shalt tell thy son in that day, saying: It is because of that which the LORD did for me when I came forth out of Egypt.

9. And it shall be for a sign unto thee upon thy hand, and for a memorial between thine eyes, that the law of the LORD may be in thy mouth; for with a strong hand hath the LORD brought thee out of Egypt.

10. Thou shalt therefore keep this ordinance in its season from year to year.

Translation of the second text:

*Parashat Vehaya Ki Yeviakha*

(Exodus, *Bo* 13:11–16)

11. And it shall be when the LORD shall bring thee into the land of the Canaanite, as He swore unto thee and to thy fathers, and shall give it thee.

12. That thou shalt set apart unto the LORD all that openeth the womb; every firstling that is a male, which thou hast coming of a beast, shall be the LORD'S.

13. And every firstling of an ass thou shalt redeem with a lamb; and if thou wilt not redeem it, then thou shalt break its neck; and all the first-born of man among thy sons shalt thou redeem.

14. And it shall be when thy son asketh thee in time to come, saying: What is this? that thou shalt say unto him: By strength of hand the LORD brought us out from Egypt, from the house of bondage;

15. And it came to pass, when Pharaoh would hardly let us go that the LORD slew all the firstborn in the land of Egypt, both the first-born of man, and the first-born of beast; therefore I sacrifice to the LORD all that openeth the womb, being males; but all the first-born of my sons I redeem.

16. And it shall be for a sign upon thy hand, and for frontlets between thine eyes; for by strength of hand the LORD brought us forth out of Egypt.

Translation of the third text:

*Parashat Shema*

(Deuteronomy *Vaethanan,* 6:4–9)

4. Hear, O Israel: the LORD our God, the LORD is one.

5. And thou shalt love the LORD thy God with all thy heart, and with all thy soul, and with all thy might.

6. And these words, which I command thee this day, shall be upon thy heart;

7. and thou shalt teach them diligently unto thy children, and shalt talk of them when thou sittest in thy house, and when thou walkest by the way, and when thou liest down, and when thou risest up.

8. And thou shalt bind them for a sign upon thy hand, and they shall be for frontlets between thine eyes.

9. And thou shalt write them upon the door-posts of thy house, and upon thy gates.

Translation of the forth text:

*Parashat Vehaya Im Shamoa*

(Deuteronomy *Ekev,* 11:13–21)

13. And it shall come to pass, if ye shall hearken diligently unto My commandments which I command you this day, to love the LORD your God, and to serve Him with all your heart and with all your soul,

14. that I will give the rain of your land in its season, the former rain and the latter rain, that thou mayest gather in thy corn, and thy wine, and thine oil.

15. And I will give grass in thy fields for thy cattle, and thou shalt eat and be satisfied.

16. Take heed to yourselves, lest your heart be deceived, and ye turn aside, and serve other gods, and worship them;

17. and the anger of the LORD be kindled against you, and He shut up the heaven, so that there shall be no rain, and the ground shall not yield her fruit; and ye perish quickly from off the good land which the LORD giveth you.

18. Therefore shall ye lay up these My words in your heart and in your soul; and ye shall bind them for a sign upon your hand, and they shall be for frontlets between your eyes.

19. And ye shall teach them your children, talking of them, when thou sittest in thy house, and when thou walkest by the way, and when thou liest down, and when thou risest up.

20. And thou shalt write them upon the door-posts of thy house, and upon thy gates;

21. that your days may be multiplied, and the days of your children, upon the land which the LORD swore unto your fathers to give them, as the days of the heavens above the earth.

## Two Types of Parchment

> *A work is eternal,*
> *not because it imposes a single meaning upon different men,*
> *but because it suggests different meanings to a single man!*
>
> Roland Barthes, *Criticism and Truth*

The four passages are written on a single parchment for the arm-tefillin, and on four separate parchments for the head-tefillin. There is a space inside the arm-tefillin box in which a single rolled-up parchment bearing four Biblical passages can be fit.

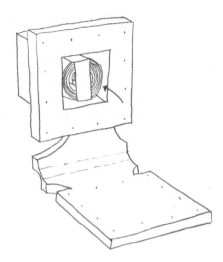

Arm-tefillin containing a scroll on which
the four Biblical passages are written.

The head-tefillin (*tefillin shel rosh*) box, which is also cubic, is actually composed of four compartments created by the folding of the leather into a coiled shape. Here, the four Biblical passages are written on individual parchments and placed in separate compartments.

151

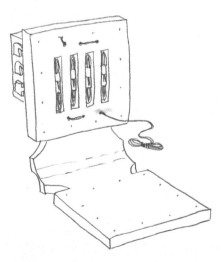

Head-tefillin.
Here, the four passages are written on four
separate parchments.

The number of lines on each parchment is identical in tefillin throughout the world. There are four lines per head-tefillin parchment and seven lines devoted to the passages on the arm-tefillin parchment.

The word "seven" in Hebrew means "oath." The arm-tefillin's seven lines therefore represent an action, a commitment, and a connection to responsibility. Tefillin initiate a way of relating to the world and to others while respecting one's own duties. In cases when it is impossible to respect one's commitments, head-tefillin, which are worn "up in the open," show the necessity to confront the situation not by running, but by dialogue and explanation. These essential concepts hold a particular didactic value for the bar mitzvah boy or bat mitzvah girl.

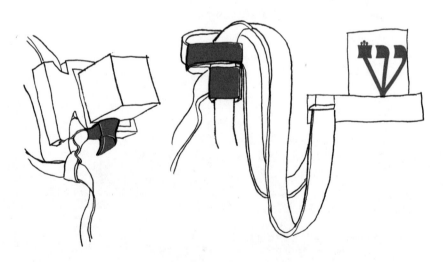

The head-tefillin and arm-tefillin are held in place by leather straps. The knots and the engraved *shin* spell the name of God, *Shaddai.*

# The Phenomenology of the Divine:
## A Dialectic of the "One" and the "Four"

> *The poetic, he says, is not vague impression, some sort of indefinable element conveniently referred to as an abstraction of the prosaic. The poetic is very precisely the symbolic capacity of a form. This capacity only has any value if it allows the form to take off in a great number of directions, thereby powerfully manifesting the infinity of the symbol, which can never be made into a final signifier, but is always the signifier of another signifier.*
>
> Roland Barthes, *The Responsibility of Forms*

The passage from the single parchment of the arm-tefillin to the four parchments of the head-tefillin reflects the symbolic system of what can be called the phenomenology of the divine in Hebraic tradition. Phenomenology refers to unveiling, expressing, revealing, and bringing to light, to clarity. In Judaism, the divine "One" always reveals itself in "fours." Examples include the divine Tetragrammaton and the river that goes out of Eden to water the garden and splits into four heads (Genesis 2:10). Similarly, any verse, word, letter, or reality has four levels of interpretation (the theory of Pardes). By comparison, it could be said that in Christianity the phenomenology of the divine is in the passage from "One" to "three," of which the Holy Trinity is the most famous example.

153

## The Mystery of the Letter Shin

*Tefillin teach a different logic, the logic of 6=7, an entirely different logic, which functions on the basis of thought association. A poetry of the living, of the strange and the astonishing, of the imagination. There is yet another logic, the logic of the heart and the emotions, and all those logics which open us up to the depths of our existence. He who does not know how to see a star in every face, will never discover the riches of his own skies!*

Mordechai Yankelevitch

The letter *shin* is engraved in the leather on both sides of the head-tefillin. On the right side, it is three-pronged, and on the left side it is four-pronged. Following the previous section, it would be logical to assume that the tefillin teach the passage from three to four. In fact, it seems that the *shins* are not different, but that one is visible black on white, and that the other is white inside the black. This double inscribing of the shin underlines the importance of having an eye for subtlety. In the words of Rabbi Levi Itzhak of Berditchev: "When the Messiah comes, we will not read the words that are written but the white spaces between the letters and the words."

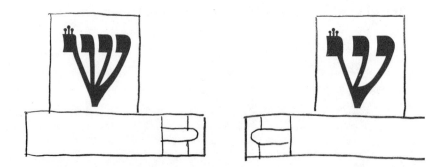

Three and four-pronged *shin* embossed on head-tefillin (Sephardic tradition).

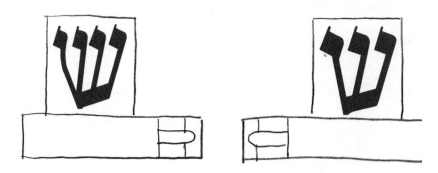

Three and four-pronged *shin* embossed on head-tefillin (Ashkenazi tradition).

## "The Day of the Tefillin"

*To have an understanding with the angel, our primary concern.*
René Char, *Fureur et Mystère* (Furor and Mystery)

The day of the bar mitzvah is the first day the child wears the tefillin. As tefillin are not worn on Saturdays (Shabbat), it is traditional to celebrate this initial donning of the tefillin on a Monday or a Thursday, days on which there is a reading of the Torah.[1] In certain traditions, the child begins to wear the tefillin a few months before he turns thirteen. This celebration is simply known as "the day of the tefillin." Following this ceremony in the synagogue, a small (or large) kiddush, a reception with refreshments, is generally served. Traditional specialty dishes are often included.

The grandfather or father begins by showing the bar mitzvah boy or bat mitzvah girl how to put on the tefillin. Then the whole family joins in. Each member of the family feels honored to help the young man or woman place the tefillin on his or her head and arms and properly wrap the straps.

## The Benedictions

Before the tefillin are put on, the following benedictions are pronounced:

בָּרוּךְ אַתָּה, יְהֹוָה, אֱלֹהֵינוּ מֶלֶךְ הָעוֹלָם אֲשֶׁר קִדְּשָׁנוּ
בְּמִצְוֹתָיו וְצִוָּנוּ לְהָנִיחַ תְּפִלִּין.

Transliteration:
*Baroukh ata, Adonai, Elohenu melekh haolam, asher kideshanu bemitzvotav vetzivanu lehaniach tefillin.*

Translation:
Blessed are You, Lord our God, King of the universe, who has sanctified us with His commandments, and commanded us to put on Tefillin.

The strap is wrapped around the arm seven or eight times. The head-tefillin are put on. In the Ashkenazi tradition, or if one has spoken after putting on the arm-tefillin, the following blessing is recited:

בָּרוּךְ אַתָּה יְהֹוָה, אֱלֹהֵינוּ מֶלֶךְ הָעוֹלָם, אֲשֶׁר קִדְּשָׁנוּ
בְּמִצְוֹתָיו וְצִוָּנוּ עַל מִצְוַת תְּפִילִין.

Transliteration :
*Baroukh ata Adonai, Elohenou melekh haolam, asher kideshanu bemitzvotav, vetzivanu al mitzvat tefillin.*

Translation:
Blessed are you, Lord, our God, King of the universe, Who has sanctified us with His commandments and has commanded us regarding the commandment of tefillin.

The hand-tefillin are wrapped once from the wrist to the point between the thumb and index finger, then three times around the middle finger (to create what looks like the letter *dalet*), then once going back down from there to the point between the thumb and index finger, and several times around the entire hand. While wrapping around the middle finger, it is customary to recite:

וְאֵרַשְׂתִּיךְ לִי לְעוֹלָם, וְאֵרַשְׂתִּיךְ לִי בְּצֶדֶק וּבְמִשְׁפָּט וּבְחֶסֶד וּבְרַחֲמִים: וְאֵרַשְׂתִּיךְ לִי בֶּאֱמוּנָה, וְיָדַעַתְּ אֶת־יְהֹוָה:

Transliteration:
*Ve'erastikh li le'olam, ve'erastikh li betzedek uvemishpat uvchesed uverachamim. ve'erastikh li be'emunah, veyadata ete Adonaï.*

Translation:
And I will betroth you to myself forever; and I will betroth you to myself in righteousness and in justice, in kindness and in mercy; and I will betroth you to myself in faithfulness, and you will know God.

## "Phylacteries"

*The true philosophical depth of a philosophy can be measured by its currency. The purest tribute to a philosophy would be to mix it with the burning issues of the day.*

Emmanuel Lévinas

In English, the word tefillin is translated as "phylacteries."

PHYLACTERIES the etymological modification (1553) of the ancient fila-tiere (c. 1155), filatire (c. 1200), an adapted borrowing from the late Latin *phylacterium*= "amulet" (the Latin amuletum was used to trans-late the Greek phulaktêrion) and, in Christendom, "shrine, reliquary." The word was also used to describe a fragment of parchment inscribed with verses from the Bible worn by Jews on their foreheads and arms

during prayer. This Latin word is a borrowing from the Greek *phulak-têrion*, "place to store, safekeeping" and "amulet," which took on the meaning borrowed by Christian Latin in the New Testament. The Greek word results in the Aramaic tefillin and is derived from *phulattein*, "to stand guard, to guard, protect, conserve," drawn from *phulax, -alios*, "guard, sentinel," and, by extension, "an object which protects," particularly, "a bandage." Despite its great age, *phulax* remains unexplained: a connection with pulê, "door," cannot be considered; the second element of the Latin *bu-bulcus*, "herdsman", *subulcus*, "swineherd" has also been suggested, placing -fulcus in relation to the Greek *phulakos* (which would therefore be prior to *phulax*). In ancient Christian liturgy, it initially referred to a reliquary holding relics of a saint. That usage no longer exists. In the sixteenth century, the word was used as a term of Greco-Roman antiquity to refer to a talisman or an amulet. In the Jewish religion, through a second borrowing from the Greek and from the Latin, it has taken the meaning "parchment on which the chapters of the Law are written" (c. 1200). Later (1861, Goncourt), it entered art history terminology as the term for the small banderoles which bore inscriptions in Medieval and Renaissance artwork (20th century).
*Le Robert* (Dictionary of history of the French language), V. II

It is always fascinating to refer to a historical language dictionary. I was not expecting to discover such rich information concerning the word *phylactère* when I opened the *Robert,* the historical dictionary of the French language. It is fascinating to see that certain Greek word relations can only be understood on the basis of Hebrew, and, more specifically, Hebraic rites. This is the case, for instance, with *phulax*, which, it seems to me, originates with *pûlé*, the "door," through the rite of mezuzah, the small parchment which serves, among other things, "to guard and protect the home and its inhabitants" and which is placed on the right hand side of the front door lintel.

Strip from the comic book by Joann Sfar, *The Rabbi's Cat*, V. I: The Bar Mitzvah .

Mezuzah case bearing the word *Shaddai*, one of God's names. According to tradition, the mezuzah protects homes.

## The Meaning of the Word "Tefillin" in Hebrew

*Can the God of the wars of religion be the God of religion?*
Léon Brunschvicg

The "in" ending of the word tefillin dates back to the implementation of the Mishna (the oral law dating back to the era of Moses). The singular of tefillin, tefillah, means "prayer." Its root, *pallal*, means "to judge," that is to draw into one's self to understand one's self and sum up one's life. In Hebrew, one of tefillah's anagrams is *petilah*, which refers to a candlewick. The tefillah of the tefillin is a foundation for the flame of the living.

## The Meaning of the Rite of the Tefillin
### The Teachings of the Father

*Man's relationship to the body of a woman*
*is always like a reunion.*
*Woman's relationship to the body of a man*
*is always like a discovery.*

Aldo Naouri, *Parier sur l'enfant* (Putting Your Faith in Children)

In the first chapter, we gave a quick general interpretation of the bar mitzvah. I showed that as a rite of passage, the bar mitzvah is what allows an adolescent to detach himself from the family cell and open himself to the community, as well as to new linguistic, cultural and emotional connections. I described the main attributes of these symbols. The essential teachings of the tefillin concern the words of the father, teachings which will allow the son's detachment and de-fusion from the body of the mother and the world of women. The four passages from the Torah reproduced on the tefillin parchments mention both the rite of the tefillin and four different teachings the father will address to the child, four different verbal expressions of transmission and transcendence, which will allow the child to discover his autonomy and freedom and to mature into adulthood. The terms for these teachings are: *Vehigadeta* (you will tell); *Veamarta* (you will say); *Veshinaneta Vedibarta* (you will repeat and you will speak); *Velimadeta* (you will teach). The context of these passages is eloquent, for it concerns birth and the flight from Egypt, and the separation/sanctification of the first-born. We therefore return to that essential and unavoidable theme found in the Bible and throughout Jewish thought, an idea previously discussed in the first chapter: the flight from Egypt as the birth of a people and a tearing away from the body of the mother, followed by the journey to the Promised Land, towards the new relationship with the woman who is no longer a mother but a wife. Between these two poles, the desert is a teaching, a body of teachings spoken by a voice from elsewhere. The desert is a teaching of Law, "the paternal voice" which explicitly speaks its role and function: "I am the Lord your God, who brought you out of Egypt, out of the land of slavery," the key sentence which opens the Ten Commandments.

## *Vehigadetah levinkha*
### The mother is also a woman!

> *On this day you shall tell (*vehigadetah*) your son, "This is because of what the LORD did for me when I came out of Egypt."*
>
> Exodus 13:1–10

First, *vehigadeta levinkha*, "you shall tell your son." This is the Haggadah, a word derived from *lehaggid*, "to tell." In the Hebrew Biblical world, telling is the way to learning gender difference and otherness. Indeed, *lehaggid* refers back to the Biblical passage in which woman is born as *ezer kenegdo*, "counterpart to Man," in contrast and as a complement to Him. As Armand Abecassis notes in *Les Temps du partage* (Times of Sharing, 1993), "*lehaggid* is to explain that life consists of encounters and that man has the ability to recognize or fail to recognize the other, that is to expose his desire to the other's desire and to simultaneously discover the necessity and the obligation to limit that desire...To be is 'to be with,' running the risk of being against, and of making war rather than making love." The father's teaching has the primary function of revealing the existence of otherness and of demonstrating that it is possible. This essential rite shows the child that though the mother is his mother, she is also, and possibly primarily, a woman, a woman who is a wife to the father and with whom the father has relations of love and respect. These words show the way to love and desire beyond function and need. In this context, it is important to underline that in the Biblical text, it is the recognition of the woman as a wife, rather than as a mother, "then he said, she is flesh of my flesh, and strength of my strength," which allows for the following verse, which is more of a commentary than a continuation of the text:

"Therefore shall a man leave his father and his mother, and shall cleave unto his wife: and they shall be one flesh" (Genesis 2:24). In the Biblical text, the word "wife" appears long before the word "mother."

The word "mother" is first mentioned in reference to Eve, following the original sin, "Eve/Chava," meaning, "the mother of all living" (Genesis 3:20). Learning about otherness and difference also demonstrates a rejection of ideologies and of all mob behavior and herd instincts. *Lehaggid* means "to oppose"; a word drawn from a story which fights stereotypes and prejudices and sets potentially stagnant patterns of thought in motion. Through this process, the father teaches his son the active dimension of thought, along with the arts of revolt and criticism. The commentaries note that in these initial teachings, the Torah orders the father to tell the story of the flight from Egypt by connecting it to the rite, but does not introduce the narrative as an answer to a question from the child. The question must arise from the rite accomplished by the parents, whose actions and example show the child their own desire to be connected to the tradition, to take their places within that tradition as irreplaceable links in assuring its continuity, and to see that the child now finds its own place in the tradition.

163

## *Veamarta*
The son does not belong to the father!

> *And it shall be when thy son asketh thee in time to come, saying, What is this? That thou shalt say unto him* (veamarta).
>
> Exodus 13:14

Then comes *amirah.* Now the teachings of the father come in response to the request/question of the son regarding the rite of sacrifice of the first-born animal and the liturgical vocation (or the buying back) of the first-born human. If the first teaching helps the child understand that he must separate himself from the mother to discover the love of a woman beyond the love of his mother, the second teaching reveals that the son does not belong to his father. "The rite of sacrifice of the first fruits and the first-born animal, according to Armand Abecassis, is a way of moving the father and son away from a relation of absolute property and replacing that idea with the notion of guardianship and tenure. In principle, at the beginning (*reishit*), everything belongs to the Creator, which is why all this *reishit* must be returned and the rest must be used to benefit the hungry and the thirsty" (op. cit.). The first fruits and the law of the first-born are a form of weaning matched by psychoanalyst Donald Winnicott's definition: "Think of the infant when it is of weaning age. The exact nature of the weaning period varies from culture to culture, but in my view the weaning period is when the child becomes able to play at letting objects fall down."[2] This is the essential gesture of opening the hand, of transforming the possessive, violent fist into a hand that opens and offers itself. The first teaching frees the child from the real or illusory/fantasized possessiveness of the mother, the second teaching from the violent possessiveness of the father.

"To consecrate the eldest son to the temple, where he must stay with God, or deliver him from it by offering his equivalent, is to remove any power of life and death the father might think he has over his son. The son does not belong to the father! To be a father cannot mean to exercise absolute power over the son, but rather the duty to educate and to love" (Armand Abecassis, op. cit.). The above is a potent reminder of the angel's gesture on Mount Moriyah to

*The Sacrifice of Abraham,* Tiepolo Gian Domenico (1722–1804).
Growing is hearing the sound made by the hand of the angel as he stops Abraham, who mistakenly
believed that one could do violence in the name of God.

halt Abraham's murderous hand. It is a reminder of the angel's request that Abraham sacrifice a ram instead of Isaac. This is where the tradition of the ram's horn, the Shofar, originated. The tradition states that a child cannot be killed in the name of God or anything else, but that on the contrary any rite proclaims: Become, live, elevate yourself.

## *Veshinantam levanekha, Vedibarta bam*
Teachings beyond the father

> *And thou shalt teach (veshinanetam) them diligently unto thy children.*
> Deuteronomy 6:7

*Veshinantam* comes from the root *leshanen,* "to repeat," "to masticate," "to digest," "to teach." Following the teachings of the separation from the mother and the non-possessiveness of the father comes the teaching of studying. The third text included in the tefillin concerns the pedagogical relationship between the father and the son, as well as the master and the disciple. The remarkable thing is that the text doesn't only state that the father must teach the son, *veshinantam,* but that he must also study for his own sake, *vedibarta bam.* He is confronted with other teachings than his own: the teachings of a text and of a God, teachings which have come from elsewhere and which transcend him.

## Velimadeta
It's your turn to teach!

> *"... and bind them for a sign upon your hand, that they (the teachings) may be as frontlets between your eyes.*
>
> Deuteronomy 11:18

The fourth passage is very similar to the third one, with the exception of a subtle difference which I will now point out. Once again, the passage relates tefillin to studying, but the word used stems from the root *lamad,* which is also the root of the word Talmud. In this case, the children have replaced the father in speaking about the Torah, "You teach them so that they in turn speak of it." We are now beyond the beyond of the father's teachings. This beyond is the personality of the child, who is discovering within himself, in his own experience, the joy of being free to think and to innovate. The father has opened his child to transcendence, to a desire for the infinite, to the continuous surpassing of one's self. The third passage is drawn from the Biblical text, and is transcendent because it stems from the tradition. The fourth passage is drawn from the Talmud, which grants the right to interpretation according to recognized and accepted collective rules. The fourth passage ushers in a transition from the passivity of learning to the inventiveness of play and the intellectual and existential construction of self.

167

## The Tefillin of Rashi and Rabenu Tam

> *The world has become infinite for us all over again, inasmuch as we cannot reject the possibility that it may include infinite interpretations.*
>
> Friedrich Nietzsche

There are two different traditions governing the order and placement of the passages in the tefillin, as well as the order in which they are written. The heart of the debate centers on whether the passages should be written

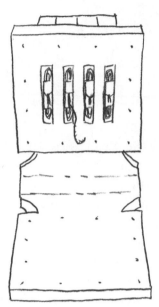

Rashi tefillin containing the four scrolls.
Right to left : Exodus, 13:1–10; Exodus 13:11–16;
Deuteronomy 6:4–9; Deuteronomy 6:13–21.

in the order of their appearance in the Biblical text, or whether the two passages beginning with the word vehayah are the central ones and should therefore be side by side, upsetting the Biblical order. According to Rashi (1040–1105), the texts should be in the order of their appearance in the Bible. When looking at the tefillin face on, the texts should therefore appear in the following order, from right to left: Exodus 13:1–10; Exodus 13:11–16; Deuteronomy 6:4–9; Deuteronomy 11:13–21. (See drawing above.) According to Rabbenu Tam (1100–1171, Rabbenu Tam was Rashi's grandson and the son of Rashbam), the order should be Exodus 13:1–10; Exodus 13:11–16; Deuteronomy 11:13–21; Deuteronomy 6:4–9. As can be seen in the drawing on the opposite page, the last two passages are inverted, so that the two *vehayah* are side by side. Today, most people only wear Rashi's tefillin, though some Jews still wear Rabbenu Tam's tefillin at the end of the prayer, to ensure they are properly accomplishing the mitzvah. Another, rarer tradition consists in wearing both at once. The ramifications of this debate are complex and cannot be adequately covered in the context of this volume.

Rabbenu Yaakov of Corbeil, one of the great medieval tossafists and a distinguished scholar, was in the habit of directing questions to "the sky" before he went to sleep. His questions were answered in his dreams. In fact, the title of his book is: *She'elot Uteshuvot Min Hashamayim,* "Questions and Answers From the Heavens." One day, he asked, which tefillin should we wear? Rashi's or Rabbenu Tam's? The answer he received went as follows: "Teachings of the few, teachings of the many, teachings of the living God" (*Elu va'elu divre Elohim Chayim*).

What can be understood is that this debate between Rashi and Rabenu Tam reflects a debate between the angels and God himself! God allegedly holds the same position as Rabbenu Tam, and the angels the same position as Rashi! Beyond his commentary's poetic and surrealist aspects, the author makes two essential points. The first is that a rite will always

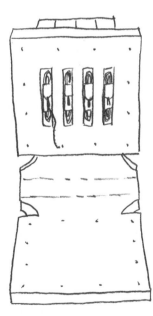

In Rabbenu Tam tefillin, the scrolls appear in the following order: (right to left) Exodus, 13:1–10; Exodus 13:11–16; Deuteronomy 11:13–21; Deuteronomy 6:4–9.

have meaning, no matter what divergences surround it. The second is that the rite achieves meaning through its divergences, for they are proof that the rite is not limited to a particular ideology or idolatry. Like thought, a rite needs two opinions to stay alive! Yet the most extraordinary thing is that the custom followed by the majority is not the one God favors, but the one the angels argue for. Custom therefore follows the opinion of the majority, the angels, against the opinion of God himself! Numerous Talmudic texts adopt this approach, giving many examples of cases in which Law is decided by human majority, despite the existence of objective theological proofs (such as a voice from the heavens) arguing a contrary opinion and presenting itself as the truth.[3] The epistemological consequences of this text on the tefillin open the door to a more general reflection on the meaning of Truth, of its place within the theological, and of its application in the city of man.

## History and Memory

> *Judaism deserves more than a moral and a bunch of well-meaning sentiments, it deserves an ethic!*
> *Indeed, one cannot be instinctively Jewish; one cannot be Jewish without knowing it.*
> *You must wish for good with all your heart,*
> *but not simply wish for it in a naive burst of heartfelt emotion.*
> *You must simultaneously preserve and destroy that burst—that may be the essence of Jewish worship!*
> *Passion being wary of its pathos, becoming conscience and becoming it again! Belonging to Judaism implies worship and science.*
> *Justice is inaccessible to the ignorant.*
> *Judaism is an extreme conscience.*
>
> Emmanuel Lévinas, *Difficult Freedom*

Sometimes, over the course of a life, one hears a voice, or even a word, that transforms one's existence. This instrument of change could also be a story, which, for reasons as obvious as they may be obscure, opens us up to our deepest being.[4]

When I read the story reproduced below, I told myself that it was my responsibility to transmit it to my readers, to pass it on. Of course, this story is not a demonstration or a commentary, but a door, which is closing, or maybe opening, yes, it is opening, on new horizons.

In the summer of 2000, Mordechai Kaler, age 16, volunteered to work at a retirement home, the Hebrew Home for the Aged in greater Washington. One of his responsibilities was to ask residents if they wanted to attend the daily services at the synagogue on the ground floor. Some accepted and others refused, but even those who refused were pleasant about it. Only one male resident stood out from the rest through his unpleasant demeanor. He had even insulted a volunteer who had asked him to join the minyan. Disconcerted by this behavior, the volunteer had stopped inviting the man to services. Mordechai decided to rise to the challenge of speaking to this difficult gentleman. He found the man sitting in the residence hall with other residents.

After having introduced himself, Mordechai firmly but respectfully told the man: "We respect your decision not to come to service, if that is your wish, but why curse a volunteer? He is only here to help and do his work." "Young man," the old man said, "wheel me to my room, I would like to tell you a story."

Once they were alone, the old man told Mordechai a terrible story, full of horror, pain, and sorrow. He had come from a prominent Orthodox family in Poland. When he was 12, he was deported with his family to a concentration camp. With the exception of his father and himself, the entire family was killed.

In their barrack in the camps, there was a man who had smuggled in the *tefillin shel rosh* (head-tefillin). Every day, each of the men would take every opportunity to put it on, even if only for a moment, whenever there were no S. S. guards in sight. The men were well aware that the mitzvah accomplished was incomplete, for they did not have the *tefillin shel yad* (arm-tefillin) but their love of the mitzvot was so great that they observed them no matter the conditions.

The old man continued: "But for my father, this wasn't enough. My bar mitzvah was coming up and my father wanted me to wear

171

complete tefillin on that day. He had heard of a man who had been killed, who had lived in a nearby barrack and had owned a complete pair of tefillin. On the morning of my bar mitzvah, my father risked his life to go to that barrack and get me those tefillin. I stayed by the window, anxiously awaiting his return. I saw my father running towards our barrack, carefully cradling a package against his body. He had nearly reached the barrack when a Nazi officer stepped out from behind a tree and shot him right before my eyes. When the Nazi left, I rushed out and took the tefillin bag, which was lying on the ground next to my father, and hid it from the Germans."

His story finished, the old man cast an irritated glance at Mordechai and vehemently asked: "How can anyone pray to a God that kills a father right before his son? I can't!" Then the man pointed to a dresser against the wall and murmured: "Open the top drawer." Mordechai did as he was told. Inside was a black tefillin bag, clearly affected by the passage of time, but showing little sign of wear and tear. It hadn't been opened in years. "Bring me the bag," the man ordered. Mordechai obeyed. The man opened it and pulled out an old pair of tefillin.

"This is what my father was carrying on that terrible day. I kept them to show the world what my father died for. Little boxes with black straps. That's all I have left of him." Mordechai was stunned. He struggled for words to comfort the man but couldn't find any. He could only take pity on this poor man who had lived in anger, bitterness and sadness since the tragedy that haunted him ever since. "I'm sorry," he finally managed to say in a threadbare voice. Mordechai left the room with the firm resolve never to come see the man again. At home that night, he was unable to eat or sleep. The next day, he went to the retirement home as usual, but avoided the old man's room. But a few days later, while Mordechai was assisting the faithful in synagogue, one of the residents told him, "I have Yahrtzeit today and need to say Kaddish. We have only nine men. Could you find a tenth man?" Mordechai had already made the rounds that morning and had had his invitation to attend service declined by numerous residents. Some hadn't properly woken up yet, and others weren't really interested in the service. The old man on the second floor was the only one

Mordechai hadn't asked. He reticently climbed the stairs to the old man's room. There could be no doubt the old man would turn him down, but he felt the obligation to try. He lightly tapped on the door and announced himself.

"You again?" the old man answered. "I'm sorry to disturb you," he answered gently, "but we need you to form a minyan so one of the residents can say Kaddish. Would you accept to join us, just this once?" The old man looked at Mordechai and said, "If I come this time, do you promise you won't bother me anymore?" Mordechai wasn't expecting that kind of an answer. "Yes," he murmured, "I won't bother you anymore."

To this day, Mordechai doesn't know where his next question came from: "Could you bring your tefillin?" This could have sent the old man into a fury. Yet instead of the withering response Mordechai had expected, the old man said, "If I bring them, will you leave me alone?" "Yes," Mordechai answered, "I promise."

"Very well. In that case, take me downstairs and leave me at the back of the synagogue so I can be the first to leave once the prayer is over." Mordechai took the old man down to the synagogue and settled him into the back of the room. "May I help you?" Mordechai asked as he removed the tefillin from the bag. The old man held out his left arm and Mordechai helped him put on the tefillin. Mordechai then left to attend to his other duties. After the service, Mordechai returned to clean up the synagogue. The old man was still there, alone, lost in thought. He was still wearing his tefillin and tears were pouring down his face. Mordechai asked him if he wanted him to get a doctor or a nurse.

The man didn't answer. Instead, he kept his eyes fixed on the tefillin straps wrapped around his left arm, caressing them with his right hand, and repeating the words, "Tatte, Tatte (Father, Father), it's so true." The old man looked up at Mordechai and confessed: "For the last half hour, I have felt so close to my Tatte, it's as if he had returned to me." Mordechai brought the man back to his room. He was on the verge of leaving him, when the man said, "Please come get me tomorrow."

From that day on, Mordechai went up to the second floor every morning. The old man would be waiting for him by the elevator with his tefillin in hand. Mordechai would wheel him to his place at the back of the synagogue, where the old man would put on his tefillin, open a siddur and retreat into his thoughts. One morning, Mordechai took the elevator to the second floor, but the old man was not there waiting for him. He ran to his room and found an empty bed. He rushed to the nurses' station, where he learned that the man had been taken to the hospital the previous evening and had later died of a stroke.

A few days later, the retirement home gave Mordechai an award in recognition of his services. Following the ceremony, a woman approached him and thanked him for the help he had given. "I'm sorry, Mordechai answered, do we know each other?"

"I'm the daughter of the man you helped," she answered. "You did so much for my father! You made his last days so peaceful. When he was in hospital, he insisted that I bring him his tefillin. He wanted to use them to pray one more time. I helped him to put them on, and then he was overcome by a stroke."

"He died wearing his tefillin. Connected to his father."

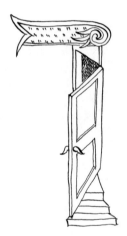

1. Reading of the first part of the parashah, which will be read in its entirety on the next Shabbat.
2. Quoted by Pierre Fédida, in *L'Absence*, pp.97-98, Gallimard, 1978.
3. See Talmud *Bava Metsia* 59b, the celebrated text of the discussion between Rabbi Eliezer and his students.
4. See Philip Roth's account in *Patrimony: A True Story,* Vintage, 1996.

# 7

# Prayer

*When the Baal Shem Tov,*
*Master of the Good Name and founder of Hasidism,*
*had a difficult task before him or saw*
*a misfortune about to befall the Jewish people,*
*he went to meditate in a certain part of the forest;*
*there, he lit a fire, lost himself in prayer*
*and what he had decided to do became possible:*
*the miracle was performed,*
*the misfortune was removed.*
*A generation later, when his disciple,*
*the Maggid of Mezeritch, had to intervene*
*with the Heavens for the same reason,*
*he would go to the same place in the forest and say:*
*"Master of the Universe, hear me.*
*I no longer know how to light the fire,*
*but I am still capable of saying the prayer."*
*And the miracle was performed yet again.*
*In the following generation, in order to save his people,*
*Rabbi Moshe Lev of Sassov*
*also went into the forest and said:*
*"I do not know how to light the fire,*
*I do not know the prayer,*
*but I remember the place and that ought to be*
*enough." And it was enough.*
*Then it was the turn of Rabbi Israel of Rijine*
*to lift the threat. He sat*
*in his gilded chair within his castle,*
*put his head in his hands*
*and addressed God in these terms:*
*"Master of the World,*
*I am incapable of lighting the fire,*
*I do not know the prayer, I cannot even*
*find the place in the forest.*
*All that I know how to do is to tell this story,*
*that ought to be enough."*
*And yet again, the miracle was performed.*

# Chapter Seven

**On the Path**

Prayer and Time

**Art and Prayer**

How Are Prayers Gathered As They Rise From Human Lips?

**An Outpouring of the Heart**

A Story

**"It Is Forbidden to Be Old!"**

The Structure of the Prayer

**Like a Meal!**

The Shema

**Toward an Ethic**

The Prayer Book, the Siddur, and the Five Books of Moses

**Reserved Seats, Choir, and Organ**

The Kaddish

**Prayer and Meditation**

Prayer and Psychoanalysis

178

## On the Path

*O God, may I be alive when I die.*

D.W. Winnicott

The ceremony of the bar/bat mitzvah is primarily based in the synagogue. Aside from being a place of prayer, the synagogue is also, as we mentioned earlier, a place to study and socialize, much like a community center. As noted by André Neher, "prayer is not a formula, but an inspiring force that constantly reminds man that his perfection resides in his perfectibility." Liturgy is precise and practically identical in synagogues throughout the world, no matter their persuasion: Orthodox, Conservative, or Reform, Sephard, or Ashkenazi.

## Prayer and Time

*This is the word of the Lord to Zerubbabel, saying: Not with an army,
nor by might, but by my spirit.*

Zechariah 4:6

Not by might, *for the foundation of might is might.*
Not with an army, *for the ally of an army is an army.*
But by my spirit, *for the spirit is the flame to the candle
and infinity to the flame.*

Edmond Jabès, *Le Parcours* (The Journey)

Three prayers are recited per day, whether one is alone or in a group, in the synagogue, at home, or on the way, according to the Biblical expression. According to tradition, the morning prayer, or *Shacharit,* was instituted by the Patriarch Abraham; the afternoon prayer, or *Minchah,* by Isaac; and the evening prayer, *Ma'ariv* or *Arvit,* by Jacob. To pray three times a day is to follow in an ancient tradition, and to recognize a trans-generational link. It is also a way of punctuating time, perhaps even of constructing time. It is to take the time to have time: time in the morning, the afternoon, and the evening.

## Art and Prayer

*Art is a wound that becomes light.*

Georges Braque

The question of time is an essential one, and one that is underlined by the Talmud itself in its opening reflection on time and prayer. "As of what time can we say the evening prayer?"
This question seeks to define the onset of night, and the passage from day to night. The issue is not night or day in and of themselves, but the passage from one to the other. This is fundamental Hebraism: Hebrew is the one who passes, the passer from one bank of the river to the other, from one

A man praying at the Kotel, the Western Wall in Jerusalem.

time to another. The moment of passage is the moment when things intertwine, and are no longer clearly defined.

Prayer is used to elucidate these moments of passage when morning hovers between the dark of night and the white of day, and evening moves from the last orange glimmers of the sun to the ever-deepening blue of night.

Time becomes a question of colors, a study of their subtlety, with particular attention devoted to light. The presence of an aesthetic dimension within the concept of time is so powerful that the word "art," *omanut* in Hebrew, has exactly the same root as *amen*, which is found throughout Jewish and, later, Christian liturgy. An artist is referred to as *oman* or *aman*.

This brings to mind Kafka's extraordinary sentence: "Art, like prayer, is a hand stretched out into the dark, seeking to catch something from grace, in order to transform itself into a giving hand."

Like art, prayer surprises the worshipper by taking him out of his daily routine, and opening him to new possibilities. The prayer must be felt, rather than read. Prayer is a rare thing. We often open the book, but we only pray on occasion, when a real event transforms us.

## How Are Prayers Gathered As They Rise From Human Lips?

> *Seeing that the Rabbi of Zans was going to the synagogue long before service, his disciples asked him:*
> *—Master, what are you doing before the prayer?*
> *—I am praying, he answered, in order to pray better!*

"Prayer rises to the superior spheres. Prayers that rise from the earth are reprised, like an echo, by the angels. At each door of the celestial palaces, watchmen relay these prayers. There are "day watchmen" and "night watchmen," responsible for the four points of the compass. The prayers of the unhappy and the persecuted rise, respectively, to the south and the north. The gates of dawn open to the west. In the east, prayer is gathered from human lips to be merged with the twelve letters of the Divine Name, which arrive dancing through the air. The more informal prayer that rises out of tears and cries is equally valuable. This type of prayer is systematically

fulfilled. The proclamation of the Sacred Name in the Shema constitutes the summit and the apogee of the prayer. The head angel "picks roses" in a sort of sacred spray and gathers them into garlands to form all of the sacred names. Finally, these roses are made into a sacred crown and offered to the Saint, may he be blessed."
(see Zohar, II, 20a)

## An Outpouring of the Heart

> *You can only write well by going toward the unknown*
> *—and not to know it, but to love it.*
>
> Christian Bobin, *Éloge du rien (In Praise of Nothingness)*

The important contribution of Hasidism, an existential Kabbalah revealed by the Baal Shem Tov (Master of the Good Name), who was mentioned in the first story of this section, should now be noted. This religious current opposes stereotyped prayer and the simple recitation of set formulas. Of course, the Hasidic masters accepted the traditional ritual, but they transformed it from the inside, and deepened it. Reciting a prayer only has meaning if it is an outpouring of the heart.

To simply repeat or imitate formulas created by others cannot satisfy the religious aspiration. To be used authentically, traditional prayer must constantly be renewed and reinvented by the person who has recourse to it, on his own behalf, like a language used to translate authentic expression of his own feelings. Hence, the Kabbalists and the Masters of Hasidism value individual prayer, personal prayer, that comes pouring out of the heart, independently of liturgical forms, of study, and of knowledge.

There are numerous examples of this high regard for simple, spontaneous prayer, as it can spring from the depths of the poorest, most ignorant of men, throughout the legend of the Baal Shem Tov.

183

## A Story

*A cage went looking for a bird.*

Franz Kafka

"One evening at the end of the day of Kippur, after prayer, the Baal Shem Tov was sitting at table with his disciples. Suddenly, he cried out, "Tell Alexei [his coach driver] to harness the horses!" He took his favorite disciple, Rabbi Nachman of Kossov, with him, got in his coach, and gave orders to be taken to a distant village.

Once he arrived, he went straight to the local inn. The innkeeper introduced himself to ask his prestigious and unexpected guests what they might like to be served, but the Baal Shem Tov responded by questioning him: "How did you recite the prayer of the holy day of Kippur?" The innkeeper began to panic. He had to make great efforts to regain his composure before he responded, stuttering, "Holy Rabbi! It is true that I have committed a great sin, for I did not pray with the community. Oh, unhappy man that I am!"

The Rabbi responded, "Tell me what happened."

"Yesterday, the innkeeper said, I took my wife and children and we started off toward the city to celebrate the holy day there and to pray with the community. Suddenly, I realized that I had forgotten to close the cellar. Worried that some passer-by might take advantage of this to help himself to my goods, I turned back and left my family to continue alone. I had barely entered my home when a messenger from the neighboring castle arrived to ask me for a few bottles required for a small feast. I gave him what he needed. Meanwhile, other customers had arrived. I should have refused to serve them and immediately caught up with my family in the city to spend the holiday with the wise and pious men of the community. It was still daylight, I thought I could still get to town before dark. But the customers kept coming, without interruption. Finally, when there was no one left in the inn and I was ready to lock up the cellar, I noticed with horror that night had fallen and that it was no longer possible for me to set off. I kept asking myself what I should do. I withdrew into a small room in the house, in order to open my heart. But I couldn't find a prayer book. My wife and children had taken them all with them.

Prayer book open to the page on which the Sabbath morning liturgy appears.

I don't know why, but I began to cry before God, saying, 'Master of the Universe, You see how heavy my heart is, for I cannot, on this holy day, unite with the community and pray with it. I don't even have a ritual to use! And I don't know the prayers by heart! But now I know what I'm going to do, the only thing within my power: I am going to start repeating the alphabet, with all my heart, like the child who doesn't yet know how to read. And you, Oh God! You will certainly take charge of assembling the letters into the words of my prayers. I ask you, sainted Rabbi, what else could I do?'

The Baal Shem Tov put his hand on the innkeeper's shoulder and said, "Be calm, God rejoiced over your prayer! It had been so very, very long since such a holy and fervent prayer had risen to the heavens!"

## "It Is Forbidden to Be Old!"

*Sleeping is another way of thinking.*
*Thinking is another way of dreaming.*
*Dreaming, another way of not being.*
*Not being, another way of existing.*

Roberto Juarroz

The word for prayer in Hebrew is *tefillah,* from the *pey, lamed, lamed* root, which means "to judge." The verb to pray is always in the pronominal form, so the judgment being referred to is judgment of one's self, a taking stock necessary to an authentic encounter with one's self and with others. Prayer is an opportunity to look into one's self, to undergo *teshuvah.*

I have often had the privilege of watching great Masters at prayer. I remember that the impression I took away was of a mixture of extreme suffering and great happiness, a struggle followed by serenity, which suddenly takes over the devotee's face. It is a strange moment which evokes an illumination, a new light.

Each time you pray, you try to be a different person, you try to truly be yourself. To pray is to learn to resist letting our habitual gestures and thoughts get old and stale. "It is forbidden to be old," according to Rabbi Nachman of Breslav. To pray is not simply "to be," but "to exist," to open one's self to a new sense of self and to new sensation. Feeling is not feeling, if one feels today how one felt yesterday. To feel the same thing today that one felt yesterday is not to feel—it is to remember what one felt yesterday. It is the living cadaver of what was yesterday's life and is now forever lost. You must face every dawn renewed, in a perpetual virginity of emotion and thought. "Today's dawn," wrote Fernando Pessoa, "is the first in the world. Never has this pink tint, so delicately turning to yellow, then to a hot white, swept across our faces."

"The man clothed with the clothing of love" is another one of Pessoa's sayings. Prayer is like art, and it is also like love. To love is a way of praying! Both for the lover and the man at prayer, everything seems to happen for the first time: this light and the existence of this God or of the beloved woman have never existed before. The manner, the intensity, the light, the joy, the tenderness, and the gentleness of the love blooming inside these men at every moment, in new, unknown ways which they lay down in tribute to the beloved, have never existed before. Though the experience of prayer may be a rare one, each day is a new opportunity to encounter it. And even once we enter the world of prayer, we must continue on the path of prayer. Just like love.

Seek love to find it, seek even once you've found it. To find it, you must seek it, for it is hidden! Once you've found it, you must still seek, for it is immense.

187

## The Structure of the Prayer

> *After Auschwitz there is no theology:*
> *the numbers tattooed on the arms of the prisoners of*
> *extermination are the telephone numbers of God.*
> *Numbers that go unanswered.*
> *That are now being disconnected,*
> *One after the other."*
>
> Yehuda Amichai

Now that we have had an overview of the spirit of prayer, we can explore its structure, which is relatively simple, for it is practically identical for all prayers. The elements that compose the structure of prayer are:

–Benedictions

–Psalms

–Anthologies of Biblical verses

–Readings from the Shema Yisrael preceded and followed by its benedictions

–The *Amidah* or *Shemoneh Esrei,* a silent prayer which is performed while standing with one's feet together (On the Sabbath and holidays there is a second prayer of this type called *musaf,* or "supplement.")

–Readings from the Torah and the Haftorah

–Rituals that depend on the holidays being celebrated, and include the sounding of the Shofar, the reading of the Megillah, the *Lulav,* etc.

The order of prayers can involve all or some of these elements.

## Like a Meal!

*Those who every day camp a little further from their place of birth, those who always pull their boat to new shores, will come to a better understanding of the indecipherable order of things with every passing day.*

Saint-John Perse

The prayer follows the same course as a meal. This similarity is not only didactic: prayer in Judaism originated as a replacement for sacrifices brought to the Temple. A meal begins with an aperitif, followed by first courses, a main dish accompanied by a side dish, dessert, coffee and, finally, a liqueur. It goes without saying that holiday meals are longer and often more copious than a regular meal: several beginners, a selection of desserts, etc.

Once the faithful have wrapped themselves in the tallith and put on their tefillin (on weekdays, and not on festivals), morning prayer begins with the benedictions, followed by a selection of Psalms and a few compilations of Biblical verses. They constitute the opening, the aperitif, and the beginners. Next, the first main dish is served, the Shema prayer. This dish is accompanied by the benedictions which precede and follow it.Then comes a second main dish, the *Amidah,* or the standing prayer spoken in a whisper, which is composed of eighteen benedictions for the days of the week. These eighteen benedictions are the source of the name *Shemoneh Esrei,* which means eighteen.

In the morning prayer, the cantor (or *chazan*) repeats the *Amidah* prayer out loud so that the assembly can answer Amen after each benediction. The *kedusha,* or "holiness," is included in this repetition, a prepared dialogue between the assembled faithful and the cantor (the rabbi or the person leading the prayer).

Following this repetition, or *chazarah,* on Mondays and Thursdays, as well as on the Sabbath and various holidays, the Torah and, less frequently, the Haftarah (not on Mondays and Thursdays) are received and read, and then the Torah is put away, a process to which we devote a chapter later in this volume. It is generally at this point, either before or after the reading, that the rabbi, the bar mitzvah boy or the bat mitzvah girl, or any other person invited to speak, address the audience. (On holidays and Rosh Chodesh, the *Hallel* is read before receiving the Torah.) After the putting away of the Torah, prayer is brought to a close, it is dessert time, with psalms and selected texts (except on the Sabbath, on holidays and on the Rosh Chodesh, on which the *musaf* is also recited). Of course, the above description is somewhat schematic, but it gives an accurate idea of the sequence of the service. With this in mind, one can easily get one's bearing upon entering a synagogue. One arrives either before or after the reading of the Torah, before or after the Shema, etc. In general, punctuality is required. People generally arrive towards the beginning of the service, and certainly before the reading of the Torah, which is considered the heart of the liturgy.

189

## The Shema

*The other is not the embodiment of God, but, through his face, where he is disembodied, is precisely the revelation of greatness where God reveals himself.*

Emmanuel Lévinas, *Totality and Infinity*

Of all the prayers, the Shema is the most well-known and the most important, for it is the only one to come from the Torah. All the other prayers come from rabbinical writings and sources. The Shema is so important that the initial chapters of the Talmud are devoted to explaining it, and describing its laws, its timing, and its significance. The Shema is therefore the centerpiece of the morning and evening prayers, but not of the afternoon prayer, when it is not recited.

שְׁמַע יִשְׂרָאֵל יְהֹוָה אֱלֹהֵינוּ יְהֹוָה ׀ אֶחָד ׃
בָּרוּךְ שֵׁם כְּבוֹד מַלְכוּתוֹ לְעוֹלָם וָעֶד

וְאָהַבְתָּ אֵת יְהֹוָה אֱלֹהֶיךָ בְּכָל־לְבָבְךָ וּבְכָל־נַפְשְׁךָ
וּבְכָל־מְאֹדֶךָ ׃ וְהָיוּ הַדְּבָרִים הָאֵלֶּה אֲשֶׁר אָנֹכִי מְצַוְּךָ
הַיּוֹם עַל־לְבָבֶךָ ׃ וְשִׁנַּנְתָּם לְבָנֶיךָ וְדִבַּרְתָּ בָּם בְּשִׁבְתְּךָ
בְּבֵיתֶךָ וּבְלֶכְתְּךָ בַדֶּרֶךְ וּבְשָׁכְבְּךָ וּבְקוּמֶךָ ׃ וּקְשַׁרְתָּם
לְאוֹת עַל־יָדֶךָ וְהָיוּ לְטֹטָפֹת בֵּין עֵינֶיךָ ׃ וּכְתַבְתָּם
עַל־מְזֻזוֹת בֵּיתֶךָ וּבִשְׁעָרֶיךָ ׃

Transliteration :

*Shema Yisrael Adonai Eloheinu Adonai echad.*
*Barukh shem k'vod malkhuto le'olam va'ed.*
*Veahavta, et Adonai Elohekha bekhol levavekha*
*uvekhol nafshekha uvekhol me'odekha.*

190

*Vehayu hadevarim haayleh asher anochi mitzavcha hayom al livavecha. Veshinantam levanecha, vedibarta bam beshivticha bevaytecha, uvelecht'cha baderech, uveshachb'cha uvekumecha. Uk'shartam leot al yadecha, v-hayu l-totafot bayn aynecha. Uchtavtam al mezuzot baytecha uvisharecha.*

Translation:
Hear, O Israel: the Lord our God, the Lord is One.
Blessed is the Name of His glorious kingdom for all eternity.
You shall love the Lord your God, with all your heart, with all your soul and with all your resources. Let these matters that I command you today be upon your heart. Teach them thoroughly to your children and speak of them while you sit in your home, while you walk on the way, when you retire and when you arise. Bind them as a sign upon your arm and let them be tefillin between your eyes. And write them on the doorposts of your house and upon your gates.

The Shema is composed of three passages from the Torah, the first two of which are also found in the tefillin and the mezuzah. These three paragraphs are: Deuteronomy 6:4–10; Deuteronomy 11:13–21; Numbers 15: 37–41. The themes covered in these texts concern the transmission to younger generations, the importance of study, the mitzvah of the mezuzah and the tefillin, the mitzvah of the talit, and the remembrance of the exodus from Egypt.

It is also the recognition of a world that exists through listening. Shema Yisrael means "listen O Israel." This is why when the first sentence of the text is recited, the faithful cover their eyes with their hands. Listening, rather than seeing.

According to tradition, Israel is the name of Jacob, the father of the twelve tribes. On his deathbed he asked his children, who were gathered around him, whether they would continue on his path and serve the name of God, his God. His children answered: "Listen Israel, listen father, the God we serve is our God, we serve him in our way, which may be a little different than yours, but that does not change anything, it is the same God."

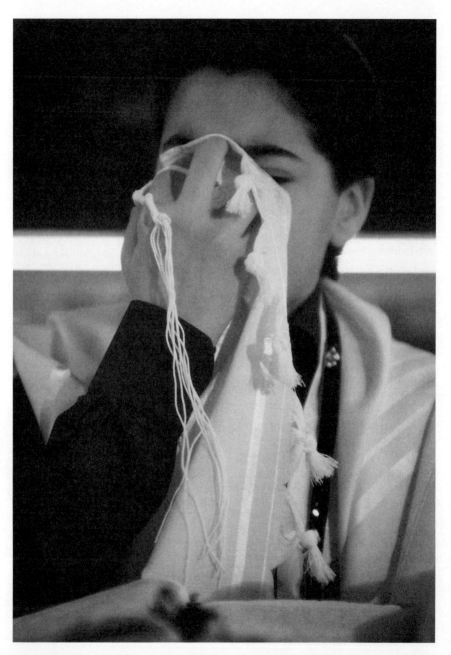

When the faithful recite the first sentence of the Shema, they cover their eyes with their hands or the tallith to concentrate on the auditory dimension.

# Toward an Ethic

*Jewish faith is in no way expressed by the phrase 'I believe in God.' It is not a question of believing in God, but of testifying to God, and testifying to God is to say 'Here I am,' in the name of God, at the service of the men who look at me!*

Emmanuel Lévinas, *Otherwise than Being: or Beyond Essence*

However, it is important to insist upon the meaning taken on by the expression "profession of faith," an expression which is often used in this prayer. I believe this is a fundamental error, which suggests that Judaism has a credo which it is sufficient to pronounce to discharge oneself. But to discharge oneself of what? As if Judaism boiled down to a question of belief! The Talmud and all the philosophical, Kabbalist, and Hasidic commentaries make it eminently clear that the key to Judaism is an ethic focused on man, rather than on God.

A story:

193

> "A highly learned man, who was also mean of heart, came to find Rabbi Abraham of Stretyn.
> –I've heard, he said, that you give people secret remedies, and that those remedies are successful. Couldn't you give me one to give me the fear of God?
> –I know of no remedy to give the fear of God. But if you want, I can give you one for the love of God.
> –Oh! That would be even more precious to me! Isn't the love of God superior to the fear of God? Quick, give it to me.
> –The remedy for the love of God is very simple, said the Rabbi, the remedy is the love of man."

# The Prayer Book, the Siddur, and the Five Books of Moses

*Without a slight touch of metaphysics,*
*it is impossible, in my opinion, to found an exact science.*

Georg Cantor

In order to allow the faithful to follow the service, every synagogue provides prayer books, which frequently include a translation and, nowadays, a phonetic transcription, which allows everyone to participate and sing with the community. The prayer book is known as the siddur, from the word *seder,* which means "order." The prayers are printed sequentially: all you need to do to follow the service is turn the pages. In Reform, Conservative, and, sometimes, Orthodox synagogues, it is common for certain passages to be recited in the local language.

It is also very common for the rabbi or the person leading the prayer to mention the page number from which the prayer is taken, so that the faithful can follow as the service proceeds. This is especially recommended for synagogues holding bar or bat mitzvahs, so that the numerous guests unaccustomed to services can still fully participate. Narrating the service with page numbers and occasional commentary is essential in minimizing boredom and inappropriate chatter, but, more importantly, it precludes the sense of a useless liturgy. In certain Reform and Conservative communities, the rabbi chooses passages and shortens the service, only keeping the most crucial texts, thereby assuring that he will not lose his audience's attention. A short, dynamic service with full participation is better than a long, drawn-out service in which nobody understands what's going on.

There is also another book that is provided for each member of the congregation in addition to the siddur, the chumash. The chumash contains the five books of Moses and includes all the *parshiot* (plural of parashah) of the year, along with the haftarot and the Sabbath prayer.

# Reserved Seats, Choir, and Organ

*Some dreams came traveling up the river. We stopped to talk to them.*
*They knew a great deal, except where they had come from.*

Franz Kafka

The faithful help themselves to prayer books and chumashim generally available at the entrance of the synagogue, and then they sit down. (In some congregations, siddurim and chumashim are found at each seat.)

In theory, one can sit wherever one wants, but it is very common for regulars to have "their" seats or even to have bought seats (a way of making donations to the synagogue). The purchaser's name is inscribed on a small bronze or plastic plaque and affixed to the seat. On the day of the bar or bat mitzvah, the family is often invited to sit at the front, near the rabbi and the important figures of the community, in order to participate and be at the heart of the event.

In certain large synagogues, the service is carried by a choir accompanied by an organ, a tradition drawn from Christianity, but which actually goes back to the Jerusalem Temple tradition by which the Leviim (men of the tribe of Levi) were charged with singing and playing a variety of instruments during the services. Numerous Psalms serve as testimony to this practice, either by referring to certain instruments, such as the harp, the cymbals, the trumpet, etc., or by indicating at the beginning of the Psalm the key in which the text was sung. Numerous Psalms were sung on the interior steps of the Temple, a practice referred to at the beginning of these texts in the expression *Shir HaMaalot*, which means "Hymn of the Degrees," or "Hymn of the Ascent."

# The Kaddish

*Books are like spring: they blossom discretely, just for one person, exactly when necessary.*

Philippe Sollers

One of the essential topics yet to be covered in this book is the Kaddish. This is one of the most well-known Jewish prayers. In Aramaic, it means saint. The Kaddish is an Aramaic prayer, a hymn in praise of God, an incantation to the coming of the Messiah. This prayer has many functions, but in general it can be said that it is used to punctuate the progression of the service, like a type of intermission or transition prayer. The Kaddish is said after each part of the service, after the benedictions, after the morning prayer, after the introductory psalms, etc.

There are four types of Kaddish:

1. The complete Kaddish *(Kaddish Shalem)*: it often follows the *Shemoneh Esrei,* the silent prayer.

2. The half Kaddish *(Chatzi Kaddish)*: it punctuates the prayer

3. The Kaddish of the Rabbis *(Kaddish Derabbanan)*: it brings the study sessions or the parts of the services that include a study text from the Mishna or the Talmud, to a close.

4. The Orphan's Kaddish *(Kaddish Yatom)*, recited by mourners at the grave of relatives and during the first eleven months following the deaths of parents. Once these eleven months are up, the Orphan's Kaddish is recited annually on the anniversary of the death. This anniversary day is referred to by a German name: *Yahrzeit*.

The Kaddish is always recited in a standing position, with the feet joined together (position of the angels), facing Jerusalem, in the presence of ten people. The Orphan's Kaddish is generally recited by men, and, particularly, by the eldest son, to the point that in some Yiddish-speaking communities the eldest son is affectionately referred to by his parents as "my Kaddish." But today, it is commonplace for women to recite the Orphan's Kaddish, including in Orthodox circles.

It has also become common for the Orphan's Kaddish to be recited in chorus by all the mourners present in the synagogue. Given that the recitation of the Orphan's Kaddish has taken on significant sentimental value, there are communities in which people are paid to recite the Kaddish every day in memory of various individuals whose children cannot come to synagogue on a daily basis.

## Prayer and Meditation

> *And the Lord God formed man of the dust of the ground, and breathed into his nostrils the breath of life; and man became a living soul.*
> Genesis 2:7

Aside from institutional prayers iterated in words and phrases, Judaism, like other spiritual practices, also includes meditation exercises. These are composed of breathing exercises and visualizations of Hebraic letters, in particular of the unpronounceable Tetragrammaton of the Divine YHVH. Several techniques are used. The one I am acquainted with, the technique I first learned and now teach, consists in visualizing each of the letters of the Tetragrammaton separately, while keeping one's eyes closed, breathing deeply and vocalizing while thinking about energizing specific parts of the body.[1]

a/o (*kamatz*) for the bones of the body
a (*patach*) for the brain
é/e (*tserei*) for the heart
é/è (*segol*) for the right arm
e (*sh'va*) for the left arm
open o (*cholam*) for the entirety of the body, in a vertical sweep from top to bottom
i (*hirik*) for right thigh and right leg
ou (*kubutz*) for the left thigh and left leg
ou (*shuruk* ) for the male sex organ
"silently" (a mixture of all the vowels) for the crown of the sex organ

This type of meditation can be practiced alone or in a group. It is useful to have one person lead the exercise in order to give it rhythm and unity. One must breathe in before each letter visualized and breathe out as the vowel is vocalized. This gives a series of four breaths for each vowel, and a total of nine series for the exercise as a whole. It is important to take a silent pause in between all the series, and when the entire exercise has been finished, it is important to keep one's eyes closed and remain quiet and empty of thought for a moment. In certain meditative practices, the Master cries out at an unexpected moment to break any habit-forming, even if the habit is merely a meditative one.[2]

## Prayer and Psychoanalysis

*For a long time, I was depressed. I was gonna kill myself, but I was in analysis with a strict Freudian analyst and if you kill yourself, they make you pay for the sessions you missed, so...*
Woody Allen

To close this chapter, or rather not to close it, it is worth noting the similarity between the structure of Jewish prayer and an analysis session. The essence of analysis is not the act of speaking, but the act of speaking to someone who is listening. The connection between the analyst and the person undergoing analysis is a "shema" connection, a connection based on listening. I believe that Freud's most brilliant accomplishment was to come up with the concept of the couch, not only because the couch makes free association and also the psychoanalyst's "drifting attention" easier, but because it allows the person being treated to stand at the end of the session, thereby allowing him to understand that having been listened to opens him to verticality. The analysis session has the structure of the Shema/amida, of the "listen/standing" of Jewish prayer. Where there is listening, there is standing! A different, but equally transcendent way of entering into the world of prayer.[3]

1. See *Meor Enayim* by Rabbi Nachum of Chernobyl, Parashat Shemot.
2. See Rabbi Nachman of Breslav, Likute Moharan, I, 21:7. Regarding this subject, also see my book *Mystères de la Kabbale* (Mysteries of the Kabbalah), Éditions Assouline.
3. Interested readers can read more on this question on the web site www.marcalainouaknin.com.

8

# Receiving the Torah

*The words of the Fathers are like embers.*
Pirkei Avot, The Ethics of the Fathers 2:10

*If you blow on embers which appear to be*
*extinguished and contain but one spark,*
*you will bring them to life by moving them*
*and you will stir them up by blowing on them.*
*And the more you blow, the more the flame will be*
*kindled, and the more the fire will spread,*
*until finally it becomes an incandescent hearth.*
*Then you will be able to take advantage of it,*
*to see by its glow or warm yourself near*
*its flickering flames...*
*But you will only be able to be near it,*
*you will never be able to take hold of it...*
*For since the embers have come alive,*
*they must be used with caution,*
*for fear that they burn you...*

Rabbi Chayim of Volozhyn

# Chapter Eight

A Book Dressed in the Clothing of Love

**The Opening of the Holy Ark**

The *Parokhet:* the Veil or the Curtain

**The Book and its Orientation**

The Book and the Unveiling

**The Book and Respiration**

The Book and Movement

**The Raising of the Torah**

203

## A Book Dressed in the Clothing of Love

> *To slander is not only to tell stories about others,*
> *or even to say bad things when we could say good ones,*
> *simply because we are jealous. It has a deeper impact.*
> *To slander someone restricts the consciousness*
> *we can have of others to the limited dimension*
> *of our own individuality as the one and only reference.*
>
> Gilles Bernheim, *Le Souci des autres* (Being Conscious of Others)

If the day of the bar/bat mitzvah marks a young man or woman's first visit to synagogue, and potentially even his or her parents and relatives' first visit, it will also be the day on which they discover the ritual reading of the Torah for the first time. As for those who are used to going to synagogue, tradition teaches that on each visit, one should behave as if it were the first time they entered this place of prayer.

The Torah is a daily part of study and liturgy. This custom goes back to the time of Moses, when passages from the Torah were read publicly every three days. Today passages from the Torah are read in synagogue four times a week: on Mondays, Thursdays, and on Saturday mornings and afternoons. During holidays, it is read from every day.

The five books of the Torah are included on a single parchment scroll attached to two wood rollers, with "handles" that make it possible to roll up and open the "Book" without touching the parchment paper. These wood rollers are called *etz chayim,* "tree of life." When the text is closed, it is "dressed" with a belt, the *mappa,* which holds it in place, and a protective jacket, the *me'il.* Fruit-shaped bells known as *rimonim* are often placed on the tops of the rollers referencing the pomegranate fruit described in the *Song of Songs.* A silver crown called the *keter* can also sometimes be found in place of the *rimonim.*

A decorative plaque is suspended from the front of the book, along with a silver hand-shaped pointer (the *yad*), which serves to read the text without touching the parchment (the *klaf*), and which was discussed in the first chapter. All of this ornamentation refers to the figure of the High Priest and the various outfits he is described wearing at the end of the book of Exodus. This reveals an essential concept: the passage from the monumental space to the space of the Book, a portable Temple of words and letters dedicated to reading, thought, and intelligence.[1]

Torah scroll ornamentation, Germany and Poland, 18th century.
The covering and ornamentation of the Book of the Torah recall the garb of the Great Priest
(Exodus 28:31).

## The Opening of the Holy Ark

*In Kyoto, there is a famous garden, the garden of the Ryoan-Ji Zen
temple. Fifteen rocks are spread out over the sand.
However, no matter where you stand, you can only ever see
fourteen rocks at a time. When the fifteenth rock appears,
the fourteenth disappears, and so on and so forth.
This invisible rock expresses the hidden center.
All that is essential is both visible and hidden.*

After the chazan repeats the *amidah*, the ceremony of the reading of the Torah
begins. A worshipper is called forth and honored by opening the Holy Ark. The
cabinet is sober and, aside from the stands holding the Torahs, or *Sifrei Torah*
(plural of *Sefer Torah*), several of which are frequently stored, it is practically empty.
The *Sifrei Torah* are donated by families in memory of loved ones or on the
occasion of an important event, either mournful or joyous. In fact, these donations are heartily celebrated at *Hakhnassat Sefer Torah*, celebrations the scale of
which can even rival those of wedding ceremonies. During *Hakhnassat Sefer Torah*,
the donor family and its guests are honored by being invited to write the last
sentences, or the last words, of the Book. They thereby realize the mitzvah, every
man and woman's ultimate obligation to write a book. The name of the donor
family and the date of the ceremony are often embroidered in gold letters on the
jacket covering the book.

## The *Parokhet:* the Veil or the Curtain

*The gentlest religious truth is already a crusade.*
Emmanuel Lévinas

A thick embroidered curtain called *parokhet* frequently hangs in front of the
cabinet. This curtain is reminiscent of the one that hung in the Jerusalem
Temple (and initially in the desert sanctuary, the *Mishkan*) to separate the "Holy
place," *Kodesh*, from the place known as the "Holy of Holies," *Kodesh*

207

Holy Ark curtain (Turkey, 18th century) recalling the separation between "Holy space" and the "Holy of Holies" in the Temple of Jerusalem (Exodus 26:33).

*Hakodashim,* in which the Holy Ark, which first appeared during the Biblical era, was found. This gilded acacia box had a solid gold cover in which two cherubs were carved facing each other.[2]

## The Book and its Orientation

*A poem is never completed, it is abandoned.*
Paul Valéry

The Holy Ark is generally found on the east-facing wall, known as the *mizrach* in Hebrew. In Occidental synagogues, the direction of prayer is the Orient, towards the Jerusalem Temple. Oriental synagogues face the west, in order to face Jerusalem.[3] The Holy Ark is a "cabinet," often built into the wall itself, which gives the exterior wall of this facade a rounded aspect. This type of architecture can be observed in many churches. A whole dimension of artistry has developed around this *mizrach,* through which artists have shown their individual takes on the concept of orientation.

It is absolutely fundamental to note the importance of the placement of the Ark. It belongs to what I refer to as the *phenomenology of the Book,* in that incredibly original, essential manner that the Book has of revealing itself, of entering into the visibility of the world, the life of men, and the community of readers.

The first function of the Book, from its place facing Jerusalem, is to vectorize man, to make him experience a tension *toward.*

This *toward,* this vectorial dimension, is central, for in Hebrew it is referred to as *el,* which is also the word for "God." Accordingly, the Divine would be the dimension which orients us *toward,* which draws us. It draws us out of our immanence through a sweep of exteriorization, of transcendence and of elevation. Man is no longer simply there, static, but turned, drawn toward an elsewhere, an "over there," referred to in Hebrew as *sham.*

On every occasion, man is another man, another life, and another existence. Man is not; he becomes. This means that it is his duty to emerge as

Torah niche. A depiction of the facade of the Temple of Jerusalem can be distinguished at the top, along with the menorah (Exodus 25:31) and the sacrifice of Isaac (Genesis 22:1).

new figures, other figures of thought and action. He must exist in constant flux. This is also true of the collective.

A society which does not engender new forms of organization would be signing its own death warrant. Man is always already *beyond* himself.

This "beyond" can be translated as "meta" in the philosophical languages originating from the Greek. Man is a "meta" animal, *metaphysical*, *metaphorical* etc.

In Hebrew, this metaphoric nature of human reality is referred to as *sham*, or "over there." *Sham* is composed of two letters which also spell out *shem*, which means "the name." *Shem* is also the source for the word *Shemite*, or "Semite." Man is fundamentally a name-bearing creature, he bears a name by which he carries himself ahead of himself: Transcendence and existence.[4] *Shem/Sham* is all the more astonishing in that its numeric value is 340, the same numeric value assigned to the word *sefer*, which means the Book!

## The Book and the Unveiling

> *To go to the sources is to enter the future:*
> *it is to make a prodigal source gush out of every dried-up source*
> *in the desert of the future.*
> Edmond Jabès

The fact that the curtain or *parokhet* must be opened before the doors of the Holy Ark can even be opened evokes a hidden dimension on the other side of the curtain and implements an understanding of a world divided into what is seen and what remains to be seen. The world is understood as "not yet being," an "upcoming" world coiled into the heart of the "still hidden." The function of the Book becomes the possibility of combining this discovery and a time being projected into the future.

The Talmud notes that in the Jerusalem Temple and even the movable sanctuary in the desert, the High Priest saw shapes like the breasts of two women, visible and invisible, appear on the *parokhet*. The *parokhet* leads the interpretive mind into an expectation of desire, borne by an erotic structure. The fact that the Book of the Torah is referred to as the "fiancée" in the Talmudic texts is directly linked to this idea, particularly given the fact that to be able to read the Book, one must remove its jacket, or *undress the fiancée*. The texts of the Kabbalah heavily insist on this eroticism of the Book and of reading. It is interesting that the implementation of this erotic structure takes place in a ritual setting when the young bar mitzvah boy or bat mitzvah girl enters the adult world, not only insofar as his or her community responsibilities, but at the moment when his or her senses are awakened to the desire for amorous and sexual encounters.

These questions prolong what was previously discussed regarding the passage from the world of the mother to the wife via the teachings of the father referring himself to the teachings of the tradition.[5]

## The Book and Respiration

> *If I am not for myself, who will be?*
> *But when I am only for myself, who am I?*
>
> Hillel

With the opening of the doors, the Book's third function comes into play. This is an opportunity to stretch out one's arms and to create an opening for breathing and the body to strive upwards, like a bird preparing for flight by spreading its wings. The body breathes and prepares for the respiration of the mind required for reading and study. It is no coincidence that the word used to refer to the basic text of the Talmud is *Mishna*, a word composed of the same letters as *neshimah*, which means "respiration" and is also the root of the word *neshamah*, the "soul." The Book allows the opening of the body and the soul, the respiration of study, and the aspiration to elevation, an essential idea accurately reflected in the French word for student: *élève*. An *élève* is a person who is elevated by contact with the spirit and study, and by contact with the Book, reading and interpretation.

A bar mitzvah boy opening the doors to the holy ark.

The image of wings being spread is not only a modern poetic metaphor. In fact, it originates with the image of the cherubs on the cover of the Holy Ark, or, in other words, on what would become the doors to the "cabinet" in which the holy scrolls are kept. The image of wings is also found in prophetic literature, specifically in Isaiah and Ezekiel, both of which describe angels with multiple wings. Personally, I like to recall the previously quoted sentence by Lévinas: "in each word, there is a bird waiting with its wings folded for the breath of the reader." To read is to allow this interior bird to spread its wings, and, ideally, to jump on its back to fly off with it. It is also a return to the idea discussed in the chapter on tallith, by which "corners" are referred to as "wings," or, in Hebrew, *kenafayim.*

At the very moment we open the doors of the Holy Ark, the Book makes the following teaching resonate within us: "If you will it, you will do it! Climb higher and higher, for you possess a powerful force, you have wings of wind, noble eagles' wings...

The Ark of the Alliance, the cherubim, and the bread table of the faces (France, c. 1280).

Do not repudiate them, for fear that they will repudiate you. Seek them and immediately they will find you..." (After the Master of Good Light, in *Orot HaKodesh*).

## The Book and Movement

*Life is only happy when it imbibes the perfume of ink.*
Qui Yuan 340–278 B.C.E.

Once the bar mitzvah boy or bat mitzvah girl has taken hold of the Book, everyone in attendance before the Holy Ark is set into motion. The procession thus formed moves around the synagogue, offering the faithful the opportunity to approach the Book and show love and respect by touching it with their tallith or kissing it as they pass by. In certain synagogues where men and women are kept separate, women do not touch the Book but show their respect from a distance by raising their hands in its direction. In a few Oriental communities, women might even release traditional cries of joy. This procession is important because it signifies that the Book is a source of movement, and of a dynamic sense of beginnings. Through the infinite interpretations offered by a text, reading gives man the possibility of reinventing himself, of eternally renewing himself. The procession finishes by placing the Book at the center of the synagogue, on the Central Table known as the bimah. The term "bimah" can refer to a stage, a place where things happen, and are displayed to be seen and heard by the people.

> One day a rich man came to see a rabbi to ask his advice. Before answering the man's questions, the rabbi asked:
> –Look out the window and tell me what you see.
> The man looked out the window and said:
> –I see a street. There are men walking and horses going by. Like the men, some horses go fast and some go very slowly.
> Then the rabbi told him:
> –Now look in this mirror. What do you see?
> The rich man looked at the mirror and said:
> –Now I see myself, yes, that is me that I see!
> –Now you understand, said the rabbi, that all you need is a thin sheet of silver stuck behind the glass and you no longer see the

After the Torah is raised, the bar mitzvah boy carries it among the assembled faithful,
so they may kiss it in respect.

street, you no longer see the men or the horses, you no longer see life! A little silver and all you see is yourself, your Me, a sad and lonely me, you understand?

## The Raising of the Torah

> God is certainly not incarnate in letters, but He is in some manner inscribed in them, and living His life therein—or a part of His life. He is in the lines and between the lines and in the exchange of ideas between readers commenting on them.
>
> Emmanuel Lévinas

When the Book is placed on the table, the Rabbi (or anyone else) begins to "undress" it. First the bells or the crown are removed, then the pectoral and the silver pointer, and finally the jacket and the belt. In certain communities, particularly in Alsace, the belt is made of a long strip of decorated fabric, the *mappah*, which is reminiscent of a baby's swaddling clothes, and which is generally donated to the synagogue on a child's third birthday. The child's name and date of birth are inscribed on the *mappah*. The *mappot* have therefore frequently served as community family records. Oriental Books of the Torah are frequently found in beautiful handcrafted boxes covered in fabric or precious metals. In this case, the "undressing" merely consists in opening the box, which stands upright without assistance.

Once the Torah is "undressed," one person is honored by being called upon to open it and raise it for display to the assembly which, at that point, is reciting a few verses. This raising of the Book is known as the *hagbah*. The person who raises the Book is chosen for his strength, for the Book is relatively heavy and a certain amount of skill is required to properly lift it, with a motion similar to that of a weightlifter lifting heavy weights. In the Sephardic tradition, during the raising of the Torah, the Rabbi, or the person who will read the parashah, shows the beginning of the passage to be read with the silver pointer. Following this opening of the Torah, it is returned to the bimah table, and the actual reading begins.

217

Silver ark for the Torah scrolls (Sephardic tradition, beginning of the 18th century).
In this case, the book stands vertically during the reading.

Before the reading of the Torah. The scrolls are held aloft and shown to the audience,
and the rabbi indicates the exact beginning of the passage to be read with a silver hand. Among the
Ashkenazi, the *hagbah* takes place after the reading of the Torah.

In Ashkenazic commmunities, the *hagbah* takes place after the Torah reading. After lifting the Torah and showing the end of the portion that has just been read to the congregation, the person honored with the *hagbah* is seated and another member of the congregation closes the scrolls and replaces its coverings. This "honor" is known as the *gelilah*. It is traditional for the parents of the bar or bat mitzvah to bestow these honors, along with the *alliyot*, or Torah blessings, on close friends or relatives on the morning of the ceremony.

1. In the *Erakhin* treatise, the Talmud explains that, like sacrifices, the clothing of the High Priest had an expiatory function. The fact that they are used as the "clothing" for the Torah gives the book and its design a meaning that goes far beyond the aesthetic dimension. It appears that the book's "jacket" has a function similar to the tallith's, i.e. to repair slander.
2. See the description of this Ark in Exodus 25.
3. It is interesting to note that in English (as well as in French) to know the direction one is going in, to not be lost, is referred to by this ability to turn to the Orient, "to orient one's self."
4. Regarding the relationship between the *Shem* and the *Sham,* see Rabbi Yossef Gikatilia, in *Guinat Ekoz, Jerusalem, 1988.*
5. See the chapter on tefillin.

9

# The Bible

*The fundamental condition of thought*
*is someone else's thinking.*
*Thought is like a brick cemented into a wall.*
*It is a mere simulacrum of thought*
*for the thinker to adopt self-reflexive mode,*
*and see a free brick rather than the price he pays*
*for that appearance of freedom:*
*he does not see the vacant lots and mounds of trash*
*which he and his brick are committed to by his vanity.*
*The mason's task, the task of assembling,*
*is the most essential of all.*
*For instance, bricks set side by side in a book*
*should not be less visible than the new brick,*
*which is the book itself.*
*Indeed, the reader*
*cannot simply be offered a single element,*
*but the whole in which the element is fitted.*
*This is the very essence of the human assembly*
*and of the human edifice,*
*both of which cannot be limited*
*to an accumulation of debris,*
*but must be self-consciousness itself.*

Georges Bataille, *The Theory of Religion*

# Chapter Nine

What is the Torah?

**The Bible: History of a Word**

General Structure of the Hebrew Bible

**How Do You Say "Bible" in Hebrew?**

The Five Books of Moses or the Chumash

**The Prophets, or *Neviim***

The Writings, or *Ketuvim*

**The *Halakhah* and the *Aggadah***

Remarks on the Christian Bible

**The Biblical "Canon"**

The Transmission of the Text from One Generation to the Next: *Sofrim* and Massoretes

**Translations Are the First Commentaries**

"The People of the Interpretation of the Book"

**The Talmud**

## What is the Torah?

> *One day when we were crossing the market, a curious bystander began to*
> *stare at you. Speaking to himself, he said, 'She is black, but she is beautiful.'*
> *I answer, 'You are beautiful because you are black.'*
> *To see you, I must close my eyes and marry the night.*
> *Your invisible voice strives towards me and I answer you*
> *with a handshake of silent words.*
>
> Edmond Jabès

The Book sits open on the bimah, the central platform in the synagogue.
What does this "Book" represent? Do we refer to it as the Bible? As a part
of the Bible? And anyhow, what is the Bible? We say "reading from the

Torah," not "reading from the Bible"! What's the difference, if any, between the Jewish Bible and the Christian Bible? And what about the Talmud, which is often mentioned in sermons or reflections on Judaism? What is the difference between the Talmud and the Bible?

Before I move on to specifically defining the parashah and describing the structure of the Torah scrolls from which the Biblical text is read during the bar/bat mitzvah, I will answer these questions by making a few general remarks on the structure of the Hebrew Bible and the nature of the Talmud.

## The Bible: History of a Word

> *It isn't because man has hands*
> *that he is the most intelligent of living beings,*
> *but because he is the most intelligent of living beings*
> *that he has hands.*
>
> Aristotle, criticizing Anaxagoras

Based on its origins in the Greek, the word "Bible" is plural. Indeed, Greek translators used the expression *ta biblia*, "The books," to refer to these ancient Hebrew scrolls. This became the singular "Bible" via the Latin *biblia*.

Greek etymology takes us back to *biblion* and *biblos*, words which initially meant "interior bark" or "papyrus core." The French word for bark, *écorce*, stems from this definition and is the root for *papier à écrire* (writing paper), *tablette à écrire* (writing tablet), *livre* (book), and *écrit* (writing).

The book therefore derives its name from the material of which it is made, material on which we make signs that leave a trace, a memory, and a meaning. According to some historians, the name *Biblos* or *Byblos* was the name of a town (which was located in present day Lebanon) specialized in papyrus culture. The interior bark of the papyrus served as a medium on which to write. (The papyrus is a plant which traditionally grows on the banks of the Nile.) Its stem served to make wicker objects and sheets on which to write. It was cut into strips which were pasted together for writing purposes. As can be guessed, the word "papyrus" is at the root of "paper."

The Latin etymology is less well known, but follows a similar track. In Latin, book (or the French "livre") is *liber,* which is a term taken from botanic jargon. The dictionary describes "a vegetal fabric composed of vessels (graded tubes) and parenchyma through which the elaborated sap circulates." The *liber* is the deep part of the bark which constitutes the sapwood. The layers of the linden tree's *liber* were used for writing. But could it be that the *liber* in trees was called *liber* because it was used to make ... books. And might the word "livre" come from *liber* because the Latin term means "free"?

## General Structure of the Hebrew Bible

> *Each atom of silence is the opportunity for a ripe fruit.*
> Louis Lavelle

The Bible is a collection of works the exact content of which differs according to the tradition embracing it. Indeed, there is a Hebrew Bible and a Jewish Bible, a Catholic Bible and a Protestant Bible.

225

The Hebrew Bible is divided into books. The books are divided into chapters and the chapters are divided into verses. When we refer to a specific passage in the Bible, we provide the name of the book, the number of the chapter, and the number of the verse. For instance, Jeremiah 3:14 refers to the Book of Jeremiah, chapter 3, verse 14.

The Hebrew Bible is divided into three major parts: the Pentateuch, or Torah, the Prophets, or *Neviim,* and the Writings, or *Ketuvim.*

The Torah scrolls from which the bar mitzvah boy or bat mitzvah girl will read are known as the Pentateuch (from the Greek penta, for "five"). These are the five books written by Moses. As mentioned earlier, in Hebrew they are referred to as the Chumash, from *hamesh* (five), or the Torah. The word Torah derives from horaah, which means "instruction," but also "parent" and "fecundity" (pregnancy is referred to as herayon). By extension, the Torah frequently refers to all three parts of the Hebrew Bible, and, in a deformation of its exact meaning, to all traditional Jewish texts.

A Pentateuch used as a volume for study (Poland, 18th century).
The liturgical reading can only be taken from this type of book.

## How Do You Say "Bible" in Hebrew?

*The Talmudic mode of thought cannot have suddenly vanished.*
*A few days ago, I was singularly captivated*
*by a small paragraph in my* Jokes. *By considering it more closely,*
*I realized that by its technique of oppositions*
*and its entire composition, it was thoroughly Talmudic.*

Sigmund Freud, Letter to Karl Abraham, May 9th, 1908.

It is interesting to note that the word Bible does not have a Hebrew equivalent. Instead, Hebrew includes the word *TaNaKH*, which is composed of the initials of the words Torah, *Neviim,* and *Ketuvim.*

The word *TaNaKH* takes us deep into the world of "Hebrew rhetoric," with all that it implies in terms of forces of connection and dis-connection. The world of Hebrew rhetoric is based on word play and the combinative potential of letters. It is a world of layered analysis, of breaks, of fragments, of permutations, of reversals, and of syntheses, etc. A world of "Witz," as Freud would have said!

The Hebrew word *TaNaKH* is interesting in and of itself, for it derives from a Hebrew root which refers to the tragus or earlobe *(tenukh).*[1]

This link to the ear is a significant one for it underlines the fact that reading immediately implies a connection between speaking and listening, and a right to the choice of which words to hear and listen to.[2] Lexicographers[3] relate the word *tenukh* to *anakh*, "vertical." *Tanakh,* the Bible, would therefore be an imperative *teanakh,* which means "Hold yourself vertical."

## The Five Books of Moses or the Chumash

> *A man turns to the man sitting next to him on the subway:*
> *—Excuse me for bothering you, sir, but which language is the book*
> *you're reading in?*
> *—In Hebrew, sir.*
> *—And which book is it?*
> *—The Bible, sir!*
> *—Oh really? So they've even translated it into Hebrew?*
>
> Thank you, Laurent Picard, for telling me this story.

The Hebrew names of the five books correspond to the first word (or one of the first words) of the first verse of each of the books. The first book, *Bereshit,*[4] relates the history of the world from the creation to Abraham, then the history of Abraham's family until Joseph's death in Egypt. The second book, *Shemot,*[5] describes the Exodus, the Revelation of the Decalogue in the Sinai, and the raising of the tent of meeting, or *mishkan,* after the incident of the golden calf. The third book, *Vayikra,*[6] is essentially composed of religious and social dictates, including the famous "thou shalt love thy neighbor as thyself," as well as all the laws concerning worship at the temple, including sacrifices. The fourth book, *Bamidbar,*[7] resumes the narrative of the Hebrew people's stay in the desert up to the announcement of the approaching death of Moses at the end of the fortieth year. This is the Testament of Moses, which is contained in the fifth book, *Devarim,*[8] as a speech which returns to most of the major themes previously covered in the Torah.

## The Prophets, or *Neviim*

*The written, printed page, like any other use of language,*
*puts a theory of language and a historicity of speech practice...*
*Any page is a spectacle... Whether the page is densely or sparsely*
*covered, the spectacle is very ancient... In the Talmud,*
*the circularity of the commentary of a text which is already,*
*in and of itself, a repetition (Mishna) of an absent-present text,*
*is transmission itself.*

Henri Meschonic

In Hebrew, the "prophet" is called a *Navi*. And as Hebrew masculine plural words end with "im." Hence, *Neviim*.[9]

## The Writings, or *Ketuvim*

*There are two cardinal sins from which all others spring:*
*impatience and laziness. They were chased out of paradise*
*because of their impatience, and they can't get back in*
*because of their laziness. But perhaps there is*
*but a single capital sin: impatience. They were chased out*
*because of impatience, and because of their impatience*
*they cannot get back in.*

Franz Kafka

Those texts which do not belong to a historical category are found in this third part of the Bible. These texts do not recount the history of the Jewish people or the narratives of that people's prophecies. These are the texts of wisdom or of the symbolic stories.

*Ketuvim* derives from *katuv*, "writing." Therefore, these are called the "Writings."[10]

## The *Halakhah* and the *Aggadah*

> *Be a scribe! Engrave this in your heart*
> *So that your name may forever live like theirs!*
> *The scroll is more valuable than the carved stone.*
> *A man is dead: his body is no longer but dust.*
> *And his people have disappeared from this world.*
> *A book will make his memory live again*
> *In the mouth of he that reads it.*
>
> Egyptian scribe circa 1300

The Torah contains two narrowly interrelated types of text. On the one hand are the texts which tell a story: the story of the creation of the world, the history of the patriarchs and matriarchs, episodes from the life of the Hebrews in Egypt and in the desert etc. These narrative texts make up the part of the Bible known as the *Aggadah,* the "story."

On the other hand, we find numerous texts which are purely legislative and prescriptive, which explain what should be done and what cannot be done. This second category of Biblical text is the *halakhah* (law). These two categories are the keys to understanding the Biblical text, the Midrash and the Talmud.

229

## Remarks on the Christian Bible

> *Despite what its etymology might suggest,*
> *imagination is not limited to the ability to form images of reality:*
> *it is the ability to form images which go beyond reality,*
> *which sing reality. It is a superhuman ability.*
> *A man is a man to the degree that he is a superman.*
> *We must define a man by the collection of tendencies*
> *which push him to go beyond the human condition.*
>
> Gaston Bachelard

Nowadays, when the word "Bible" is used, it is used both to refer to the Hebrew canon and to the Christian canon, which was based on the model of the Septuagint, to which the New Testament was added.

The Bible therefore consists of three parts:
–Hebrew Biblical canon: 24 books
–Deuterocanonica: 11 (or 12) books
–New Testament–Second Testimony

## The Biblical "Canon"

> *The letters are sparks and the word is a flame!*
> *At every syllable, the reader's eye might start a fire!*
> Edmond Jabès

The stories, and the history, told in the Biblical text cover a period ranging from the creation of the world to the return from the Babylonian exile in 520 B.C.E. The Hebrew Bible ends with the Book of Chronicles, the last verse of which reports the words of Cyrus, King of Persia, as he reports that he has received an order from God to build Him a house in Jerusalem in the country of Judea, "he who is there among you of all his people (desires it), The Lord his God be with him, and let him go up."

The events recorded in Genesis take place around the eighteenth century before Christ, the exile from Egypt told of in Exodus takes place around the fourteenth century B.C.E., and the monarchy of David and Solomon around the tenth century B.C.E.

Given that the various books were written after the events described had taken place, there has been much discussion aimed at determining the period during which these Biblical texts were written. However, readers of the Bible are practically never faced with the question of when it was written, for everything is related in a timeless mode, or in the simple opposition of present, past and future. Readers who belong to the religious community that follow these books read them to discover founding events which are the source for their community's identities, and, especially, its narrative identity. These texts are "myths," in the sense of identity-founding teachings. The question of the meaning of Judaic historiography remains as current as it is fascinating, but is beyond the scale of this introductory work.[11]

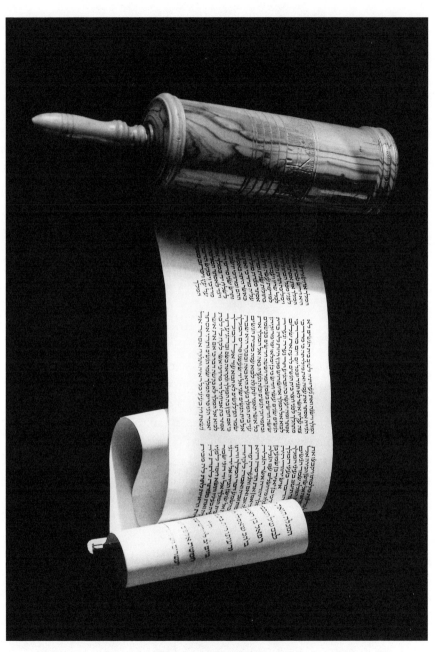

The Megillah of Esther.
It is read twice during the Purim carnival festival.

The canon of the Hebrew Bible was set very late, during the Talmudic period of the first centuries of the Christian era. This is made clear by the fact that we can still find discussions of certain books in the Talmud (such as whether certain books, like the Book of Esther, should or should not be included).[12]

## The Transmission of the Text from One Generation to the Next: *Sofrim* and Massoretes

> –*Where are you going, Master?*
> –*I don't know, I answered. I only want to leave here, always leave here, that is the only way I can reach my goal.*
> –*So you know your goal?*
> –*Yes, I answered, haven't I told you before? I want to leave here, that is my goal...*
>
> Franz Kafka

The first official transmitters of the text are known as the *Sofrim*, the "scribes," or counters. They undertook a task which was later taken over by the Massoretes. The *Sofrim* were the first masters of the oral tradition following the closing of the Hebrew canon (sixth century B.C.E.). For instance, they came up with the following counts for the Pentateuch:
669 paragraphs
5845 verses
79,976 words
304,805 consonants

In the Jewish tradition, structure is significant in and of itself. A flaw in the form of a scroll would render a public or liturgical reading invalid. If a letter is missing, or if there is an additional letter or symbol, or if the separation spaces (open or closed) are not respected, the book is considered *pasul*, "unfit for reading," despite the fact that the text's meaning is entirely legible and unencumbered. The masters had to use various techniques to maintain the Biblical tradition's undisputed unity. This conservation effort is known as the Massorete, or *Massorah*, which means the "usages of transmission." The wise men who were charged with this science were known as the Massoretes, a term which referred both to individuals and, more frequently, to entire schools.

## Translations Are the First Commentaries

> *"To leave men without food is a sin which cannot be attenuated by any circumstance; we cannot attribute the voluntary and the involuntary to it,"* according to Rabbi Yohanan.
> *A quote which Lévinas was quick to comment upon, without the slightest ambiguity:*
> *"Facing the hunger of men, responsibility can only be measured objectively. It is incontestable."*
> Emmanuel Lévinas *Totality and Infinity*

During the third century B.C.E., in Alexandria, the five books of the Torah, or Pentateuch, were translated into Greek. This extraordinary event was followed over the course of the next generations by the translation of the other Judaic books—Psalms, Book of Prophets, historical and poetic books—until, by roughly the first century, the Greek translations constituted a whole known as the Bible of the Septuagint, or simply the "Septuagint." The Talmud hailed the miraculous aspect of this endeavor. Rabbi Shimon Ben Gamliel authorized the reading of the Bible in Greek, but underlined its character as benediction, quoting verse 27, chapter 9 of Genesis: "God shall enlarge Japheth, and he shall dwell in the tents of Shem; and Canaan shall be his servant." In the Bible, Japheth is the ancestor of the Greeks and Shem is the ancestor of the Semitic Hebrews. According to Rabbi Shimon Ben Gamliel in the Talmud, the most beautiful thing Japheth owned was the Greek language, which must have resided in the tents, in other words in the Shem's places of study and of prayer![13]

233

הדרן עלך יש בערכין

הדרן עלך יש בערכין

Page from the Talmud;
this is an excerpt from the *Erakhim* Treatise, which deals with the
question of "slander," among other subjects.

## "The People of the Interpretation of the Book"

> *To be Jewish is to believe in the intelligence of the Pharisees and their*
> *masters. To accede to faith in the Bible through the Talmud.*
> *If there were no Talmud, there would be no Jews today.*
>
> Emmanuel Lévinas

"The people of the Book" is a famous expression, but it is not entirely accurate. The Jewish people are not the "people of the Book" but the "people of the books"! We must indeed insist upon this point: Judaism is not based on a single book, for, aside from the Bible, there is another book: the Talmud. The Bible, also known as the Torah, must be properly shed light on and interpreted by the Talmud to introduce the reader into a Jewish deciphering of Scriptures. The Jewish people are not only the people of the Book but also, to quote Armand Abecassis, "the people of the interpretation of the book"!

235

## The Talmud

> *You bought books and filled the shelves, oh lover of the Muses.*
> *Does this mean you are now a wise man?*
> *If today you buy stringed instruments, lyres and plectrum,*
> *Do you think that tomorrow the kingdom of music will belong to you?*
>
> Ausone, Gallic poet, quoted by Alberto Manguel in *Histoire de la lecture*
> (History of Reading)

So Judaism rests upon two original sets of teachings: written teachings, or *Torah she-bikhtav,* which would become the Bible (or *Tanakh,* in Hebrew), and oral teachings, or *Torah she be-al-pe,* literally "the law which is on the mouth," which would become the Talmud, the Midrash and certain Kaballistic texts from the Talmudic era.

The Talmud is the oral commentary on the Biblical text. It was transmitted from one generation to the next. In principle, the oral law was intended to be exclusively disseminated by word of mouth; yet "one day" (which actually lasted several hundred years) it was written down. This transcription of the oral law constitutes the Talmud.

This "oral-written" law became the preeminent book of Judaism. For fifteen centuries, it has been the true fundamental text of the Jewish people, an obligatory element in any interpretation of Scripture, a decisive authority regarding the rules to live by, and the ultimate reference concerning the understanding of Revelation.

The Talmud governs daily and ritual life, along with the intellectual life of practicing Jews, by discussing and codifying them. Aside from the vast body of rabbinical literature connected to it, the Talmud represents the work done in the name of Judaism from Ezra the Scribe, in the sixth century B.C.E., to the sixth century of the Christian era, an uninterrupted task which was contributed to with all the energy of the wise men and the spiritual and intellectual activity of a nation. Along with its subsequent commentaries, the Talmud added up to a monumental set of twenty enormous volumes in the first edition, which was known as the Bomberg edition (named after the printer), and published in Venice in 1523. This edition defined the definitive pagination and formatting of the Talmud for all editions up to the present day.

1. According to the Kabbalah, the tragus (earlobe) is one of the three points of desire (amorous and sexual), along with the right big toe and the right thumb. See Charles Mopsik, *La lettre de la sainteté* (The Letter of Holiness), Verdier, Paris, Note p. 89. See also Exodus 29:20, Leviticus 8:23-24, and Leviticus 14:14 and following.

2. Indeed, the tragus (earlobe) is symbolically what allows us to close the auditory canal by applying light pressure with a finger.

3. Such as Mendelkern, see *Concordance*, p. 1249.

4. Literally, "In the beginning," or Genesis.

5. Literally, "Names", or Exodus.

6. Literally, "He called", or Leviticus, the law of the priests.

7. Literally, "In the desert", or Numbers, for it begins with the enumeration of the tribes.

8. Literally, "Teachings" or Deuteronomy, in other words, "repetition of the Law."

9. The *Neviim* consist of: The First Prophets: - Joshua: *Yehoshua*. – Judges: *Shoftim*. – Samuel: *Shmuel I* and *II*. – Kings: *Melakhim I* and *II*. The Three Great Prophets: Isaiah: *Yeshayahu*; Jeremiah: *Yirmiyahu*; Ezekiel: *Yeheskiel*. The Twelve "Minor" Prophets: Hosea: *Hoshea;* Joel: *Yoel;* Amos: *Amos;* Jonah: *Yona;* Micah: *Mikha;* Obadiah: *Ovadia;* Nahum: *Nachum;* Habakkuk: *Habakkuk;* Zephaniah: *Tsephania;* Haggai: *Hagaya;* Zechariah: *Zekharia;* Malachi: *Malakhi*. Note: the term "minor" in the expression "minor prophets" does not refer to the quality of the prophecy but the length of these prophets' prophecies, which in some cases, such as Obadiah's, can be limited.

10. The *Ketuvim* include: The Psalms: *Tehilim;* The Proverbs: *Mishlei;* Job: *Iyov;* The five scrolls: The Song of Songs: *Shir Hashirim;* Ruth: *Rut;* Lamentations: *Eicha;* Ecclesiastes: *Kohelet;* Esther: *Esther;* Daniel: *Daniel;* Ezra: *Ezra;* Nehemia: *Nehemiah;* Chronicles (two books): *Divrei Hayamim*.

11. Regarding this question, see Yosef-Hayyim Yerushalmi, *Zakhor, histoire juive et mémoire juive*, (Zakhor, Jewish History and Jewish Memory) Verdier, 1984.

12. See *Bava Batra*, 14 and 15.

13. There is also "the *Targumim*, or Aramaic translations, are the first link between Scripture and various forms of its interpretation." The Aramaic versions were the first used to understand the Scripture. Indeed, the *Targum* (particularly the so-called Onkelos Targum, named after its translator) was linked to Synagogue liturgy. It needed to be heard and immediately understood. The Aramaic translations are introduced as "the simplest state of Scriptural exegesis". They are on the threshold joining Written Law and Oral Law. They are particularly close to Written Law because they are the closest to the era of Ezra (6th century B.C.E.). They influenced the Mishna – the Oral Law – and its language. The teachers consider them exegetic works, for a translation is already an elaboration, a construction of meaning, an *interpretation*.

# 10

# The Ascent to the Torah

*Everything moves and ascends. Any step is an ascent.*
*Even descents are interior ascents.*
*Everything moves, everything flows and everything*
*ascends...*
*Any true poet, any man who knows how to get inside*
*things, anybody who can hear the spirit of Holiness*
*perceives the dynamic ascent within any reality...*
*Man must experience the world not as a constructed,*
*finished thing, but as something that is always*
*happening, rising, developing and rising even further.*
*Everything renews itself.*
*This is what we call the* chiddush hatemidi.

Based on Rav Kook, *Orot Hakodesh*, Volume II

# Chapter Ten

The "Weekly Parashah" and the Parashah of the Bar/Bat Mitzvah

**Public Reading of the Torah**

The "Book" and the "Name"

**The Blessings of the Torah**

The Seven "Ascents," *Mashlim, Maftir,* and *Musaf*

***Barukh Shepetarani:* "The Relief of the Father"**

Parchment, Ink, Quill, and Reed Calamus

**A Few Fundamental Rules of Writing**

The Two Meanings of the Word "Parashah"

**Remarks Regarding the Expression "Consonantal Writing"**

The Lack of Vowel Notation: A Fundamental Ambiguity

**The Cantillation Signs: the *Taamim***

The *Tikkun Kor'im* and the Synagogue Prompter

# The "Weekly Parashah" and the Parashah of the Bar/Bat Mitzvah

*If you think you are capable of destruction,*
*you should also think that you are capable of reconstruction.*
Rabbi Nachman of Breslav

The parashah, or "weekly parashah," is the text from the Torah (the Pentateuch or Five Books of Moses), which is read in the synagogue every week on the Sabbath.

Today, the liturgical text of the Torah is read publicly four times a week, on the Sabbath (Saturday morning and afternoon), on Monday morning, and on Thursday morning. Aside from these set days, it is also read on Rosh Chodesh (the first day of the month), and on holidays. Given that the reading of the Torah is an important part of the bar mitzvah ceremony, bar/bat mitzvahs are always scheduled for one of these days.

Initially, the custom was for the Torah to be read over a cycle of three years. To do so, the Torah was divided into 153 (or 155 or 167, depending on the year) *Sedarim* or *sidrot* (plural of *sidrah*). Later, the triennial cycle became annual (and continues to be practiced as such). The Torah is therefore divided into 54 *sedarim* or *sidrot*.

A different sidrah is read on each Sabbath. The cycle begins on the Sabbath following the Simchat Torah holiday, which brings the autumn holidays (Rosh Hashanah and Yom Kippur) to a close. It ends with the following year's Simchat Torah. From one week to the next, the Biblical story follows the Jewish people from Creation to the death of Moses and the entry into the "Promised Land."

Each of the 54 parts takes on the name of "sidrah of the week," and is given a specific title, which is the first word (or one of the first words) of the first verse of the week's sidrah. For instance, the first sidrah of the Torah is called *Bereshit*, which is the first word of the first verse in Genesis.

Zodiac wheel with the names of the astrological signs in Hebrew (Germany, 1341).

Every Sabbath (Saturday), a sidrah is read aloud. The Sabbath takes its name from the day's sidrah and is referred to as *Shabbat Bereshit, Shabbat Noah,* etc. The bar/bat mitzvah Sabbath is frequently referred to by its sidrah. Therefore, when a child is asked when he or she will have his or her bar/bat mitzvah, he or she can respond by saying *Shabbat Bereshit* or *Shabbat Noah,* etc.

I have previously defined the parashah as a text passage between two blank spaces. Over time, the word parashah has developed a secondary meaning and has often come to replace the term sidrah. Today, the parashah refers to those passages from the Torah read on the Sabbath. It is commonplace to refer either to the "sidrah of the week" or the "parashah of the week," an expression which translates as the classic Hebrew phrase *Parashat HaShavua.*

## Public Reading of the Torah: The Ascent to the Torah, or the *Aliyah*

> *To interpret the Book is, first and foremost, to rise up against God in order to seize both a voice and a writing implement from His power. We must detach ourselves from the divine part within us, in order to return God to himself and to enjoy our freedom as men.*

Edmond Jabès, *Elya*

After the reading of the Psalms, the Shema, and the repetition of silent prayer (*amidah*), the Torah is taken out of the Holy Ark or the cabinet set in the front of the synagogue, in which all the scrolls are stored. As explained in a previous chapter, the Book is carried around the assembly, the members of which honor it with a symbolic kiss. It is then set down on the *tevah,* or bimah, the synagogue's central table, and opened to the passage to be read. One of the faithful is then called forward to hold up the open scroll and display it to the assembly. In Ashkenazi synagogues, the raising of the Torah takes place after it has been read from. This presentation, as was mentioned in a previous chapter, is known as the *hagbah,* or "raising." Following the *hagbah* several people are called by turn (the exact number varies depending on the occasion) to pronounce a blessing before or after the reading of the passage. Being called to the Torah is known as an *aliyah,* an "ascent."

## The "Book" and the "Name"

*When I was born, he wrote, it crossed my parents' minds that I could perhaps become a writer. It would therefore be preferable that it not be immediately clear to all and sundry that I was Jewish. That is why, along with my everyday first name, they gave me two other, unused names, which were not obviously Jewish, or clearly my own. Forty years ago, a couple of parents could not have been more clairvoyant. What they considered a distant possibility has come to pass...*

Walter Benjamin, *Angelus novus*

The person who ascends to the Torah is called by his or her first name and the name of his or her father or of both parents, depending on the community. This is significant because it is a continuation of what I have referred to as the phenomenology of the book. After all the impact the book has had by opening, moving and elevating the faithful, it returns them to a genealogical continuity. It is no coincidence that the word "book," in Hebrew *sefer*, has the same numeric value as the word "name," *shem*, namely 340.

This idea is all the more significant on the day of the bar/bat mitzvah, for though young men and women are taught to detach themselves from the parental link, they also learn that maturing does not imply breaking all ties. A new adult manner of maintaining the connection between the generations is thereby installed.

In general, the first person to ascend to the Torah is a Cohen, the second is a Levi, and the third person is a Yisrael. If the bar mitzvah boy or bat mitzvah girl is reading the haftarah, he or she is called last. A person of honor is often called third, or sixth. On the day of the bar/bat mitzvah, an effort is made to call all the family members to the Torah. As there are often over eight people to be honored, the same passage can be read several times in order to ensure everyone is called.

If the person called does not know his or her first name in Hebrew, he or she can be called by his or her regular name. In certain communities, the family name is added to the first name.

## The Blessings of the Torah

בָּרְכוּ אֶת יְהֹוָה הַמְבוֹרָךְ.

בָּרוּךְ יְהֹוָה הַמְבוֹרָךְ לְעוֹלָם וָעֶד.

בָּרוּךְ יְהֹוָה הַמְבוֹרָךְ לְעוֹלָם וָעֶד.

בָּרוּךְ אַתָּה יְהֹוָה, אֱלֹהֵינוּ מֶלֶךְ הָעוֹלָם, אֲשֶׁר בָּחַר

בָּנוּ מִכָּל־הָעַמִּים, וְנָתַן לָנוּ אֶת תּוֹרָתוֹ. בָּרוּךְ אַתָּה

יְהֹוָה, נוֹתֵן הַתּוֹרָה.

Transliteration:

The one who is called: *Bareku et Adonai hamevorakh.*
The assembly: *Barukh Adonai hamevorakh le'olam va'ed.*
The one who is called: *Barukh Adonai hamevorakh le'olam va'ed.*

*Barukh ata Adonai Elohenu melekh ha'olam, asher bachar banu mikol ha'amim, venatan lanu et Torato. Barukh ata, Adonai, noten Hatorah.*

In English:

The one who is called: Bless God who is worthy of blessing!
The assembly: Blessed are you eternal, Who is eternally worthy
of blessing!
The one who is called: Blessed are you eternal, Who is eternally worthy
of blessing!

Blessed are you Adonai our God, ruler of the universe, Who has chosen us
among all people and given us his Torah.
Blessed are you Adonai, Who gives us the Torah.

The chazan (or the person called) reads the passage from the Torah without
reciting a single word by heart.

After the reading, the person called says:

בָּרוּךְ אַתָּה יְהֹוָה, אֱלֹהֵינוּ מֶלֶךְ הָעוֹלָם, אֲשֶׁר נָתַן
לָנוּ (תּוֹרָתוֹ) תּוֹרַת אֱמֶת וְחַיֵּי עוֹלָם נָטַע בְּתוֹכֵנוּ.
בָּרוּךְ אַתָּה יְהֹוָה, נוֹתֵן הַתּוֹרָה.

Transliteration:
*Barukh ata Adonai, Elohenu melekh ha'olam, asher natan lanu (torato) Torat
emet vehayei olam nata betokhenu. Barukh ata Adonai, noten Hatorah.*

In English:
Blessed are you Adonai our God, ruler of the universe Who has given us (His
Torah) truthful Torah, and who implanted in us an eternal life; Blessed are
you Adonai who gives us the Torah.

## The Seven "Ascents," *Mashlim, Maftir,* and *Musaf*

> *One day a rabbi gathered all his disciples and invited them to question
> him and even to criticize him. The disciples said:*
> *–Master, your behavior stuns us, you never do as your father,
> your master, did before he chose you as his successor.
> How are you treating his legacy, where is your faithfulness?
> The rabbi looked at his disciples very seriously,
> but his eyes could not hide a spark of joy and malice. He answered:
> –I'll explain it to you, it's very simple. No one is more faithful than I
> am! I follow my father to the very last word, in every way: in the same
> way that he did not follow his father, I do not follow him.*
>
> Traditional history of Hasidism.

On the Sabbath, seven people are invited to "ascend." The parashah of the
week is therefore divided into seven parts. An eighth person is called to
read the last verses of the sidrah and a text drawn from Prophets, the
haftarah, once the scrolls have been rolled up in a ceremonial moment
known as the *gelilah,* the rolling up. On weekdays, there are only three

"ascensions" to read a text which corresponds to one seventh of the text read on the Sabbath.

In general, the bar mitzvah boy or bat mitzvah girl reads the entire sidrah or parashah, but it occasionally happens that he or she only reads part of it, or doesn't read from the parashah at all, choosing instead to read only the blessings before and after his or her *aliyah* to the Torah. In numerous communities, the bar mitzvah boy or girl is called to read the last passage of the parashah, known as the *maftir*, along with the haftarah.[1]

## *Barukh Shepetarani:* "The Relief of the Father"
### A surprising but important blessing

> *We are all in possession of a mystery,*
> *since we have all had a childhood.*
>
> Philippe Labro

The link between the name and the importance of filiation in the ascent to the Torah gives rise to a tradition known as the blessing of *Barukh shepetarani*. During the ascent to the Torah, the father says *Barukh shepetarani meonesho shel zeh.* "Blessed are You who has spared me the punishment of this one." The meaning of this strange blessing relates to a father's relief at having properly carried out his son's education up to that point. This underlines the importance of the conscience of the educational responsibility taught in the Shema and the four *parshiyot* of the tefillin.

It means that the father has crucially contributed to the preparation of the bar mitzvah, so that his son could accede to a good Jewish education including Hebrew, the Torah and its blessings, the reading of the parashah and of the haftarah, etc. It is the blessing of a happy father who has fulfilled his fundamental and foundational pedagogical obligations, who has not only conceived a child but has given it the foundations for a beautiful, strong participation in life, the city of man, and the community. The faithful respond to this blessing by saying amen, and adding "mazel tov," congratulating the child, but also the father, and thereby joining in the family's happiness.

Bat mitzvah girl reading the Torah, with the rabbi and her father at her side.
Today, in Orthodox communities, if the bat mitzvah girl reads it is before a minyan entirely
composed of women.

## Parchment, Ink, Quill, and Reed Calamus

> *How did He combine them? Two stones build two houses,*
> *three stones build six houses, four stones build twenty-four houses,*
> *five stones build one hundred and twenty houses,*
> *six stones build seven hundred and twenty houses,*
> *and seven stones build five thousand forty houses.*
> *From that point on, what appears and what counts is what the mouth*
> *cannot speak and the ear cannot hear...*

The Book of Creation

Before closing this chapter, I would like to give the reader a better idea of what the Torah scrolls from which the bar mitzvah boy reads look like. In their original form, the holy texts were initially disseminated as scrolls made of tanned leather or leather with a parchment finish. This continues to be the practice for texts used in the liturgy. These rolls made of layers of animal hide, sewn together and finished with an awl, reproduce the holy texts vertically and horizontally. In the Orient, the texts are copied with a reed calamus, and in the Occident with a goose quill. These copies are painstakingly realized following all the customary regulations. There are no specific signs or vowels to instruct the reader how to vocalize the text, and therefore to interpret it or divide it into logical or semantic sections, in order to make the reader more sensitive to the act of reading.

## A Few Fundamental Rules of Writing

*The space starts like this, with nothing but words, signs traced on the blank page. Before, there was nothing, or nearly nothing; after, there isn't much, just a few signs, but enough to provide an up and a down, a beginning and an end, a right and a left, a front and a back.*

Georges Perec, *Species of Spaces*

At this point, it is necessary to mention two important rules of writing: first and foremost, two letters cannot be in contact. Each letter must be autonomous. Each letter is a world, a universe. The scribe is particularly careful to avoid having letters touching each other. If any letters should touch, the book is considered *passul,* unfit for liturgical reading.

The second rule deals with the position of the letters in relation to the guide line. Indeed, as with calligraphy in most other languages, the Hebrew scribe traces a straight line before beginning to write, so the letters will be properly aligned. These guide lines are known as *sirtut* (or *sirtutim* in the plural).

These lines are etched with a dry awl. The fact that they are made without ink renders them practically invisible from a distance. One particularity of liturgical writing concerns the positioning of the letters in relation to these guide lines. As Rabbi Tsadok Hakohen of Lublin remarked, there is an essential difference between the proper way of writing Hebrew characters and Latin characters.

The bar mitzvah boy reads the Torah with a *yad*.
While reading aloud, he follows the text in order to find his place if necessary.

In Latin calligraphy, the letter rests on the bottom line, such as:

However, in Hebrew writing, the letter is literally suspended from the top line, such as:

The upper guide line is the limit for script. This limit also has a symbolic meaning, for it traces the boundary between writing and what is beyond writing. It is also worth noting that none of the 22 letters of the Hebrew alphabet go beyond this limit, with the exception of the letter *lamed:*

The name of this letter, *lamed,* includes the very meaning of its form: *lamed* is a root which means "study" and "education," a meaning which echoes the move beyond the writing line, or, in the words of Emmanuel Lévinas, "beyond the verse."

## The Two Meanings of the Word "Parashah"

> *The position of a man at his work table is similar to the position of a fisherman holding his fishing rod on the banks of a river.*
> *One man spends hours looking at a blank page, the other watches the water and that circle of clearer water at the surface where the fish is the center of attraction. One man is on the watch for words, the other, for fish. This shows what an essential role the pen plays and how the fingers which hold it must be careful to avoid disrupting those moves and shifts of the pen which track and sometimes even precede the appearance of their prey with the discretion of a shadow.*
>
> Edmond Jabès

The Biblical text, and particularly the Five Books of Moses, does not show any vowels. Additionally, there is no punctuation. There is nothing to reveal the rhythm of the text or the shift from one sentence to another. The text is devoid of periods and of commas. Nothing interrupts the flow of words aside from the occasional blank space, those writing voids that, to the untrained eye, appear like holes within the writing.

The text between two blank spaces is known as parashah, or "passage." The word "parashah" derives from the Hebrew letter root *pey, resh, kaf,* which means, "separate," to be cut off, like the Mishnaic proverb which states, *al tifrosh min hatzibbur,* "do not separate yourself from the community, do not cut yourself off." There are two types of *parshiyot* (plural of parashah), depending on the blank space preceding the text. When the blank space is at the center of a line, shut in by writing to its right and to its left, the passage that follows is known as *parashah setuma,* "closed." However, when the blank space is open on the margin, the following passage is *parashah petuha,* "open." The length of the blank space is equivalent to at least nine letters for the closed parashah and indefinite for the open parashah. As can be

253

noted, the passage bears the name and description of the blank space preceding the opening blank. It should also be noted that the margins between the columns are half an inch wide, the upper margin is three quarters of an inch high, and the lower margin is one inch high. Four blank lines indicate the separation between the books.

This notion of the "open" or closed parashah is fundamental to the point that a failure to respect it leads to the book being considered unfit for liturgical use.

If the scribe accidentally reverses the nature of a blank space, making it "open" instead of "closed" or vice versa, the entire book cannot be used for public reading.[2]

יא אַחֶ֖רֶת יִֽקַּֽח־ל֑וֹ שְׁאֵרָ֛הּ כְּסוּתָ֥הּ וְעֹנָתָ֖הּ לֹ֥א יִגְרָֽע׃ וְאִם־שְׁלָשׁ־

יב אֵ֖לֶּה לֹ֣א יַעֲשֶׂ֖ה לָ֑הּ וְיָצְאָ֥ה חִנָּ֖ם אֵ֥ין כָּֽסֶף׃ מַכֵּ֥ה

יג אִ֛ישׁ וָמֵ֖ת מ֥וֹת יוּמָֽת׃ וַאֲשֶׁר֙ לֹ֣א צָדָ֔ה וְהָאֱלֹהִ֖ים אִנָּ֣ה לְיָד֑וֹ

יד וְשַׂמְתִּ֤י לְךָ֙ מָק֔וֹם אֲשֶׁ֥ר יָנ֖וּס שָֽׁמָּה׃ וְכִֽי־

יֵזִ֥ד אִ֛ישׁ עַל־רֵעֵ֖הוּ לְהָרְג֣וֹ בְעָרְמָ֑ה מֵעִ֣ם מִזְבְּחִ֔י תִּקָּחֶ֖נּוּ

טו לָמֽוּת׃ וּמַכֵּ֥ה אָבִ֛יו וְאִמּ֖וֹ מ֥וֹת יוּמָֽת׃ וְגֹנֵ֨ב

טז אִ֤ישׁ וּמְכָר֙וֹ וְנִמְצָ֣א בְיָד֔וֹ מ֥וֹת יוּמָֽת׃ וּמְקַלֵּ֧ל

When there is a space in the heart of a line, the following passage forms a *parashah setuma*, "closed."
When the space opens on the margin, the following passage is known as *parashah petucha*, "open."

## Remarks Regarding the Expression "Consonantal Writing"

*Before signifying something, language is significant to someone.*
Jacques Lacan

Hebrew writing is composed of twenty-two consonants. However, it is inaccurate, though common, to claim that there are no Hebrew vowels. Vowels do exist, and in fact their vocalization follows grammatical rules of rigorously mathematic precision.

Nonetheless, vowels do not always appear in the written text. Indeed, despite the undeniable existence of these vowels, a reader is likely to read a Hebrew text without encountering a single one. The liturgical text of the Torah only features the consonants.

Today Hebrew newspapers and the majority of Hebrew books published both in Israel and around the world are purely consonantal. Only children's books, beginners' publications, and certain poetry books also include the vowels.[3]

255

## The Lack of Vowel Notation:
## A Fundamental Ambiguity

*Everyone knows that God is a writer. His masterpiece is called the Bible. Often imitated, it has never been equaled. God, who is never short of inspiration, is barely acquainted with the anxiety of the blank page. Indeed, his pages are beautifully, densely filled, and you need only lift your eyes to the starry night sky to read, black on white, what Mallarmé called "the alphabet of the stars," and to learn the latest news from across the universe...*

Stéphane Zagdanski

Originally, vowels were entirely avoided. Hebrew script only included the consonants, and it was up to the reader to add the appropriate vocalization by recognizing words and expressions. Hebrew script therefore requires a prior knowledge of the language, and of its syntax and phonology. A single word can frequently have several potential vocalizations, and hence several potential meanings. In this case, the context determines the meaning of the word. Midrashic and Talmudic interpretations frequently play on these ambiguities to construct a commentary. For instance, the *zayin, kaf, reish* root can be vocalized as *zakhar,* meaning "masculine," or *zekher,* "memory."[4]

## The Cantillation Signs: the *Taamim*

> *I allowed myself to be seduced by the femininity of the words.*
> *My reverie followed the inflections of sweetness.*
> *The feminine in a word accentuates the pleasure of speaking.*
> *But one must have a certain love for slow sounds.*

Gaston Bachelard

The public reading of the Torah follows extremely precise rules, for each word is accompanied by musical notations known in Hebrew as *taamim,* which means "what gives taste" or "what gives meaning."

This form of musical notation is different from our occidental systems of musical notation. In Hebrew, the notes are small signs placed above or below the letters. The names of these signs vary a little based on their geographic origin or the threnody of the reading.

For instance, Sephardic reading, which originated in Spain and was subsequently influenced by Arab culture, includes singing that resembles Arab music, while Ashkenazi readers—with ancestry in Alsace, Germany, or Eastern Europe—have a far more western style of singing.

The Zohar comments: What does the *Song of Songs* mean by the expression "We will make thee earrings of gold with studs of silver" (1:11)? The earrings of gold are the cantillation signs suspended from the letters like the decorated earrings hang from the ear...words without cantillation signs would be like the ears of a young bride without earrings or jewelry."

Placed above or below the letters, the cantillation signs (shown here in red)
indicate how to vocalize the text.

The scribe's workshop.
Three types of parchments can be recognized in this photo:
the mezuzah (bottom), the tefillin (center), the Torah (background).

## The *Tikkun Korim* and the Synagogue Prompter

*The tree can become a blazing flame, man a speaking flame...*
Novalis, *Fragments.*

Liturgical reading requires serious preparation, both to learn the exact vocalization and the exact cantillation for the texts to be read from scrolls which do not include vocalization and cantillation signs. For this purpose, there are preparatory books known as *tikkun korim,* which feature pages with two columns: one, for practice, includes the text with all signs, vowels and music, while the other, which can be used to test yourself, has the text without any additional indications for vowels and music, just as it will appear in the liturgical scroll.

Nonetheless, given that memorizing this information is difficult, an assistant stands next to the reader during the liturgical reading in the synagogue and occasionally prompts him or accompanies the reading with coded sign language indicating the cantillation signs, thereby making the task of reading much simpler.

1. In many communities, a passage can be repeated as many times as necessary, provided the assembly is not exhausted, to allow all the bar mitzvah guests to ascend to the Torah. The passage repeated is known as the *hosafah* (addition.

2. In his *Mishnah Torah, Hilchot Sefer Torah*, Chapter 8, Maimonides lists all the *parshiyot petuchot* and *setumot* based on a body of texts he was able to consult in Egypt, a body of texts which was corrected by no less an authority than Aaron ben Moses of the Asher tribe, also known as Aaron ben Asher, who was rector of the Tiberian Academy (*Rosh Yeshiva*), which specialized in Massoretic study. Maimonides concludes by providing the following data: there are 290 "open" *parshiyot* and 379 "closed" *parshiyot* in the Pentateuch, for a total of 669 *parshiyot*.

3. In the liturgical writing of the Torah text, caps known as *taigim* are placed on certain letters (13 letters in all, seven with triple-pronged caps and six with single-pronged caps). The seven letters which have triple-pronged caps are: *shin, ayin, tet, nun, zayin, gimel,* and *tsadi.* There is a mnemonic expression to remember these seven capped letters: *Shaatnez-gats.* The six letters with single-pronged caps are: *bet, dalet, kaf, het, yod,* and *hey.* This leaves nine unornamented letters: *alef, vav, kaf, lamed, mem, samekh, pey, resh,* and *taf.* These letters form the eloquent mnemonic expression: "the art of the scribe" (literally "the work of the scribe"): *melekhet hasofer.*

4. In the ninth century C.E., after long, arduous work, the Massoretes of the Tiberian Academy perfected a new system for vocalization known as *nikud,* which literally translates to "punctuation", for this system of vocalization is based on the use of points primarily placed beneath consonants, and in a few cases, to represent certain vowels, above or in the middle of the consonant. This Tiberian system of vocalization which remains in use to the present day, and is also referred to as the inferior vocalization system due to the fact that most of the vowel-signs are beneath consonant-letters. (This system did not appear suddenly but was the fruit of a slow evolution and maturation from the sixth to the ninth century, a process which resulted in a system of practically mathematical precision. For instance, in the system's initial phase, there was only one sign for "ei" and "ê," and a single sign for the "open a" and the "closed a." The system's initial phase did not include distinctive signs for the vowels, but tiny consonant-letters which were placed above or below the actual consonants (at the very beginning, mostly above). This was the case with the upside down *ayin* which was placed over a consonant to make the sound "a". The *ayin* is probably the source of the shape of the *kamatz.*

# 11

# The Haftarah

*In Krakow, there lived a Jew by the name of*
*Rabbi Isaac, son of Rabbi Yankel.*
*One night, he dreamed that a man told him,*
*"Go to Prague, to the bridge that leads*
*to the royal castle, dig under the third pillar*
*and you will find a treasure."*
*Rabbi Isaac didn't really pay attention to the dream.*
*But when it recurred not only once, but twice,*
*he took out his bag and his walking shoes*
*and set off for Prague. [...]*
*Once he arrived under the royal bridge,*
*he wanted to start digging, but the royal guard*
*was on watch and kept looking over*
*at Rabbi Isaac with surprise.*
*The captain of the guards called to him and said,*
*"What are you doing? What are you looking for?"*
*And Rabbi Isaac, as straight-talking as ever,*
*told the guard his dream. The captain of the guards*
*burst out laughing.*
*"My poor friend, he said, you came all the way*
*to Prague from Krakow for a dream?*
*Imagine what would happen if I also listened*
*to my dreams! Last night I dreamed*
*that I had to go to Krakow, to the home of Isaac,*
*son of Yankel, so that I could find a great treasure*
*beneath his furnace. Forget about it!*
*I'm not going to go all the way to some town where*
*half the Jews are called Isaac and the other half are*
*called Yankel!" Rabbi Isaac, son of Yankel, smiled,*
*thanked the captain and returned to Krakow,*
*where he found the treasure buried under his furnace.*

Martin Buber, *The Way of Man: According to the*
*Teaching of Hasidism*

# Chapter Eleven

A Passage from Prophets

**The Detour Man**

Man in Revolt

## A Passage from Prophets

*In the happiest of cases, the poet can succeed at two things:
representing, representing his time, and presenting something
whose time hasn't yet come.*

Ingeborg Bachmann

As was stated in the previous chapter, the *Tanakh* is divided into three parts:
the actual Torah, or "the Five Books of Moses," which make up the text of the
parashah; the *Neviim,* or Prophets; and the *Ketuvim,* or Writings.

The haftarah is a text drawn from "Prophets." It relates to the content of the
parashah being read on a given day. There are two hypotheses regarding the
origin of the haftarah. The first assumes that the anti-Jewish laws decreed by
Antiochus Epiphane in 165 B.C.E. forced Jews to find an alternative to reading
the Torah in public, which had become illegal. The era's Masters therefore
decided to replace the parashah with the reading of a prophetic text with similar
subject matter to the Torah, but contained in lighter, less ostentatious parchments. It may even have been a question of telling the prophetic tales, or reciting them by heart, which was not possible in the case of the "written Torah,"

for it could only be read in the liturgical text. The second hypothesis regarding the origin of the haftarah is linked to the Masters' desire to separate themselves from the Samaritans who did not recognize any canonical value in the prophetic writings.

The source of the word "haftarah" can be related to the Hebrew root *pey, tet, resh,* "to take leave," insofar as the reading of the Torah on the morning of the Sabbath ends with the haftarah. Some take it to mean *patur,* or "settlement," for in reading the haftarah one accomplishes one's duty to listen to the Torah. Others interpret it to mean "opening," on the basis that it is permissible to open one's mouth during the haftarah to speak to a neighbor while it is theoretically forbidden during the reading of the Torah. It is unknown when the haftarot corresponding to each Sabbath were chosen, or who wrote them. It is known, however, that once Antiochus's decree was abolished, the custom continued, for the wise men wanted to preserve the prophetic message for all the future generations. In fact, its trace can be found in the Gospel: "as his custom was, he went into the synagogue on the Sabbath day, and stood up for to read. And there was delivered unto him the book of the prophet Esaias" (Luke 4:16).

In Sephardic communities, the privilege of singing the haftarah can be granted to a minor, and it is a significant honor to read it on the day of one's bar/bat mitzvah. Today it is common for the bar mitzvah boy or bat mitzvah girl to read only the eighth part of the parashah, the *maftir* (a very short text), which is read in conjunction with the haftarah. Since it is read from a book containing vowels, it is far less strenuous to learn the haftarah than to learn the entire parashah.

The haftarah is generally at least 21 verses long. This is the number of verses in the book of Ovadiah, the shortest book in the Prophets. One can also interpret this number to be a reference to the name of God, YHVH, the numeric value of which is 21. This name means "I will be" and has been interpreted as a divine promise by God to always be there for his creatures. According to this theory, the reading of the haftarah would be a prophetic promise by its form alone.

Today, certain customs divide the haftarah into less than 21 verses. As with the parashah, there are different sung melodies, which vary according to location. Oriental modulations are heard among the Sephardic Jews, and more

*The Vocation of Ezekiel,* (1952–1956), Marc Chagall.
An astonishing prophet who was ordered to "eat the Book."

occidental sounds can be heard among the Ashkenazi Jews. The style and lexicon of the Prophets is complex. A Talmudic custom therefore recommends that the haftarah be translated into the language of the audience so that those present can follow the text and understand what is happening on the liturgical level. Today, in certain communities, the rabbi introduces the haftarah with a brief commentary, resituates the Prophet in his historical context, and explains the connection with the parashah. Then the rabbi reads a few verses of the haftarah, or, if it isn't too long, the entire text, in English. It is only once the rabbi has been through this procedure that the reading is done in Hebrew. At the time of the Talmud, the text was translated every three verses. The essential idea was to make this liturgy comprehensible and to allow the maximum amount of participation from the public.

In the context of the bar/bat mitzvah, the commentary and the translation can be made by the bat mitzvah girl or bar mitzvah boy, and are considered part of his or her speech.

## The Detour Man

> *The Bible warns us away from false prophets. The result is that prophecy is wary of prophecy and that he who devotes himself to Revelation runs a risk.*
> *There is a call to vigilance herein, which probably belongs to the essence of Revelation: it does not separate from disquiet.*
>
> Emmanuel Lévinas

The prophet is the man who takes a detour.

The third chapter of Exodus reads:

1. Now Moses kept the flock of Jethro his father in law, the priest of Midian: and he led the flock to the backside of the desert, and came to the mountain of God, [even] to Horeb.

2. And the angel of the LORD appeared unto him in a flame of fire out of the midst of a bush: and he looked, and, behold, the bush burned with fire, and the bush [was] not consumed.

3. And Moses said, I will now turn aside, and see this great sight, why the bush is not burnt.

4. And when the LORD saw that he turned aside to see, God called unto him out of the midst of the bush, and said, Moses, Moses. And he said, Here [am] I.

5. And he said, Draw not nigh hither: put off thy shoes from off thy feet, for the place whereon thou standest [is] holy ground.

This is a crucial passage, for it sets forth the structures of God's revelation to Moses. Revelation only takes place because Moses is able to be open to the event, to the vision which provokes his surprise, and to be sensitive to the reason why *(ma'duh)* God is addressing him. It is only because Moses is able to go "out of his way," to take a detour from the straight path to go see the contradiction of "what burns but is not consumed," that he is apt to hear the word of Revelation.

The willingness to go out of the way or take a detour allows for an encounter, and the encounter is revelation. This is the capacity to be open to the event and what is unpredictably new. The man who is capable of events is open to his own becoming, he is on the path to his name, though he will never be able to reach it. The event does not take place in the world, but the world opens from the event at every occurrence. And since every event transforms our very being, we say: *hineni*, "Here am I."

267

## Man in Revolt

> *What best reminds us of a person is precisely what we had forgotten*
> *(because it was insignificant and we had therefore left it with all its*
> *power untouched).*
> *This is why the best part of our memory is outside of ourselves, in a*
> *rainy breath, in the stuffy smell of a room or in that first smell of a*
> *fire, everywhere we rediscover those parts of ourselves which our*
> *intelligence, having no use for them, disdained: the last reserve of*
> *the past, the best...*
>
> Marcel Proust, *In the Shadow of Young Girls in Flower*

The prophet is man in revolt!

Some years ago, I came across a biography of Anatoly Sharansky, then a Russian dissident and *refusnik,* who had been arrested on March 15th, 1977, for requesting a visa to Israel and was subsequently sentenced to three years in prison and ten years in the Gulag on July 14th, 1978!

"He remained in the KGB's prison cells for nine years. For nine years, he said no to the Soviet authorities, without making a single concession. The day before his early morning release on Monday, February 10th, 1986, Anatoly still had no idea he was going to be released. He was busy reading the German classics, Goethe and Schiller, in his jail cell. Suddenly, the door opened, and he was brought a stack of old civilian clothes. 'Get dressed!' This was the first time such a thing had happened. Anatoly became convinced that something exceptional was going to happen. He put on the clothes, which were far too big for him, gathered the few books he had always managed to keep by his side, and followed the four men who had come to get him. They traveled to the Moscow airport in a black Volga, via familiar streets. A plane was waiting for Sharansky. When he got out of the car, one of the KGB men took his package of books and told him it was forbidden to take it on the plane. Anatoly insisted on keeping a single one of them, the small collection of Hebrew psalms which his wife Avital had given him many years before, but the agent refused. So Anatoly lay down in the snow and said he wouldn't move until his book had been returned to him. He could feel that his liberation was near, but he could not give up on leading his dedicated battle against the KGB to the last moment. The four men swore at him and threatened him, but it was useless, and they finally had to return his book. Once Anatoly had boarded the plane, it took off. During the flight, he was told that as 'an American spy,' he was being expelled from the Soviet Union. He replied that he was satisfied that after thirteen years had passed since he had requested to be stripped of his nationality, his request was finally being acceded to. The plane landed in East Germany. The KGB men explained to him that due to certain diplomatic regulations they could not set foot in East Germany, and he would therefore have to exit the plane alone. 'Do you see that car over there, one of the men asked, pointing to a limousine with tinted windows parked on the landing strip, just go straight to it, agreed?' 'You know, I never agree with the KGB, so if you tell me to go straight, I'll go off in the other direction.' The KGB man told him that could prove to be dangerous. 'We'll see,' answered Sharansky. He exited the plane and zigzagged all the way to the car..."[1]

269

1. In Anatoly and Avital Sharansky, *Such a Long Journey,* 1986.

12

# The Speech

*One day Rabbi Levi Yitzhak was asked*
*why each treatise in the Babylonian Talmud*
*is missing the first page and starts instead on page 2.*
*The Rabbi responded that the wise man,*
*no matter how many pages he has read and meditated*
*upon, must never lose sight of the fact*
*that he hasn't yet reached the first page...*

# Chapter Twelve

To Read and Interpret

**The Jewish Individual and Gratitude**

Intelligence to Accompany Faith

**Learning to Question**

Denial of Dogmatism and Fixed Thought

**Proposition Rather Than Imposition**

Protect Critical Thought

**A Short Story Regarding Study**

Preparing the Speech

## To Read and Interpret

*Written philosophy consists in thinking about every aspect of a given*
*question worth considering. It is to go to the depths of these thoughts,*
*no matter the cost. Philosophy consists in untangling the inextricable*
*and keeping going until you have reached the point where it is*
*absolutely impossible to go any further.*

Vladimir Jankélévitch

273

The previous chapters outlined the reading of the Torah, from the unveiling
of the scrolls in the Holy Ark to the end of the reading of the haftarah. Now
it is necessary to explain the significance of a reading that exists not only
in a ritual context, but in a specific philosophical horizon. Why are the Book
and the reading at the heart of the rite of initiation, the passage from childhood to maturity? Preparing for the bar/bat mitzvah reading makes the
young person on the verge of entering the community aware of the crucial
importance of a tradition and a civilization which has placed the book,
reading and interpretation, or, in other words, study, at the heart of its spiritual concerns.

In the Jewish religion, the construction of the individual and of society takes place through the book, through study and exegesis. The relationship to the book is not simply an accident, but one of the indispensable conditions for life itself.

## The Jewish Individual and Gratitude

> *I am not making this alliance and this entreaty with you alone*
> *but with whomever else is here with us today in the presence of God...*
> *and with whomever is not here with us today.*
> *All those who will be born in the future until the end of all generations*
> *were with them on Mount Sinai.*
>
> *Pirkei of Rabbi Eliezer,* chapter 41

The young person preparing for a bar/bat mitzvah discovers the idea of the Talmud, of study and of interpretation by being asked to prepare a speech. The speech is not only an opportunity to display one's intelligence and eloquence, but to become conscious of the way Jewish thought functions on the basis of the art of interpretation.

Intellectually, the speech is a crucial moment, but it is first and foremost an opportunity to thank the loved ones who have gathered for the ceremony: parents and family, friends, the faithful, and those who helped to prepare the bar/bat mitzvah. This expression of thanks does not only have a social purpose, for it also places the bar mitzvah boy or bat mitzvah girl in an essential aspect of Judaism. Indeed, as was stressed in the second chapter, a primary aspect of the Jewish character can be found simply by analyzing the etymology of the word "Jew." The word derives from the adjective *yehudi,* which derives from the noun "Yehuda," which is in turn derived from the verb *lehodot,* "to thank." A Jew is therefore, first and foremost, an individual capable of gratitude! The bar mitzvah boy or bat mitzvah girl enters the world of his or her Judaism through this acknowledgement of the importance of gratitude towards the other.

A bar mitzvah boy reading his speech. The speech most frequently consists of
a commentary of the text the bar mitzvah boy has just analyzed.
It is also customary for young men or women to take advantage of the speech to thank the rabbi,
their parents, and all their guests.

## Intelligence to Accompany Faith

> *The ability to doubt the existence of the spirits and the gods,*
> *to separate words from objects, and to contest those theories*
> *which close in on the world as if it was transparent*
> *is inherent to the homo sapiens.*

Edgard Morin, *Le Paradigme perdu* (Paradigm Lost)

The speech is the moment where faith is put on the line, for its own good, so that it does not get shut into self-satisfaction, which would lead it to fall prey to credulity based on fables, fictions, myths, and children's tales. The speech does not dismiss faith, but balances it with intelligence.

The bar mitzvah boy or bat mitzvah girl could be led to believe that, in our day, in the context of a relatively codified ceremony, Judaism amounts to a series of right moves and wrong moves, of pat formulas, of texts repeated thousands of times, and of multi-secular blessings. He or she could be tempted to believe that Judaism is a faith with little consciousness of reason and intelligence.

I believe it is salutary to underline that the reality is something else entirely and that though the texts presently read during services do address theological and prophetic issues, one should always remember the following sentence from the Talmud: "The wise man is preferable to the prophet."

The speech reminds that aside from the recited and dictated text, there is a freedom to speak, to question and to comment.

## Learning to Question

> *Each generation must preserve the strength to question the world in*
> *new ways. It is not a matter of rejecting what was said in the past*
> *out of principle, as if the past should simply be passed over.*
> Eric Weil

It is no coincidence that the Sanctuary, which became the Temple, followed by the Book, was built by Betsalel, a man capable of questioning, of critical thought and of knowledge: of *chokhmah*, *binah*, and *da'at*. According to

Rashi's commentary, *chokhmah* is the capacity to be open to another's words. It is the dimension of listening and openness. Dogmatism is nothing other than the opinion according to which the real consists in a proposition which has a fixed or immediately known result. *Chokhmah* opens instead of closing, it asks instead of proving, it expresses a question instead of striving to possess an answer. Moreover, the masters of the Kabbalah analyze the word *kokhmah* as *koach-mah,* or the power of what.

## Denial of Dogmatism and Fixed Thought

> *Interpretation exists to show that, contrary to the pretense of ideology,*
> *meaning is built patiently, that it does not identify*
> *with a prefabricated truth that can simply be appropriated*
> *once and for all and imposed on the rest of the world.*

Catherine Chalier

A dynamic, interrogative attitude can be subjected to changes necessary to insertion in the human reality of the world. Intelligence objectifies itself into a type of knowledge referred to as *daat* in Hebrew, and particularly Kabbalistic, tradition. *Daat* can be faith, the belief into which we shut ourselves so as to avoid being troubled. But *chokhma,* critical intelligence, and *daat,* positive knowledge, are not two static poles of consciousness. There is a dialectic to and fro between the question and the answer referred to in Hebrew as *binah. Binah* derives from *bein,* which means *between.* It is literally the "in-between" thought.

The speech is an opportunity to discover the Talmudic idea by which man experiences the abandonment of sovereign coincidence with himself and of the loss of rest and complacency. This experience of calling faith into question immediately transforms Talmudic man to his very core, for he becomes a "question-man" rather than a man merely asking questions. By refusing to succumb to "definitive" time and by preserving the greatness of "infinitive" time, the Talmud stresses questioning and the dynamism of meaning versus the dogmatism of Truth. Talmudic thought therefore begins with this questioning which is the very foundation of Jewish thought.

## Proposition Rather Than Imposition

*The spiritual images of the universe which are available to us through knowledge, art, or language do not consist of passive reception and recording but are acts of the mind, and each of these original acts introduces us to a specific, original picture.*

Ernst Cassirer, *Essais sur le langage* (Essays on Language)

The speech is the moment when the young man or woman discovers through Talmudic thought that interpretation always contains an essential reference to the question that has been asked of us. To understand a text, the world, or the other is to hear this question! This is an ethic of listening best expressed by the Hebrew saying Shema Yisrael, "Listen Israel." Anything, whether a word or an event, is an answer. One must hear it and apprehend it as such, or, in other words, on the basis of a question to which it is the answer. By finding that question which predates the world appearing in the present, we notice that there are numerous potential answers to the question and that the world or the text we interpret are in fact simply a single potential answer among many others. As much as possible, the world and the texts are only propositions. Any answer is simply a choice. And any definition is an answer to a question.

Studying the holy texts is accompanied by the hand gestures
punctuating deep thought and reasoning.

## Protect Critical Thought

*And there was evening and there was morning, the first day.*
Genesis 1:5

The speech is not a secondary part of the ceremony, but the fruit of the long preparation through study of a specific knowledge. It is also the moment the young person becomes aware of the Book as foundation of the culture, of reading and of interpretation. The speech is the moment when one uses study, the generic term for which is Talmud, to make use of one's reason, in a public manner, within the community. I am particularly fond of one of the first verses in Genesis: *And there was evening and there was morning, the first day.* In Hebrew, the word evening, *erev,* means "mixture," and morning, *boker,* which means "discernment," led to *bikoret,* which means critical thought. It is only once we have used knowledge, questioning and emotion to discover the "morning," which follows the "evening," that we see the "first day," or the dawn of countable, counted time, the inscription of man in a veritable temporality.[1]

## A Short Story Regarding Study

*The manner in which the texts and the Scriptures are treated by Talmudists is already extremely complicated and scholarly, yet Chouchani knew how to take it further, into new horizons of the text, to allow a constantly uneasy dialectic to keep moving.*

Emmanuel Lévinas, On his master Monsieur Chouchani, *Qui êtes-vous?* (Who are you?)

Thinking about this incompletion and this openness, I am reminded of a story set somewhere between a fairy tale and a joke, which I once read in a Gérard Haddad book about the Talmudic sources of psychoanalysis.

"One day a man entered the house of study. A complete novice regarding Judaism, he watched these passionate students in surprise and learned they were studying the Talmud.

Intrigued, he came back that night, and found the same students, still studying.

This field of study probably holds great secrets, he thought. Jews, who are so practical and know how to value their labor, would not devote so much effort to studying for naught, he reflected. There must be amazing riches to be garnered here...

To be certain of his conclusions, the man approached the Rabbi and began to question him.

The Rabbi answered:

–You are absolutely correct, amazing riches, a real treasure: Paradise.

–Paradise?

–Yes, study opens the gates to Paradise!

–This Paradise must be marvelous, the man said. Could I visit it?

–Of course, said the Rabbi, this very night, in the heart of your dreams, I will come to find you and I will take you there.

That night the man was led along tortuous paths, through the snow, the rain, and the wind.

–Is this your Paradise?, the man asked.

–How impatient you are!

They arrived before a small house in a thick forest.

–Here is Paradise, the Rabbi proudly announced, go in and look around!

The man went in and discovered an old man reading a voluminous treatise by candlelight.

–That is Rabbi Akiva, said the Rabbi. He is the greatest master of the Talmud. He is in Paradise.

–Are you mocking me?, the man burst out. This Paradise is pathetic! This man spent his whole life studying and now he's still studying. And he's probably already read and reread this treatise!

–Yes, said the Rabbi, but now he understands it..."

## Preparing the Speech

*Inventing a tale. A story. It won't be written for a child, nor will it be written for an adult. Written for nobody. The story of nobody. It will start anywhere, any old way. With this word: God. The rest will follow, by itself...*
Christian Bobin

To prepare the speech, the bar mitzvah boy or bat mitzvah girl chooses a verse from the parashah or the haftarah and uses it to construct an "essay" in which he or she will discuss one or several questions raised by the verse, using quotes from the Talmud commenting on the verse and showing several aspects of interpretation. The most important thing is probably to avoid falling into the morality of good and evil, for beyond this admittedly significant Manichaeism, there are texts, ideas, and authors who offer modern reflection based on complexity, reflection which avoids the sometime unfortunate impression that entering a synagogue is a regressive action both for the emotional and intellectual aspects of the mind. Of course, it requires work, but isn't that the whole reason we prepare for the bar mitzvah?

It would be good for the speech to always be prepared in the spirit we have just described: a search for meaning, for life, for self-construction, for maturation, and for elevation. One must always ask oneself how the texts read in the parashah and the haftarah are significant not only as historical texts, but in relation to the contemporary reader. The question is no longer simply to understand the text, but to understand one's self before the text. Such as in the brief story in which a disciple tells the Master, "I have been through the Talmud three times," and the Master responds, "but has the Talmud been through you?"[2]

1. The speech is the critical, vigilant part of the ceremony of reading the Book. There is a natural tendency for objects to return to their original states. The Book, which is, after all, an object, follows this rule. Like everything else, the Book would like to return to its original state, would like to return to what it once was: a monument, a stone, a Temple. Yet the Book becoming a stone would be something "petrified." And if venerated and adored, wouldn't it become an idol? Wouldn't we then run the risk of textolatry?

Study and the bar mitzvah speech are what prevent us from succumbing to this textolatry.

The text implies reading and readers. The Jewish reading of the Scriptures, like the Jewish conception of God, is not a fideist reading, the passive repetition of a text permanently fixed into a single meaning. The reading immediately implies exegesis, interpretation, hermeneutics, study, and commentary on the commentary, all of which combine to renew the immutable letters and breath of the Living God.

2. The act of interpreting, of passing from one text to another, from one idea to another, proves the vitality of the spirit, and the dynamic which also has impact on bio-cognitive functions such as logic, memory, and intellectual creativity. Interpretation allows for the liberation from certain habits of thought and for the disruption of cerebral determinism. It allows one to reach "the freedom to invent to invent freedom" (Paul Ricoeur).

The child is born with an unfinished brain, rather than an unoccupied brain. The opposite of the unfinished is not the "finished," which would be understood in the sense that one "finished off" an animal or a condemned man. The mind follows a maturation cycle which does not necessarily lead to a "finished" brain, but to a brain which is constantly open to other transformations and maturations. The brain is an open organism, the organism of open psychic functions.

The interpretation of the texts and hermeneutic activity in general, and the interpretative activity of the Talmud in particular, specifically follow this search for openness... Interpretation is a journey "somewhere into the unfinished," according to the beautiful Rainer Maria Rilke quote repeated by Vladimir Jankelevitch.

# 13

# The Sabbath

*In every remote corner of the world, at every instant,*
*every particle of every being is in motion,*
*being attracted and repelled, repelled and attracted,*
*going up, going down, always going up*
*even if it outwardly appears to be falling,*
*infinitely coming and going according to the expression*
*of the prophet Ezekiel: And the creatures came and*
*went ... Each particle of being, no matter how small,*
*holds a spark of holiness which aspires to return*
*to its source and produces existence's fundamental*
*motion of elevation and dynamism.*
*Rising and falling is uninterrupted in man,*
*and in the cosmos in its entirety. Any movement,*
*even a fall, a collapse, or a psychological depression,*
*is an elevation. Changes of state, of mood,*
*even heavy depressions, have their positive values.*
*It is the near-invisible sliver moon right before*
*the new moon, it is low tide before the return*
*of high tide, it is sleep which rejuvenates us*
*and gives us the strength to wake and be aware...*
*Falling down is not an accident, but a natural*
*movement of our inscription in the world.*
*Wasn't the world born of a descent of light*
*and the Infinite?*
*According to a famous expression in the Kabbalah,*
*there is a state of yerida letsorekh haaliya, of a*
*"descent which can only lead to ascending again."*

Rav Kook, *Orot Hakodesh, Volume II*

# Chapter Thirteen

The Sanctification of Time

> The Day of Rest
> Holiness: Construction of the Interior Temple
> Preparation and Duration of the Sabbath
> Come, My Beloved: *Lekha Dodi*

The Lighting of the Candles

> Time and Light
> Mothers and Daughters: A Rite of Initiation
> A Metaphysics of Light
> Light and Bouquets of Flowers

The Blessing of the Children

The Kiddush

The Purification of the Hands

The *Motzi*

> The Challah, or the Sabbath Bread
> The Bread, the Salt, and the Dream
> The Guest: Light and Fragrance
> Breaking Bread!

The Songs of Sabbath, the Meal and the *Dvar Torah*

> The *Zemirot*
> Eating and Talking
> To Thank
> Accompanying the Guests

The Havdalah

> The Sabbath Schedule
> The Havdalah Ceremony

## The Sanctification of Time

*One day, Rabbi Nachman noticed one of his disciples rushing home.*
*He asked him,*
*—Did you look at the sun this morning?*
*—No, Rabbi, I didn't have time.*
*—Believe me, in fifty years, whatever is here now will have disappeared.*
*There will be another fair, other horses, other carts, and different*
*people. I will no longer be here, and neither will you. So what could*
*be so important that you don't have time to look at the sky?*

### The Day of Rest

The Sabbath is the seventh day of the Creation of the world described in
Genesis: "Thus the heavens and the earth were finished, and all the host of
them. And on the seventh day God ended his work which he had made; and
he rested on the seventh day from all his work which he had made. And
God blessed the seventh day, and sanctified it: because that in it he had rested
from all his work which God created and made" (Genesis 2:1–3).

There are innumerable commentaries of this passage, which is also reprised in the Friday night liturgy at synagogue, following the whispered prayer, the *amidah*. The passage additionally constitutes the first part of the kiddush blessing, the "sanctification" enacted over bread or wine, which signals the beginning of the Friday night Sabbath dinner.

The Sabbath ritual is so important that it is described in the fourth of the Ten Commandments: "Remember the Sabbath day, to keep it holy. Six days shalt thou labor, and do all thy work: But the seventh day is the Sabbath of the Lord thy God: in it thou shalt not do any work, thou, nor thy son, nor thy daughter, thy manservant, nor thy maidservant, nor thy cattle, nor thy stranger that is within thy gates: For in six days the Lord made heaven and earth, the sea, and all that in them is, and rested the seventh day: wherefore the Lord blessed the sabbath day, and hallowed it."
(Exodus 20:8––1, also see Exodus 31:13–17).

The Masters therefore consider that there are two Sabbaths: God's Sabbath, the seventh day of Creation, which he blesses and sanctifies, the day "work ceases" (literal translation of Sabbath); and the Sabbath of men, when time is set aside for spending time with one's family, for socializing, for welcoming strangers, for friends, for love, for study, for prayer, for chants, for meditation, for taking a walk, and for enjoying a festive meal.

### Holiness: Construction of the Interior Temple

Holiness in Judaism, and particularly on the Sabbath, gives meaning to life and orients one's existence. The Sabbath is not an opportunity to withdraw from the world, but to call ourselves into question and examine whether our actions over the days of the week truly correspond to our desires and our life choices.

The notion of rest, which is crucially linked to the Exodus from Egypt and the end of enslavement (see Deuteronomy 5:15), is set forth in the Talmud in a completely original manner. The Talmud does not forbid physical or mental effort on the Sabbath, but asks the faithful to avoid reproducing those gestures which were used to build the Sanctuary (the *mishkan*) in the desert. All the gestures used and the tasks accomplished in the construction of the Sanctuary are therefore prohibited. These gestures and tasks include thirty-nine principal tasks which are subdivided into a large number of secondary tasks. The masters interpret this prohibition to build exterior space as an opportunity to allow us to build our inner space.

In Hebrew, *mishkan* is spelled with the four letters M-SH-K-N, *mem, shin, kaf, nun,* which stand for the king, *melekh,* the judge, *shofet;* the priest, *kohen;* and the prophet, *navi.* These characters symbolize the "political" (the king), the "legal" (the judge), the "ritual" (the priest) and the "liturgical" (the prophet) spheres necessary to balance personal and social space. These are the four spheres which must be worked upon, for the sake of the individual and of the community, on the Sabbath.[1]

### Preparation and Duration of the Sabbath

In order to give the bar mitzvah boy some advance idea of the Sabbath, I have outlined the events that make up this day, from its beginning one hour and ten minutes before the sun sets on Friday, until the appearance of three stars on Saturday night. The Sabbath therefore lasts twenty-five hours.

However, the Sabbath atmosphere starts long before its official beginning, especially on the eve of a bar/bat mitzvah. Preparation for the Sabbath consists of a comprehensive, meticulous housecleaning, the purchase of the necessary food products, and the preparation of all three Sabbath meals, which generally include fish (in traditional homes, the famous *gefilte fish*), a meat or poultry dish, soup, vegetables, cakes, and a special bread called challah.

I am sure that, like me, many Jews have clearer childhood memories of the preparations than the actual Sabbath. It is that odor of a specific type of cooking which comes over us when we walk into school: "it smells like Sabbath!" With time, the Sabbath acquires colors, odors and tastes, which mark a child's life and are fondly and nostalgically recalled in adulthood. I must recommend the wonderful little book Abraham Joshua Heschel devoted to the Sabbath, *The Sabbath*, which takes us on a journey to discover the Sabbath as celebrated by Eastern European Jews, an opulent celebration prepared through great sacrifice by Jews who otherwise lived in poverty.

**Come, My Beloved:** *Lekha Dodi*

The Friday night prayer which opens the Sabbath is characterized by a song-heavy service. In addition to the classic blessings recited on the other nights of the week, a series of psalms precedes the reading of the Shema. The *Lekha Dodi* chant is the central element of the Friday night liturgy. The Hymn was composed by Rabbi Shlomo ben Moshe Halevi Alkabetz. This great mystic, who was born in 1505 in Turkey and settled in Israel, in Safed, in 1535. He became one of the disciples, as well as the brother in law of the great Kabbalist Moses Cordovero. Alkabetz participated in the Kabbalist renaissance Cordovero launched in Safed. Along with the Shema Yisrael, *Lekha Dodi* may be Judaism's most popular liturgical text. Over a period of 350 years, more than 2,500 different tunes have been written for this beautiful hymn. The world of the poem is the world of the Judaic liturgy *Song of Songs,* a love story between a woman and her beloved, with the woman representing the Sabbath and the beloved representing the community of Israel. The rural atmosphere of the text evokes a custom which arose in Safed, probably due to Alkabetz himself, which consisted in going out into the fields to meet the Sabbath bride. This love metaphor is partially due to the fact that the word by which the Bible explains that God "ended" the creation *(vayekhal)* and the word "bride" *(kallah)* have the same root. Every Sabbath, communities and families around the world recreate this festive atmosphere replete with dancing, socializing and love, all reminiscent of a wedding ceremony.

לְכָה דוֹדִי לִקְרַאת כַּלָּה, פְּנֵי שַׁבָּת נְקַבְּלָה.

Transliteration:
*Lekha dodi likrat kallah*
*Penei Shabbat nekabbela*
Translation:
Come, my beloved, to meet the bride
The face of Sabbath we shall receive.

# The Lighting of the Candles

> *A woman dressed in red, lit by the candle before which she held her hand, in such a way that the light was reflected onto another woman, who watched the first one as her body took on a glow of silence and gold.*

Pascal Quignard, *Petits traités II* (Little Treatises II)

## Time and Light

The Sabbath is a celebration of light. It begins with the lighting of two candles and ends with the lighting of a single candle braided with several wicks. The Friday night candles are known as the *nerot shel Shabbat*. Several chapters of the Talmud are devoted to them. In many families, oil lamps are used, and are most frequently lit by the lady of the house, who covers her eyes and pronounces the following blessing:

בָּרוּךְ אַתָּה יְהוָה, אֱלֹהֵינוּ מֶלֶךְ הָעוֹלָם, אֲשֶׁר קִדְּשָׁנוּ בְּמִצְוֹתָיו
וְצִוָּנוּ לְהַדְלִיק נֵר שֶׁל שַׁבָּת.

291

Transliteration:
*Barukh atah Adonai, Eloheynu, melekh ha'olam asher kideshanu bemitzvotav vetzivanu lehadlik ner shel Shabbat.*

Translation:
Blessed are you, Lord, our God, king of the universe Who has sanctified us with His commandments and commanded us to light the candles of Shabbat.

The lady of the house then removes her hands and looks at the candles. The Sabbath has then been received, it is said that it has entered. Every Jewish calendar provides the times for the beginning and end of Sabbath in various major cities around the globe, based on time zones, daylight saving time, etc. Today, travelers arriving in Jerusalem by car are greeted on one of the last curves before the road enters the city with a beautiful large clock which indicates the times the next Sabbath will begin and end.

## Mothers and Daughters: A Rite of Initiation

On a young man's and, especially a young woman's, bar mitzvah or bat mitzvah Sabbath, extreme attention must be paid to the lighting of the candles, for it is the first time that the girl will light the two candles, just like her mother. This is a crucial moment of transmission between two generations. The bar mitzvah boy can also light the candles on this special occasion, though his mother and sisters will later resume responsibility for this task.[2] When a family includes one or several girls, the girls light the *nerot* with their mother: they light two candles if they have already been bat mitzvahed, or only one if they haven't. Certain family or social gatherings hold off until all the guests have arrived to light the candles as a group and welcome the Sabbath together. Among the most liberal, the candles are sometimes lit after the beginning of the Sabbath.

## A Metaphysics of Light

One of the most important words of the Sabbath is undoubtedly the word *light.* Light is the first visible sign of material Creation. "And God said, Let there be light: and there was light" (Genesis 1:3). As the first sign and first word of Creation, and as the first and highest reality of the universe, light is the first path to the Divine, and the greatest metaphor for infinity. The Sabbath is a world of light, a conception of light, and, most importantly, it is all the behaviors, thoughts and actions, the studies and rituals which allow man to receive the light of infinity. A very famous Sabbath chant sung during the three meals has a chorus which goes *orah vesimchah,* "light and joy."

The moment of lighting the candles, along with the synagogue chants and entire ritual that go with it, is referred to as *Kabbalat Shabbat,* or "Kabbalah of the Sabbath," the "reception" or "welcoming of the Sabbath." After the lighting of the candles, on the way out of synagogue, and throughout the following day, the faithful greet each other with *Shabbat shalom* or, in Yiddish, *gut Shabbes* or *a git Shabbes.*

## Light and Bouquets of Flowers

Could it be a coincidence that the Hebrew word for "light," "*or,*" has the same numeric value of 207 as the expression *"Ein-Sof,"* "Infinity"? "*Or*" is spelled *alef, vav, resh* (1 + 6 + 200 = 207) and "Infinity" is spelled *alef, yod, nun,*

The lighting of the candles is a key moment in the passing of traditions from mother to daughter.

*samekh, vav, pey* (1 + 10 + 50 + 60 + 6 + 80 = 207). The Masters also note that 207 is the numeric value of the word *raz,* the "mystery," or, the "secret." And *zer,* an anagram of *raz,* means "bouquet of flowers." To offer flowers is to offer a secret and a light. This is where the lovely tradition of bringing flowers for Sabbath on Friday afternoons comes from. I may now have a better understanding of why my sister is a florist in Lakewood, New Jersey, and why my father gives my mother a bouquet of flowers and a single rose every Friday afternoon...

## The Blessing of the Children

> *The Torah is a task to be accomplished every day and every night.*
> *It is a task rife with danger [...] To interrupt one's studying*
> *to admire the beauty of a tree would be such a severe wrong*
> *as to endanger one's life. Yet the man for whom looking at the tree*
> *is an interruption rather than a continuation of study*
> *endangers his life!*

### The Angels of the Sabbath

After returning from the Synagogue and before sitting down to eat, the faithful sing the song of welcome to the angels, or *Shalom Aleikhem.* This song originated with a Kabbalist tradition which holds that each worshipper is accompanied and protected by two angels on the return from the synagogue and throughout the beginning of the evening. During the *Shalom Aleikhem,* the angels are therefore thanked for their benevolent presence. Following the angels song, which also has a wide variety of melodies customarily danced to in a family round, the family moves on to the blessing of the children.

The imposition of the hands is first encountered explicitly as a ceremony of transmission and of blessing with the story of Jacob, who had Joseph and his grandchildren called to his deathbed so he could speak his last words to them (Genesis 48).

This tradition has continued to the present day through the blessing parents give their children on Friday or Saturday evening at the beginning or the end of the Sabbath and the holidays.[3] It is customary to repeat the phrasing of the priests' blessing, referring to Ephraim and Manasseh for boys, and to the matriarchs for girls. The father and the mother take turns laying their hands on the heads of their children, from the oldest to the youngest, while pronouncing the following blessing:

Transliteration:
For boys:
*Yesimkha Elohim*
*k'Efraim vekhiMenashe.*
*Yevarekhekha Adonai veyishmerekha.*
*Ya'er Adonai panav elekha vichuneka.*
*Yisa Adonai panav elekha veyasem lekha shalom.*
For girls:
*Yessimekh Elohim*
*keSara Rivka Rachel veLeah.*
*Yevarekhekha Adonai veyishmerekha.*
*Ya'er Adonai panav elekha vichuneka.*
*Yissa Adonai panav elekha veyasem lekha Shalom.*

יְשִׂמְךָ אֱלֹהִים כְּשָׂרָה     יְשִׂמְךָ אֱלֹהִים
רִבְקָה רָחֵל וְלֵאָה:     כְּאֶפְרַיִם וְכִמְנַשֶּׁה:

יְבָרֶכְךָ יְהוָה וְיִשְׁמְרֶךָ: יָאֵר יְהוָה פָּנָיו אֵלֶיךָ, וִיחֻנֶּךָּ:
יִשָּׂא יְהוָה פָּנָיו אֵלֶיךָ, וְיָשֵׂם לְךָ שָׁלוֹם:

Translation:
For boys:
May God make you like Ephraim and Manasseh
May God bless you and protect you
May God light his face for you and be favorable to you
May God turn his face to you and grant you his peace:
Shalom!

For girls:
May God make you like Sarah, Rebecca, Rachel, and Leah
May God bless you and protect you
May God light his face for you and be favorable to you
May God turn his face to you and grant you his peace:
Shalom!

This blessing is particularly important on the bar mitzvah Sabbath and can be a second opportunity to give the bar mitzvah boy or bat mitzvah girl presents.

*Jacob Blessing the Children of Joseph* (1656), Harmensz van Rijn Rembrandt (1606–1669).
Jacob blesses his grandchildren Ephraim and Manasseh in Joseph's presence.

# The Kiddush
## The blessing of time

*Holiness makes a distinctive break with this conception of the sacred.
It introduces and pronounces doubt and questioning, even risking
atheism. Yet this risk must be taken. It is only through this risk that
man can elevate himself to the spiritual notion of Transcendence.*

Emmanuel Lévinas, *Difficult Freedom*

The meal always begins with the ceremony of the kiddush. The entire family
and all its guests stand around the table. The head of the family holds a
cup of wine (preferably red wine) and speaks the following blessing:

יוֹם הַשִּׁשִּׁי, וַיְכֻלּוּ הַשָּׁמַיִם וְהָאָרֶץ וְכָל־צְבָאָם: וַיְכַל
אֱלֹהִים בַּיּוֹם הַשְּׁבִיעִי מְלַאכְתּוֹ אֲשֶׁר עָשָׂה, וַיִּשְׁבֹּת
בַּיּוֹם הַשְּׁבִיעִי מִכָּל־מְלַאכְתּוֹ אֲשֶׁר עָשָׂה: וַיְבָרֶךְ
אֱלֹהִים אֶת יוֹם הַשְּׁבִיעִי וַיְקַדֵּשׁ אֹתוֹ, כִּי בוֹ שָׁבַת
מִכָּל־מְלַאכְתּוֹ, אֲשֶׁר בָּרָא אֱלֹהִים לַעֲשׂוֹת:
סַבְרִי מָרָנָן,

בָּרוּךְ אַתָּה יְהֹוָה, אֱלֹהֵינוּ מֶלֶךְ הָעוֹלָם, בּוֹרֵא פְּרִי
הַגָּפֶן:

בָּרוּךְ אַתָּה יְהֹוָה, אֱלֹהֵינוּ מֶלֶךְ הָעוֹלָם, אֲשֶׁר קִדְּשָׁנוּ
בְּמִצְוֹתָיו וְרָצָה בָנוּ, וְשַׁבָּת קָדְשׁוֹ בְּאַהֲבָה וּבְרָצוֹן
הִנְחִילָנוּ, זִכָּרוֹן לְמַעֲשֵׂה בְרֵאשִׁית, תְּחִלָּה לְמִקְרָאֵי
קֹדֶשׁ, זֵכֶר לִיצִיאַת מִצְרָיִם. וְשַׁבָּת קָדְשְׁךָ בְּאַהֲבָה
וּבְרָצוֹן הִנְחַלְתָּנוּ. בָּרוּךְ אַתָּה יְהֹוָה, מְקַדֵּשׁ הַשַּׁבָּת.

Transliteration:

*Yom hashishi Veyekhulu hashamayim veha'aretz vkhol tzevaam. Vayekhal Elohim bayom hashevi'ie melakhto asher asa, vayishbot bayom hasheviie mikol melakhto asher asa. Vayevarekh Elohim et yom hashevii vayekadesh oto, ki vo shavat mikol melachto asher bara Elo-him laasot.*
*Savri maranan,*
*Barukh Ata Adonai Elohenu Melekh Ha'olam, Borei peri hagafen.*
*Barukh Ata Adonai Elohenu Melekh Ha'olam, asher kideshanu bemitzvotav veratzah vanu, ve'Shabbat kodsho be'ahavah uveratzon hinchilanu zikaron lema'aseh bereshit;*
*Ki hu yom techilah lemikraei kodesh, zecher liyetziat Mitzrayim; Ki vanu vacharta ve'otanu kidashta mikol haamim, v'Shabbat kodshekha be'ahavah uveratzon hinchaltanu;*
*Baruch ata Adonai Mekadesh HaShabbat.*

Translation:

Of the sixth day. And creation of heaven and earth were completed with all of their array. On the seventh day God completed all of His creative activity, And He withdrew on the seventh day from the creative activity which He had done. God blessed the seventh day and made it holy, for on it He abstained from all the creative activity which God had created, to be developed.
With the permission of our masters.
Blessed are You, Holy Master, our God, King of the Universe,
Who creates the fruit of the vine.
Blessed are You, Holy Master, our God, King of the Universe, who sanctified us with His commandments and desired us, and His holy Shabbat with love and pleasure He gave to us as an inheritance, as a remembrance of the Act of Creation. For Shabbat is the first of the holidays, which are remembrances of the Exodus from Egypt. For You have chosen us, and made us holy from all the nations, and You gave us Your holy Shabbat with love and pleasure; Blessed are You, Holy Master, Who sanctifies the Shabbat.

Silver Kiddush cup.
The Masters of the Kabbalah noted that the numeric value of the word "cup" (*kos*) is 86, the same numeric value assigned to Elohim, God the Creator, who is cited at the beginning of the Kiddush.

On the day of the bar/bat mitzvah, in many communities, it is customary to honor the young man or woman being bar/bat mitzvahed with pronouncing the above blessing. Following the blessing, the person pronouncing it drinks a little wine, then distributes wine to the other celebrants. The cup is known as the *kos*. It is frequently made of silver, but this is not obligatory. It must be filled to the brim, or even spill over, to represent abundance. Some put water in the wine, as a Kabbalist symbol which represents rigor and mercy through the mixture of white and red.

The kiddush represents sanctification, or, in a second meaning of the word, "separation." A famous saying by Rashi, which is repeated by the masters of the Talmud, specifically states that "there is no holiness outside of separation." Since the Sabbath is considered a unique, privileged moment, the kiddush opens a door into time. It therefore allows to attain holiness, through a space of meditation and study which leads us to reflect on our condition as living beings, and on our goals, and the goods and happiness to which we want to aspire.

301

## The Purification of the Hands
*Netilat Yadayim*

> *You say:*
> *It is tiresome to frequent children.*
> *You are right.*
> *You add:*
> *Because you have to come down to their level, lean down, lower yourself, bend over, make yourself small.*
> *Here, you are wrong. That is not the most tiring. It is rather that you must elevate yourself to the height of their feelings. You must stretch yourself, extend yourself, push yourself up on the tips of your toes so as not to offend them.*
>
> Janusz Korczak

After the kiddush comes the ceremony of the purification of the hands known as *Netilat Yadayim*. Even those who have clean hands must go through *netilat yadayim* before they can eat the bread. The *netila* is carried out in the following manner: water is poured into a *keli,* a type of glass or carafe, without a spout, which has two handles and is often specifically made for this purpose. The *keli* is used to pour water three times on each hand, sequentially or in alternation with a celebrant's other hand. Following this, the blessing is pronounced:

בָּרוּךְ אַתָּה יְהֹוָה, אֱלֹהֵינוּ מֶלֶךְ הָעוֹלָם, אֲשֶׁר קִדְּשָׁנוּ
בְּמִצְוֹתָיו, וְצִוָּנוּ עַל נְטִילַת יָדַיִם.

Transliteration:

*Barukh atah Adonai, Eloheynu, melekh ha'olam asher kidshanu bemitzvotav vetzivanu al netilat yadayim.*

Translation:

Blessed are you, Lord, our God, king of the universe, Who has sanctified us with His commandments and commanded us concerning washing of hands.

Pewter *Keli.* The *netilat yadayim* consists of pouring water on each of one's hands three times, as a sign of purification.

This gesture of purification reminds us that the man who is about to sit down and eat is in the same situation as the priest who could only make sacrifices at the Temple when he was "pure." The question of what the Judaic concept of purity is naturally arises.

The masters explain this ritual with an example drawn from the geography of the country of Israel. They ask the question, what is the difference between Lake Tiberias and the Dead Sea? If you look at a map, the Mediterranean is on the left, and on the right there is a river, the Jordan, which flows from the North to the South and into Lake Tiberias. It then comes back out south of the Lake and flows further south into another lake, the Salt Sea, known in English as the Dead Sea. Why is it called the "Dead Sea"? What definition should we provide of something that is dead? The answer is extraordinarily simple but formidably wide-ranging. Lake Tiberias, known in Hebrew as the *Kinneret,* is a lake of life, for it receives the Jordan, fills itself with its waters and releases it a little further along. On the contrary, the "Dead Sea" receives the Jordan, "takes" its water but doesn't give anything back. No river comes out of it. This results in a very existential, concrete definition of death as what is capable of receiving, but cannot give. This idea of receiving-giving can be found in all aspects of life, but particularly regarding table manners. Eating is an important rite which consists in doing the *tikkun,* or the reparation of the breaks in the world through the purification of the hands and the sharing of the bread. The *netilat yadayim* and the blessing pronounced during the meal are part of the above concept of receiving-giving. For instance, the *keli,* in which the water for washing the hands is initially poured, is a symbolic reminiscence of Lake Tiberias filling up with the water of the Jordan and letting it continue its course from its southern side. The ritual teaches us that "purity" is not a "magical" notion, but an ethic which can be translated as receiving-giving, or, in other words, sharing!

303

## The Motzi
## Sharing the Bread

> *Now the bread takes its turn to break the man,*
> *to be the beauty of the breaking day.*
> René Char

Following the "purification of the hands," the celebrants take their places around a decorated table generally covered with a white tablecloth.

### The Challah, or the Sabbath Bread

The three Sabbath meals (Friday evening, Saturday noon and evening) are served with *challot,* a braided or round bread, depending on the tradition. The *challot* can be purchased, but it is customarily prepared by the lady of the house. When more than two and a half pounds of flour is used, a piece of the dough must be removed and burned in its entirety, to ensure that it is not consumed. This piece is known as the challah, and has passed its name on to the Sabbath bread as a whole. (Regarding the source of this sample, which was initially intended for the Kohen, see Numbers 15:17–21).

When the challah is removed, the following blessing is pronounced:

בָּרוּךְ אַתָּה יְהֹוָה, אֱלֹהֵינוּ מֶלֶךְ הָעוֹלָם, אֲשֶׁר קִדְּשָׁנוּ בְּמִצְוֹתָיו וְצִוָּנוּ לְהַפְרִישׁ חַלָּה תְּרוּמָה.

Transliteration:
*Barukh atah Adonai, Eloheynu, melekh ha'olam asher kideshanu bemitzvotav vetzivanu lehafrish challah min haterumah.*

Translation:
Blessed are you, Lord, our God, king of the universe Who has sanctified us with His commandments and commanded us concerning levying of challah.

At the beginning of the meal, the master of the house takes two braided breads from a dish which is reserved for this specific task, and is covered with a Sabbath doily or decorative cloth. These two breads recall the two manna which appeared in the desert on Fridays. He (or she, as the blessing over the bread may also be made by a woman) then lifts the two breads and says the following blessing:

בָּרוּךְ אַתָּה יְהֹוָה, אֱלֹהֵינוּ מֶלֶךְ הָעוֹלָם, הַמּוֹצִיא
לֶחֶם מִן הָאָרֶץ.

Transliteration:
*Barukh atah Adonai, Eloheynu, melekh ha'olam hamotzi lechem min ha'aretz.*

Translation:
Blessed are you, Lord, our God, king of the universe, Who brings forth bread from the earth.

### The Bread, the Salt, and the Dream

Then the master of the house cuts the braided bread with his hands or with a special knife and dips the pieces in salt before giving them to each of his guests... He begins by giving bread to his wife and his parents, followed by any guests, and finally the children, from the oldest to the youngest. On the bar/bat mitzvah Sabbath, the young man or woman pronounces the blessing. He or she distributes the bread, first to his or her parents and grandparents, then to the guests, then finally to his or her brothers and sisters, from the oldest to the youngest. Some people also say a brief passage from the Zohar before the blessing. Others sing the *Hashem Melekh* during the distribution of the bread. This is a song which states that "God rules, God has ruled, God will rule," and which is repeated until everyone has received a piece of bread.

The bread is dipped in salt because the dining table serves as a symbolic replacement for the Temple altar, where a pinch of salt was added for every sacrifice. There is a beautiful play on words involving the word for bread, *"lechem,"* and the word for salt, *"melach,"* two words which are composed of the same letters and which lead to a third word, *"chalom,"* the dream.

Some people are mistakenly in the habit of throwing the bread out instead of distributing it. This seems to me to be a serious mistake. This practice originates with the prohibition to directly give the bread hand to

305

hand, to show that it is not us, but God, who is giving. In fact, the bread must be passed around on a plate or a dish, or it must be set down in the celebrants' plates.

## The Guest: Light and Fragrance

According to Talmudic tradition, celebrants must make sure that domestic animals have been fed and must break bread, even when eating alone, before the meal can begin. This is an extraordinary symbol of a daily ethic: I can never begin eating unless I am ready to share my bread.

In Hebrew, a guest is called an *oreach,* a particularly beautiful word the root of which also means the path, *orah.* One can also read the words or and *reah* in *oreah,* "light" and "fragrance."

Anybody with whom we break bread, even a close relation, is considered a guest. This is why the word "meal" is pronounced *arucha* in Hebrew, from the same *oreach,* guest root. In fact, it is the act of sharing which confers the status of a guest upon the other person. Breaking bread opens one's house to light and to the fragrance of life. It is by welcoming the other that one is in turn welcomed by the other, and by light and fragrance.

The act of sharing bread is one of the most essential ones in the Jewish faith. It shows that man is always already engaged in a relationship with others, and that this connection is ontological. As a verse in Genesis puts it: "It is not good that the man should be alone; I will make him a help meet for him." The sharing of bread and of dialogue are signs of friendship and love.

## Breaking Bread!

There is an important Talmudic text concerning this beautiful Friday evening ceremony which I would like to reproduce and comment upon below.

Rav Ashi, one of the great Masters of the Talmud, gave a lesson about those Kings of Israel—Jeroboam, Ahav, and Menashe—who, according to the Talmud, do not have a share in the future world.

Sabbath breads are braided and covered with poppy seeds and sometimes aniseed.
Many woman have their own "personal" recipes, passed on through the generations.

One day when Rav Ashi did not have time to finish his lesson, he told his students, who were all great scholars: "Tomorrow I will continue my study by inaugurating the lesson with a discussion of my friends." By friends, Rav Ashi was referring to the three kings. That night, King Menashe came to Rav Ashi in a dream and said, "You referred to my father and me as 'your friends'! The implication was: 'I am a king and you are a rabbi! How dare you call me friend!" King Menashe went on to say: "I will give you a chance to make up for your error in protocol! Tell me from what part of the bread you must cut when you break bread?" Rav Ashi replied that he did not know...

Menashe was surprised: "You don't know from what part of the bread you must cut to break bread and you dare to call us your friends?" Rav Ashi answered: "Teach me this law, tell me the secret of this place of sharing and tomorrow, in your name, I will teach it and comment upon it during the lesson." Menashe answered: "From the part where it is most baked! (which implies that it is from the crust, and not the white of the bread). And in the crust itself, the most baked!"

Rav Ashi then told Menashe: "If you are so wise, why were you an idolater (which excluded him from the future world!)?"

Menashe answered: "If you had been there, you would have picked up the tails of your coat and run even faster than I had!"

The next day Rav Ashi began the lesson by saying: "We are going to start by talking about our Masters!"

What does this text tell us? Why "break bread"? How did the crooked king who does not share in the future world suddenly become a Master? Isn't it extraordinary that this law governing the breaking of bread, a law which we have practiced for centuries, was taught in a dream? I cannot answer all these questions in the context of this book, but I will summarize the main idea as follows: At the beginning, man was as soft as dough, the flexibility and malleability of which is underlined by the making of two braided breads for the Sabbath. These braids are reminders that according to tradition, Adam, the first man born of the dust of the earth, was originally a malleable mixture of water and clay. Reminding man of his provenance confronts him with his capacity for change, to avoid getting stuck into habits. The Midrash also states that these braids refer to the ones Eve made with her long, beautiful hair for her first meeting with Adam, thereby showing him that her "ribbed birth" would not be an obstacle to her capacity for change and reinvention. The crust is what has hardened, it is habit! Eating is to break bread, to "break the crust." In other words, it is a refusal to get bogged down, to get stuck, in a word, to get encrusted by layers of habit.

## The Songs of the Sabbath, the Meal and the *Dvar Torah*

> *There comes a time when the philosopher must return to music...*
> Vladimir Jankélévitch

### The *Zemirot*

Aside from a festive menu and a variety of culinary specialties, the Sabbath meal includes traditional songs known as *zemirot* and a short speech on the parasha of the week, known as the *Dvar Torah*.

Small books known as *zimronim* or *birkonim* reproduce all these songs, which are the same throughout the world. This allows a New York Jew and a Paris Jew, for instance, to join a Jerusalem family for their Sabbath dinner, and to know all the words and the tunes, most of which go back to the Middle Ages and the Renaissance. As with the reading of the Torah, the influence of the geographic context is strongly felt: tunes known as Sephardic airs resemble Arab chants, while Ashkenazi threnodies resemble Russian waltzes and folk songs.

It is customary to have several copies of this small book specially printed for the bar/bat mitzvah, with the name of the bar mitzvah boy or the bat mitzvah girl printed on the cover along with the date and the name of the parashah. These books are distributed to guests during the Sabbath meals and the ceremony, as a souvenir of this essential moment in the young person's life.

## Eating and Talking

The presence of the Holy Ark containing the Tables of Law in the Temple is recalled during the meal by "words from the Torah," or *Dvar Torah*. This is an opportunity for the bar mitzvah boy or bat mitzvah girl to rehearse the speech he or she will make the next day at Synagogue. This is also the point when parents and even their guests will take the floor, raising their glass to make a short personal commentary or a commentary on the weekly parashah.

## To Thank

After the meal, the *Birkat Hamazon,* or actions of grace, is recited. Introduced by an invitation to the blessing, or *zimun,* this text is frequently sung. It has the same tune practically all over the world and has been made popular by youth groups (scouts, *Bnei Akiva,* etc.) On this special day, the bar mitzvah boy or bat mitzvha girl recites the *Birkat Hamazon,* with the rest of the celebrants joining in for certain passages. The *Birkat Hamazon* is an opportunity to thank God for the food received, but also to celebrate all the spiritual and material resources which make up a life.

## Accompanying the Guests

After the meal, it is customary to accompany the guests on a short stretch of their trip home. It's important to make sure the Sabbath candles don't set fire to the house during this short absence.

*David at the Harp* (1956), Marc Chagall (1887–1985).
King David was a musician and a composer. His psalms remain an extraordinary source of inspiration for artists the world over.

# The Havdalah
## The Ending of the Sabbath

> *We possess the past: we have no fear of the future.*
> *We know where we come from.*
> *By remembering the beginning, we believe in the end, so much so*
> *that we live between two historical poles: the Sinai and the*
> *Kingdom of God...*
> *What will be the outcome of our history?*
> *Born of the wonderful, we will return to the wonderful.*

Abraham Joshua Heschel

### The Sabbath Schedule

The rest of the Sabbath follows a simple schedule. The morning is devoted to synagogue. At noon, the faithful go home or stay at synagogue for the second of the three Sabbath meals, inaugurated by a kiddush different not only in its textual but also in its posture, for it is generally said sitting down rather than standing up. This second meal does not include any songs, or any blessings from the parents. The afternoon, or what is left of it, is devoted to napping and studying, which is followed by the afternoon prayer and a third meal, which is relatively light and does not include a kiddush. The Sabbath ends when the first three medium-sized stars "come out," with the evening prayer and the havdalah ceremony.

### The Havdalah Ceremony

The Sabbath, which began with the lighting of the *nerot,* ends with the lighting of a single candle with a braided wick. The commentary generally given regarding this ritual is as follows: the Sabbath is a day of initiation to meetings. It starts at a time when the candles are two, and are separated, like two hearts which may not yet know each other, but are searching and yearning for one another, until they reach the moment when they are but one intertwined light.[4]

The havdalah consists of four blessings (once again, the famous four!): blessings of the wine, the perfume, the light and the separation between the holiness of the Sabbath and the rest of the week. In the same way that a rite is necessary to enter the Sabbath, a rite is necessary to leave it,

312

Begun through light, the Sabbath also comes to a close through light.
The havdalah candle braided with several wicks speaks of love and friendship and evokes the spleen
caused by the end of the Sabbath.

for, when experienced following the tradition, the Sabbath is such an intense day that our way of perceiving the world is profoundly modified by it. At the end of the Sabbath, we must return to a normal state of consciousness, a little as if we were coming out of a mystical trance. The Kabbalah says that it is not enough to know how to rise; one must also know how to come down. This modification of the Sabbath state of mind has a name, which is the extra soul, or *neshamah yetarah*. It is this soul which leaves, and therefore needs to be accompanied by this extremely beautiful ritual. With the havdalah, the extra soul leaves the simple soul, and produces a moment of weakness. The perfume is there to support the simple soul and fortify it in this separation from its extra soul. There is an authentic existential pain in this passage from the holy to the profane. This Saturday night *spleen* is overcome by a series of joyous ceremonies, of songs and of dances, which are particularly lively in Hassidic communities. This period immediately following the Sabbath is known as *melaveh malkah,* or "the accompaniment of the queen" Sabbath.

Following the blessing of the wine and the perfume, the blessing of fire comes. The tradition is to extinguish all lights and to contemplate the reflections of the flames on one's fingernails, which are momentary mirrors of the future. It is an ideal point to make wishes for the week and, more generally, for a happy life. In these moments, one has the impression of stepping into a Georges de la Tour painting in which the light illuminates faces with a warm clarity...

The blessing of separation ends the Sabbath officially, despite the fact that this part of the ceremony can happen as late as Tuesday morning. At this point, a song dedicated to the prophet Elijah is sung and people wish each other *shavua tov,* which means good week. On the day of a bar/bat mitzvah, it is once again the young man or woman who conducts this closing ceremony, which frequently takes place Saturday night after the Sabbath...

1. Note that, once again, the idea of a Hebrew phenomenology of the divine as the dialectic of "One" and "Four" is present.

2. If a man lives alone, he follows the same steps to light the candles himself. It is worth mentioning that the Sabbath candles are still lit among the Marranos, Jews who converted to Christianity during the Inquisition and at the time of the expulsion of Jews from Spain in 1492, while continuing to secretly practice Judaism and pass on its fundamental principles. In Portugal, a vast crypto-Jewish liturgy exists today due to five centuries of exclusively oral transmission, as written records of the Jewish faith were punishable by death. To this day, many women in highly Catholic Portugal continue to light candles on Friday evenings in the privacy of a basement or a storage room, without exactly knowing why they are doing it beyond the fact that their mothers and grandmothers taught them to.

3. See *Sefer Hachinukh* numbers 118 and 119.

4. In fact, the night of the Sabbath is traditionally considered a time to devote to lovemaking.

14

# The Bar Mitzvah Party

*Mr. Berstein had decided to impress his friends*
*by throwing a truly original Bar Mitzvah,*
*an ex-cep-tion-al party.*
*He invited all his friends on an African safari,*
*and, sure enough, all his guests wound up*
*riding elephants in one long, festive procession.*
*Suddenly, the procession came to a halt,*
*and stayed still for hours. Guests became impatient*
*and began asking what was wrong.*
*Mr. Berstein dismounted and went to see*
*the organizer of the safari at the head of the column:*
*"What's the problem here?"*
*"Oh, nothing serious, Mr. Berstein, we just have to let*
*the elephants for the Katz Bar Mitzvah by!"*

# Chapter Fourteen

The Third Phase of the "Rites of Passage"

**Dances, Chair, and Video**

Joy and Pedagogy

**"Eating Is Great": Towards a Bar Mitzvah Ethic**

**Ethics and "Diet-ethics"**

The Symbolism of Kashrut

## The Third Phase of the "Rites of Passage"

*Any philosophical system in which the body does not play a fundamental role is unfit and inept.*

Paul Valéry

The preceding chapters and, particularly, the first chapter, showed how the bar mitzvah serves as a "rite of passage," which allows the child to grow up harmoniously and enter the responsible life of adults, by successfully forgoing strictly familial connections in favor of creating new links with the religious, cultural, and social community.

I have also shown that the bar mitzvah includes three phases which are found in any "rite of passage" as defined and analyzed in the fields of anthropology or ethnology. The celebration precisely matches the third phase of this system, which posits that the child is reinserted and returned to the community, which in turn applauds him for the task accomplished.

In fact, the celebration does not achieve its significance unless the two first parts of the bar mitzvah, the preparation and the synagogue ceremony, have laid the path to initiation and growing.

Unfortunately, oftentimes parents and their children expend too much effort concentrating on "the party," and fail to give the preceding events all the significance and attention they deserve.

A bat mitzvah girl surrounded by her family and friends. These traditional dances are frequently danced in a circle. They require some prior knowledge...and powerful lungs!

## Dances, Chair, and Video

*Your knowledge is great. You love.*

Reb Racah, in *Le livre des questions* (The Book of Questions) by Edmond Jabès

As the true hero of the celebration, the young man or young woman is often presented to the celebrants the moment they enter the party hall, through an amusing photo or video montage.

The custom of gift giving remains central, though it evolves from decade to decade, following various fashions. There was the "watch" period, then the "gold fountain pen" one...

These presents are not unfounded. In fact, they have a specific meaning. The young man or young woman must be given something which relates to the idea of maturity, of responsibility and of adequately managing time and laws. The watch obviously has a logical relationship to time, as does the pen, in an era when it is less and less frequent to write by hand rather than with a computer. In traditional circles, the bar/bat mitzvah is an opportunity to constitute a basic Judaic library. In these cases, the young person is given books such as the Mishnah, the Talmud, the Bible, a special edition of the Haggadah, works of Jewish philosophy, etc.

Another highlight of the bar/bat mitzvah celebrations is the dancing.

A highlight of the evening takes place when the bar mitzvah boy or bat mitzvah girl sits on a chair and is triumphantly lifted up and carried through the middle of the room filled with people dancing.[1]

Hasidism places a lot of emphasis on the importance of dance as a way to implicate the body in this ritual joy, combining the engagement with the community with the sacred aspect of the celebration.

## Joy and Pedagogy

*In the country where one is always right,*
*flowers do not bloom in spring...*
Yehuda Amichai

In some circles, parents try to maintain the spirit of the bar mitzvah by organizing the tables so that they have names related to Judaism or ancient and contemporary Jewish history. Guests may be seated at the "Rabbi Akiva" table, the "parashat hashavua" table, or even the "Ben Gurion" or "Yitzhak Rabin" table. One could even imagine a game which pedagogically explained the different parts of the bar mitzvah process. Questions would be prepared and left on each participant's dish, or handed out as people came in. In this way, as the orchestra played and the guests danced, an intellectual element would be added to the party.

## "Eating Is Great"
### Towards a Bar Mitzvah Ethic

> *Before the hunger of men,*
> *responsibility cannot be objectively measured.*
> *It is indisputable.*
>
> Emmanuel Lévinas, *Totality and Infinity*

There is a concrete ethic within Judaism which underlines one's "indisputable responsibility" before another man's hunger. This is a concrete, limitless responsibility, which is placed at the very beginning of the Talmud: "As of what point do we hear something of the Revelation? As of the moment the priests go home to eat!" Listening to the word of God is subordinated to man's hunger! The ethical revelation makes us enter a time span which is not measured in hours and minutes, but in the number of mouths I can feed and in the vigilance of my own attention to others' suffering!

Lévinas frequently quoted the Talmudic author Rabbi Yohanan's statement that "eating is great."

The Talmud is justly referred to in Hebrew by the eloquent expression, *Torah she- be'al pe.* Generally translated as "oral law", this expression literally translates to, "the Torah which is on the mouth." This expression does not primarily refer to spoken words—which would then be in opposition to written words—but to the "mouth which eats," and which cries when it is hungry. The *Torah shebe'al peh,* the "Torah on the mouth," the words of the commentary, and the exegesis of the texts are a Torah, a Law, which order us to be just.

Oral law in the sense of the law of what is oral, a law which teaches us to speak and reminds us of our responsibility to a concrete ethic of sharing the bread, as was described in the section discussing the Sabbath bread.

It is important to note that the God who reveals Himself in the Ten

Commandments introduces Himself as "the One who brought you out of the land of Egypt, out of the house of slavery," and that the commemoration of this liberation (which is central to the bar mitzvah, as I have underlined several times) takes place through a ritual, *Pesach,* the Passover, which is inaugurated by the opening of the door to the house and the following statement: "Here is the bread of misery, whomever is hungry, let him come and eat, whomever is hungry, let him come and talk to us!"

Let him eat and let him talk! For the ethic of "the law on the mouth" cannot, after all, simply be reduced to the regulation of an economy of bellies, for growing is also crucially linked to the possibility for men to communicate amongst themselves.

We cannot therefore close this chapter on the bar mitzvah celebration without mentioning that in Hebrew the word "bar" can also mean bread, food, and that it is clear that this celebration must be prepared with the sensitivity required by the day's spiritual content. One cannot consider extravagant expenses without thinking of children and adults throughout the world, and particularly in Israel, who, at that very moment, do not have enough to eat. It is good to set a personal bar mitzvah ethic which consists of giving ten percent of the amount spent on this party to institutions or foundations which will help young people throughout the world to be associated with the joy and the celebration of the bar/bat mitzvah.[2]

## Ethics and "Diet-ethics"

*It is because the act of eating is so fundamental to mankind that it can serve as the most concrete vector of transmission for the highest values.*

Gilles Bernheim, *Le Souci des autres* (Caring For Others)

Before closing this chapter, it is necessary to discuss the meaning of *kashrut,* the rules governing diet in the Jewish faith. The bar mitzvah provides an ideal opportunity to reflect on this question, as families preparing a bar mitzvah celebration frequently hesitate between choosing a Beth-Din approved, kosher caterer or a regular caterer. The grounds for this hesitation are often simply financial ones: for "strange" reasons, kosher caterers are far more expensive than traditional caterers.

What is the meaning of the word "kosher"? The Hebraic term means "to be fit"—in this case, fit to be eaten—and can more generally be used to refer to something which conforms to a defined norm. It is therefore not limited to food, but to any situation or object. For instance, someone who is particularly good at a certain sport or art form will be said to be *mukhshar*. One could also mention that fitness rooms, which are currently all the rage, are referred to in Hebrew as *Makhon Kosher*, or, literally, "institute to get fit," the place where one goes to become fit to run, dance, or lift weights. In terms of nutrition, kosher food is therefore food that Jewish law considers fit to be eaten.

The kosher laws are relatively simple, though they can also be looked at in a more complex light for the sake of thorough, detailed study. The "Torah on the mouth" which was previously mentioned becomes the "Torah of the mouth." As Gilles Bernheim notes in his book *Le Souci des autres* (Caring For Others), "the fact that man cannot exist without eating is the foremost reason he thinks of himself humbly, as a creature which recognizes itself as such; in other words, excluding any idea of omnipotence or self-sufficiency." Food is such an important question that it is the subject of the first law imposed on man, "Of every tree of the garden thou mayest freely eat; but of the tree of the knowledge of good and evil, thou shalt not eat of it" (Genesis 2).

As a "law of the mouth," kosher law implies a simultaneous relationship to food and to speech, as underlined by the verse, "man doth not live by bread only, but by every thing that proceedeth out of the mouth of the Lord doth man live," (Deuteronomy 8:3). According to Gilles Bernheim, this double relationship should be interpreted as showing that eating, "must be testimony of the divine presence, and therefore of justice, or, in other words, of a relationship to one's fellow man which implies a responsibility towards him."

## The Symbolism of Kashrut

*Thou shalt love thy neighbour as thyself.*

Leviticus, 19:18

The kosher laws are highly symbolic. They serve as a way of teaching, transmitting and daily living the shared experience of those highest values which make up the human race. We will look at the laws in the order which they appear in the Torah. The first law concerns the ban on eating blood *(dam)*. *Dam* is clearly an important word, given that it is composed of two of the three letters that make up the word man *(adam)*. The first law stipulates that only meats which have been thoroughly drained of blood be eaten. It teaches that the vital principle, blood, should not come from any other being than one's self, and that it must come through a long and arduous process of intellectual, spiritual, and emotional elaboration. Though others can help us to construct ourselves, it is from ourselves and within ourselves that we develop the principle of life, in order to avoid the illusion that another's blood is the source of our life. This stipulation could be interpreted as a refusal of vampirism and parasitic behavior.

The second law forbids the mixing of meat and milk, or of any meat product with any dairy products, in keeping with the verse, "Thou shalt not seethe a kid in its mother's milk," (Exodus 23:19). Interpretation of this law is particularly relevant to the bar mitzvah, given the bar mitzvah's insistence on the necessity of tearing one's self away from the world of the mother, of not repeating her history, and of finding one's own path and freedom. One cannot "grow in the milk of one's mother." One cannot grow in the same parental values, without personally reinterpreting them and bringing them up to date. Parents are therefore responsible for offering their children the possibility to find their way through a constantly reinvented creativity.

The third law names those animals which are fit to be consumed. Quadrupeds must have cloven hooves and chew their own cud. Marine animals must have fins and scales.

Mollusks, reptiles and crustaceans are therefore forbidden. As for birds, no bird of prey is kosher.

325

As an example, one could explain that the cloven hoof expresses the impossibility of the single way of thinking or the single path, by demonstrating that every situation or idea has at least two aspects. This openness is explored in the Talmudic practice of the *machloket*, or conversation between masters. Ways of thinking can be discussed and exposed but cannot be imposed!

As for rumination, it teaches us what the philosopher Alain expressed so well, "that a thought, even a true one, becomes false once we are satisfied with it." A thought should always be reconsidered and retooled. Studying requires infinite labor. This painstaking approach to thought is the only way to escape ideology. Pigs, for instance, may have cloven hooves, but they do not ruminate. They aren't kosher!

Let us continue our short journey into the world of kashrut interpretation. Fins allow a fish to guide itself and to avoid being at the mercy of the currents. Eating kosher fish makes us aware of our responsibility to make our own way and of the possibility of deciding things for ourselves, without excluding the possibility of asking for advice and soliciting help. Scales allow fish to take hold. This evokes the ability to face events without running from them.

The concepts we have just rapidly explained deserve greater depth and development. We have attempted to suggest how the kosher laws, particularly in the context of the bar/bat mitzvah, contain an essential pedagogical dimension and have a powerful effect on the transmission of the highest values. We turn once again to Gilles Bernheim, who stresses that, "Kashrut must not be considered solely on the basis of its quality and taste, but also because it invites us to think justly! Any food which could lead human thought astray would be considered inedible."

The above statement allows us to appreciate the importance of including the bar mitzvah in the context of this transmission of the principles and values which are at the very heart of "growing."

1. This reminds me of the hilarious Gad Elmaleh skit entitled "The Bar Mitzvah," in which the chair holds a central place.
2. See the list at the end of the bibliography.

# 15

# Bar Mitzvahs Throughout the World

*Truth for a man is the thing
that makes him a man.*

Antoine de Saint-Exupéry, *Wind, Sand, and Stars*

# Chapter Fifteen

Sephardim and Ashkenazim

**In Hasidic Communities**

In Ashkenazi Communities

**In Morocco**

Algeria

**In Tunisia**

Libyan Community (Tripoli)

**In Iraq**

In Iran

**In Kurdistan**

In Yemen

**In France, the United States, and Israel**

The Secular Bar Mitzvah

**Personal Account**

The *Kotel*

## Sephardim and Ashkenazim

*Anthropology modestly contributes to the elaboration of that logic of the concrete which appears to be one of the major concerns of modern thought, and which draws us closer to forms of thought very foreign to our own, far more than it estranges us from them.*

Claude Lévi-Strauss, *Structural Anthropology II*

This final chapter will take the reader on a journey throughout the world to discover the different bar mitzvah customs found in various countries. This should be considered an interactive chapter, and I encourage readers to write to share their communities' or families' traditions, so they can be included in the next edition. My sources throughout this chapter are multiple, though the *Yalkut Minhagim*, a collection of descriptions of various customs, stands out as a particularly essential reference.

The Jewish people can be divided into two major, global groups, the Sephardim and the Ashkenazim, both of which can be further subdivided into numerous smaller groups. The Ashkenazim are Jews originating from Northern and Eastern Europe. The Ashkenazim's primary languages were essentially German and Yiddish, in addition to local languages and dialects. The various Hasidic communities belong to the Ashkenazi community. It is worth noting, for instance, that numerous twelfth-century French words can be found in Rashi's medieval commentary, making his writings inestimable sources for the study of ancient French.

Sephardim are originally Spanish Jews, but since the expulsion of the Jews from Spain in 1492, the term came to refer to all the Jewish communities around the Mediterranean and, eventually, by extension, to Iraqi, Ethiopian and Yemenite Jews, despite the fact that they have strictly no relation to fifteenth-century Spain. Today, the Ashkenazi community is the larger of the two communities. It is particularly strong in the United States. The situation in France is quite particular. Though there is a significant Ashkenazi community in Eastern France, the vast majority of French Jews are Sephardic. This is due to the repatriation of the Algerian Jews and the migration of Moroccan and Tunisian Jews to France in the 1950s and 1960s.

The creation of the state of Israel gave rise to a new and very powerful Jewish identity, the Israeli identity, which, due to Israel's language and its central position in contemporary Jewish consciousness, plays a very significant role in the dissemination of Jewish values and cultural habits.

A chapter on the history of the Jews would be useful at this point, but is beyond the scope of this volume.

## In Hasidic Communities

*When the rabbi dances, all the Hasidim dance...*

Traditional Yiddish song

Hasidism is a mystical movement founded in the eighteenth century by Rabbi Israel ben Eliezer, known as the Baal Shem Tov, or "Master of the Good Name" (1700–1760). This movement translates the major themes of the Kabbalah to an existential level. It is connected to a search for the "light of Infinity" as a means of discovering a joyful path of life. Hasidism's specificity notably resides in the democratization of the Kabbalist concepts experienced thanks to a Master referred to as the Rabbi or *Tzadik*. The Master becomes the pillar of the group and the world, the individual who comforts, councils and heals his followers. Hasidism became the way of life of an entire people who had discovered the marvels and profound secrets of this hidden tradition (the Kabbalah). The great masters responsible for the birth and development of this movement were the Baal Shem Tov, the founder, and his disciples, including Rabbi Levi Issac of Berditchev, the Clairvoyant of Lublin, the Maggid of Mezeritch, Rabbi Nahman of Breslav, Rabbi Schneur Zalman of Lyadi, and many others. Hasidism has probably been one of the greatest socio-religious revolutions to appear within the Jewish community since the beginning of Christianity. The movement remains very much alive today. In Hasidic communities, the bar mitzvah boy goes to the mikvah on the day of the tefillin ceremony and on his bar mitzvah Sabbath, to symbolize a rebirth. It is also customary for the bar mitzvah boy to go to the rabbi's home to receive his blessing.

Among the Lubavitch Jews, the same speech is pronounced at every bar mitzvah. It is a speech originally made by Rabbi Rashav (Rabbi Shalom Dov Ber, the fifth rabbi of the Chabad lineage) on the occasion of his bar mitzvah on 20 Marheshvan (October-November) 5632 (1873), and later repeated by Rabbi Yosef Itshak Shneersohn on the occasion of his own bar mitzvah on 12 Tamuz (July-August) 5653 (1893). In these communities, a honey cake is served during the celebratory meal.

Another somewhat surprising but widely spread custom consists of bothering and obstructing the bar mitzvah boy during his speech, and the prayer, if the bar mitzvah boy is conducting the service. This custom allegedly aims to help anxious children who find it hard to appear in front of an audience. The hubbub makes it difficult to distinguish between those who are at ease in front of an audience, and those who are more awkward...

The bar mitzvah is always followed by a light meal during which salted or

333

pickled herring is served, along with cakes and egg kichel, a type of bowl-shaped dry crêpe inside which vegetables or herring can be placed. One person is selected to pour each of the guests a glass of alcohol. As guests receive their drinks, they say *lehayim* (to life!) and are answered with *lechayim u livrakha,* "to life and for the blessing." Then one of the participants, gene-rally the rabbi, raises his glass, says *lechayim* twice and makes a small commentary (the *Dvar Torah).* The guests then rise to sing and dance in a circle, before it all starts all over again: a little drink, *lechayim,* speech, dances, and a little drink...

## In Ashkenazi Communities

> *Yéde pekele findt seine tékele*
> **Each little pot finds its cover...**
>
> Alsatian Jewish saying

In Ashkenazi communities, and particularly in the old community in Jerusalem, it is customary to give the bar mitzvah boy a tallith and a silk or velour case on which his initials or name are printed along with the date of the ceremony. The bar mitzvah boy is also given engraved tefillin cases. In these communi-ties, it is traditional to have the bar mitzvah boy "ascend" to read the haftarah on the Sabbath preceding his thirteenth birthday, even if he is also "ascen-ding" for his Sabbath bar mitzvah, which could take place much later. On the bar mitzvah Sabbath, a kiddush, or light meal, is served. The kiddush may include traditional dishes such as *lekakh,* a sweet cake, as well as the famous *kugel,* which can be made from potatoes or sweet noodles. *Chulent,* a stew of meat, beans, barley, and potatoes cooked overnight is another Ashkenazic dish. The kiddush fare is always accompanied with pickles dipped in vinegar. Once again, there is a tradition of "preventing" the bar mitzvah boy from making his speech. He is interrupted by the chants of his classmates and other members of the community. Gifts largely consist of Torahs and Jewish commentaries, as well as cash.

# In Morocco

*—What do we call a classic?*
*—A book that everyone is talking about and no one has read!*
Ernest Hemingway

In Morocco, the bar mitzvah is celebrated when the boy turns thirteen. Emphasis is placed on the *drush,* or speech, which largely consists of verses about the tallith and the tefillin. During the *drush,* the young man pays particular attention to lavishly expressing his gratitude to his parents, his family, and his teachers. In general, the young man does not read the haftarah on the day of his bar mitzvah, for by then he will already have been invited to read it. Indeed, it is extremely common for children to read the haftarah as of seven, or even earlier. When children read the haftarah for the first time, candy is thrown at them, after which a special family dinner is held in the synagogue.

The evening before the bar mitzvah, the father and son have their hair done at home, surrounded by poets and musicians.

The bar mitzvah tends to take place on Mondays, or on Thursdays, when the child can put on the tallith and the tefillin, and ascend to the Torah.

The bar mitzvah boy goes to synagogue in a procession of family and friends holding decorated candles and singing and reciting poems... The same procession forms to accompany the bar mitzvah boy as he returns from synagogue. As in many other communities, the bar mitzvah boy puts the tallit and tefillin on for the first time on the day of his bar mitzvah. The ceremony is planned to ensure that the bar mitzvah boy speak after he has put on the arm-tefillin, so that he must bless the head-tefillin.

Once the tefillin have been put on, the father pronounces the *Barukh Shepetarani* blessing (without pronouncing God's name).

Some put the Rashi and Rabbenu Tam tefillin on at the same time, rather than one after the other, as is the custom in certain communities. Bar mitzvahs celebrations remain rare in Morocco or among Jewish communities of Moroccan background.

335

Traditional musicians accompany the celebratory meal with songs and music. A wide variety of wines and hard liquor is served, providing the guests with opportunities to make numerous toasts.

Moroccan Jews in traditional garb.
In our day, it is common to add folkloric elements from the celebrants' homeland to the bar/bat mitzvah.

## Algeria

*I left my country*
*I left my home...*
*The sun! The sun of my lost country*
*Of the white cities I loved*
*Of the girls I used to know...*

Enrico Macias

Algerian customs are very similar to those of Morocco and Tunisia, though there are certain dishes and songs specific to the Algerian Jewish tradition.

The most characteristic trait of Algerian bar mitzvahs is that they are referred to as "communions." This is probably due to the fact that Algerian Jews became French with the Crémieux decree of October 24th, 1870.

Doctor Aldo Naouri has shared the following account with me: in Algeria, the bar mitzvah boy has two *chochbim,* who are like two best boys chosen among his younger friends. In the days preceding the placing of the tefillin, the bar mitzvah boy is constantly accompanied by his *chochbim.* They join him at the *hammam,* which serves as a ritual bath, and sleep over at his house the night before the ceremony. I have often been told of another, somewhat grotesque, detail, which is that in certain families, particularly rich ones, the father of the bar mitzvah boy entrusts him to older young men, providing them with money to take his son to a brothel as soon as the ceremony is over.

## In Tunisia

> *I bear your name, your nose, and sometimes your luggage.*
>
> Achille Talon

In Tunisian communities, bar mitzvahs only take place on Monday and Thursday. The date of the ceremony is not chosen in relation to the child's birthday, but simply to fall during his thirteenth year. The evening before the ceremony, the bar mitzvah boy's friends join him at home for a joint haircut session. The hairdresser also serves as a waiter for a light meal during which friends and family members can enjoy egg and tuna briks, boiled fhava beans, meat-based appetizers, and, of course, the traditional *araq.*

On the morning of the bar mitzvah, the young man puts a small tallith, the *tallit katan,* on for the first time and pronounces the *sheheyanu* blessing over it. He is then accompanied to the synagogue by his family, his guests, and Talmud-Torah singers. Once the group has arrived at the synagogue, the father places the larger tallith on his son.

The bar mitzvah boy's mother or other women decorate the tzitzit, the fringes of the tallith (this is also done for the groom before a wedding). Tzitzit decoration, which is an art in and of itself, differs from one tallith to another. Tunisian tefillin are smaller than those worn in Ashkenazi countries. The most fervent believers wear both Rashi and Rabbenu Tam's tefillin.

The tefillin case, which is often shaped like a little box, can also serve as a "*tzedakah* box." Children form the habit of placing a coin inside the "*tzedakah* box" on a daily basis, to collect funds to be donated to people living in poverty or various humanitarian associations. The money is donated on a regular basis, either once a year or every month.

As the culmination of the ceremony, the ascent to the Torah is greeted with songs and numerous poems. Cologne, perfume or even jasmines are distributed to the audience, and as many people as possible are invited to ascend to the Torah. Most of these people have made generous donations to the synagogue. After the synagogue ceremony, a small buffet is set up, and when lunchtime rolls around the entire community feasts on the obligatory traditional couscous.

## Libyan Community (Tripoli)

*Art is an anti-destiny.*

André Malraux, *The Voices of Silence*

In Jewish communities in Libya, or of Libyan background, the bar mitzvah boy has his hair cut in the presence of his friends and family and of musicians on the Thursday before the Sabbath preceding the ceremony. He also invites his friends to join him in getting a haircut. While the boys have their hair cut, guests sing and play music, and women chant festive calls and serve cakes and sweets to the celebrants.

The first time the child goes to the Talmud-Torah to learn to read and prepare his bar mitzvah, the mother takes the first egg laid by a chicken (I assume the first egg of the day), hard boils it, and brings it to the teacher. The teacher peels the egg and carves the initials of the verses *Torah tzihva lanu Moshe, morashah kehilat Yaakov* ("a law Moses commanded us, a heritage for the congregation of Jacob") and *gal enai vaabita niflaot mitoratekha* ("I raise *ratekha* ("I raise my eyes and see the wonders of your Torah") on it. The child eats the egg, after which the teacher places a chumash (Pentateuch) on his head and repeatedly but lightly hits him, thereby symbolizing the easy absorption of the teachings into his mind. Under the teacher's supervision, older students follow the same procedure, in order to ensure that this custom does not serve as a pretext to bully or humiliate the new student.

On the day of his thirteenth birthday (or the day he puts on the tefillin), the young man is dressed by his family and close friends. Before he goes to synagogue, he visits with his mother and asks her to forgive him for any trouble he may have caused her during his childhood. The young man then shows her his hands, which she washes as a sign of having granted him her forgiveness, while wishing him happiness and success. According to most accounts, this is one of the happiest moments in a mother's life. Following the ritual washing of the hands, the father places the tallith on his son, and the whole group accompanies him with songs and poems as he heads to the synagogue directly surrounded by personal friends who take turns being at his side on this important trip. The ceremony of the ascent to the Torah only takes place on the Sabbath. If the boy is an orphan, the ceremony can take place on Monday or Thursday, and everyone accompanies him to the synagogue for the donning of the tefillin.

It is customary to organize a bar mitzvah in which the bar mitzvah boy invites a poor or orphaned bar mitzvah boy to join him. The second boy dresses like his host and is considered his twin brother. Both boys receive the same honors and are given the same gifts.

In a similar spirit, it is common for the community to fund collective bar mitzvahs for all the children of struggling families. Ideally, these collective bar mitzvahs are celebrated on the Shavuot holiday, one of the three pilgrimage holidays which commemorate the giving of the Torah.

## In Iraq

*The spirit lives on difference.*
*Disparity excites it, plenitude leaves it inert.*

Paul Valéry, *Autres rhumbs*

Iraqi Jewish communities are particularly fond of songs and sung poetry. Numerous collections of their verses have been printed in Baghdad, India, and Jerusalem.

The bar mitzvah ceremony is not markedly different than in other communities. After ascending to the Torah, the reader comes back down and addresses the audience with *Kulekhem berukhim,* "you are all blessed," to which the assembly responds, *Hazak ubarukh,* "be strong and be blessed." After the meal, guests say *lehan berakha el betekha,* "may the blessing come upon your house," to their host, who answers, *Uvetekha lo yehsar,* "may your house not lack for anything."

## In Iran

*Mr. Rabinovitch wanted to change his name to a less Jewish-sounding name: Julius Schmidt. As he headed to city hall, he kept repeating the name to himself: Julius Schmidt, Julius Schmidt, Iulius Schmi, Schulius Midt...When he arrived in front of the registrar, he was asked to state the name he wanted to take. Confused, he blurted out: Schmilius Yid!*

In Iran, the father writes his son's name in the margins of the prayer book. The tefillin are worn on Monday, Thursday, or Rosh Chodesh (the first day of the month). The ascent to the Torah is accompanied by songs, festive calls, and, occasionally, the ringing of the shofar. Candy is thrown at the bar mitzvah boy. On the Sabbath, sweets are given to the other children, and following the bar mitzvah ceremony, neighbors prepare a meal and bring it to the bar mitzvah boy's family home.

# In Kurdistan

*I only exist in so far as I exist for others.*
*At most, being is loving.*

Emmanuel Mounier, *Personalism*

In Kurdistan, there was a time when the bar mitzvah was not celebrated. Later, certain customs made their way into tradition: new clothes were bought, houses were whitewashed, new furniture was made, and people danced, sang and celebrated late into the night.

In these communities, the moment the young man takes his tefillin off for the first time is considered to augur well for a successful match in life. For this reason, a young woman who has already had her bat mitzvah is chosen to be present among the young man's friends and family to witness the "untying" of the tefillin. This custom is particularly significant in the context of my analysis of the bar mitzvah as a "science of the knots to be undone," in which the tefillin is seen as the symbol of new links outside of the family and the departure from the mother's world to move towards a wife.[11]

An initial celebration is held on the evening after the tefillin has been put on. Traditional dishes are served, and each guest receives a dish with meat, an egg and salads. The wine flows freely.

On the bar mitzvah Sabbath, when the head of the family ascends to the Torah, the entire family and all the guests rise in his honor. When he returns to his seat, everyone comes to kiss his hand. When a young person ascends to the Torah, he must go to kiss the hands of all his family members and guests, starting with the *Hakham* (the rabbi), as he returns to his seat.

Generally, anybody descending from the bimah after having ascended to the Torah, addresses the assembly with *kulekhem berukhim,* "May you all be blessed."[12]

341

## In Yemen

*If we don't change, we don't grow.*
*If we don't grow, we are not really living.*
*Growing requires a temporary relinquishing of any sense of security.*
Gail Sheehy

In Yemen, the custom of the *tallit katan* did not exist, for the entire community wore clothing with tzitzit (ritual fringes). This community's characteristic trait was the importance placed on covering one's hair. Children wore *karkush,* a type of large kippah, from infancy, and their hair was kept long until they reached the age of three, at which point a ceremony similar to the Hasidic ceremony of cutting the child's hair was performed. The child's head was entirely shaved, with the exception of two long curls left dangling from each side. At this stage, boys' *karkush* were replaced with hats, while girls continued to wear *karkush,* sometimes long after their weddings. When a woman became a grandmother, she replaced her *karkush* with a *tsuna.* In Yemen, nobody ever went out with their head uncovered. Doing so would have signified that the person in question had converted to another religion, or, in any case, would have been considered to have done so.

It appears that there are no bar mitzvah customs specific to Yemen and communities of Yemenite origin. Fathers are simply responsible for telling their sons how to put on the tefillin, so that they may in turn pass this knowledge on to their own children.

Yemenite Jews during a holiday meal.

Meals begin with the purification of the hands, with one person coming around to pour water on each of the participants' hands. The first person to have his hands washed is always the *Maari* (Yemenite term referring to the head of the family, or the rabbi), followed by those sitting next to him. The person receiving water says *yaavdukha amim,* "may the people be obliged to you," to the person pouring the water, who replies *veyishtachavu lekha leumim,* "may the nations have great respect for you." Then the *Maari* pronounces the *motzi,* the blessing over the bread, dips the bread in salt, eats a little, and distributes it among the guests. (In the case of a wake, he distributes the bread first, then eats it.) After the meal, the *Maari,* or another wise man, pronounces a commentary on the parashah, known as the *kishur,* or "link."

## In France, the United States, and Israel

> *An authentic voyage of discovery does not consist in searching for new horizons but in having a new way of looking at things.*
> Marcel Proust

In France, the United States, Israel, and throughout the world, we are witnessing something of a standardization of the bar mitzvah ceremony, with variations and combinations of the Diaspora customs described above as the norm.

Another new phenomenon is the rise of "neo-traditions" which never existed previously but have arisen as nostalgic evocations of the home country, whether it is Morocco, Algeria, Tunisia, Russia, England, or any other Jewish homeland. For instance, young Jews born in France and now living in Israel, might wear traditional Moroccan clothing, have their hair hennaed and provide their bar mitzvah guests with a *"nargileh* lounge," complete with traditional Arab music and a stereotypical belly dance. (Which, in fact, does have psychological significance when seen in the context of our general commentary on the bar mitzvah...)

344

Bar Mitzvah boys of the Ethiopian community.
Ethiopian Jews claim to be descendants of the Queen of Sheba.
They made aliyah to Israel, over the course of two spectacular operations:
Operation Moses (1984) and Operation Solomon (1991).

# The Secular Bar Mitzvah

*In every man, you will find the positive*
*Even those who appear to you as the worst miscreants.*
*Tirelessly,*
*generously, search, harvest,*
*Listen...*
*They are musical notes.*
*Dance.*
*Clap your hands.*
*Let the melody rise up!*
*Write the joyous song of healing,*
*The precious song of deliverance...*

Rabbi Nachman of Breslav

Our world tour of bar mitzvahs would not be complete without mention-ing secular bar mitzvahs. For several years now, secular Jewish centers have attempted to introduce a new type of approach to Judaism. Upon reading my outline of this new approach, readers will note that it is not significantly different from liberal or conservative Judaism, or even from a form of tradi-tional Judaism open to modernity. The main differences reside in the defi-nition of who is Jewish, in the mixing of Jews and non-Jews for certain ceremonies, such as secular weddings, for example, and in the strict appli-cation of traditional customs. However, the traditions described in the previous fourteen chapters can all be found in the secular bar mitzvah cere-mony, notably the parashah, the speech, the party and the preparatory studying. The only exception may be in the reduced emphasis placed on the tefillin and the tallith, which remain central aspects of a more traditional approach to the bar mitzvah. At first glance, the synagogal dimension also seems to be largely absent, but if we consider that the synagogue is, first and foremost, a community center intended as a place for people to get together, we realize this is not necessarily true. Secularism invites us to reflect on the meaning of the religious, a process we have attempted in the introduction to this volume.

Though the figure of the rabbi is also missing from secular Judaism, his role is filled by the community leader, and the *Bnai Mitzvah* celebrants and their

345

families are probably far more involved in the organization of the ceremonies.[13] "A one-year bar mitzvah program for boys and girls" called "Year of Judaism for *Bnai Mitzvah* celebrants" is offered.

The program has a triple objective: to develop young people's sense of belonging to the Jewish community and people, to allow them to discover their own potential, and to make them aware of Jewish values.

To reach these objectives, the collective and individual lessons offered over the course of the school year are divided into three parts:

1. *Exploration of contemporary Jewish history* through each student's study of his or her own family history. By interviewing the oldest members of the family, as well as by making family trees and albums containing photos and documents, students will feel directly implicated in the transmission of Judaism and the history of the Jewish people. This is also a unique, moving opportunity for intergenerational bonds to be strengthened. (This type of assignment seems to be inspired by classes for bar mitzvah age children in Israel. These are known as *avodat shorashim,* "work to find one's roots.")

2. *Volunteering in the community.* The traditional bar mitzvah marks the welcoming of the young Jew as an integral part of the community. He is recognized as an adult from the religious point of view and must assume the rights and duties of this new position. However, given that twelve or thirteen year-olds are in many respects still children, we consider it absurd to consider the bar mitzvah as the passage to adult status. Nonetheless, this year of study and of reflection, in conjunction with the natural processes of adolescence, will lead the students to greater maturity. How can we translate the newfound desire to be entrusted with greater responsibility into actions? By helping those who need help. Becoming an adult means devoting one's time to others and no longer giving priority to satisfying one's own desires. Each bar mitzvah student will therefore select a Jewish institution (retirement home, school, nursery, memorial foundation, newspaper, radio station, social services...) to devote several days' work to.

3. *Analysis of Biblical texts,* and, in particular, of the student's parashah. It is traditional for bar mitzvah students to study the part of the Torah which corresponds to their birth date. Why should we deprive ourselves of a fantastic heritage, which continues to convey relevant moral values? The Torah is not

only a religious text, it is the founding text of Judaism and, as such, it carries the history of a whole people."

To complete this year of study, an annual weekend devoted to the Holocaust is organized. Over the course of this weekend, students listen to the accounts of a Holocaust survivor, of a hidden child, or of a resistance member. They also visit a Memorial and a Holocaust Museum...

Future *bnai mitzvah* celebrants are also invited to participate in the celebration of Jewish holidays at the Secular Jewish Community Center. These special events are extremely important, for they allow the students to understand the cycle of a Jewish year and to take in the values and meaning of each holiday. The history of the Jewish people becomes their history.

The closing ceremony held in June is the culmination of a year of work. The students present the fruits of their research and training to their friends and families. They thereby symbolically make their entrance into the adult Jewish community.

## Personal account

347

> *For he who is lost, there is the sky or there are books. In both cases, his solitude is invaded and appeased by the most beautiful voices in the world.*
> Erri de Luca

"As a child, I always found the family celebrations of Jewish ceremonies magical. This certainly contributed to my desire to learn more about the Jewish people, the Jewish religion and Jewish thought. During our study of Judaism, I discovered that the community aspect was important: studying in a group allows you to avoid being alone, and to share and think as a group...We worked and studied hard, but we also laughed a lot and enjoyed discovering our Jewish identity."

Noémie G., Bat Mitzvah in 1998.

# The Kotel
## The Western Wall in Jerusalem

*From the beginning, a father's love for his child is destined*
*to renunciation and disappointments. This means that parents*
*must grow at the same time as their children grow.*
Geneviève Bersihand

Another significant contemporary aspect of the bar mitzvah is the beautiful new custom of holding bar mitzvahs in Jerusalem at the Kotel (the Western Wall or Wailing Wall).

Even when the bar mitzvah is celebrated in the Diaspora, parents, or sometimes just the father or mother, take their son or daughter to Jerusalem, to pray and put on the tefillin at the Wall. The young man or woman constructs his or her entry into the community with a strong connection to the people of Israel, thereby making good on the ancestral prayer recited during Passover: "Next year in Jerusalem..."

The Western Wall has become the symbol of the memory of the Temple, illustrating the following statement by Rav Kook: "When you are in prayer before this wall, you must remember that there are men with hearts of stone but the hope is that within some of those stones the heart of a man still beats."

"Next year in Jerusalem," a phrase that expresses hope and faith, closes the book of the Pesach Haggadah, a central, fundamental text on the question of separation and "growing."

349

1. Department of religious education, Ministry of Education and Culture, Israel, 1993.

2. The word "Ashkenazi" is a Hebrew word which means "Germany." The word "Sephardi," which is also from the Hebrew, means "Spain." Through the tricks of history, these terms have taken on broader meanings.

3. In general, *Parshat Noach*, or *Ki Tetzei*, because the *haftarot* are short.

4. In cases where the Bar Mitzvah boy does not speak, only one blessing is made for the arm and the head.

5. The texts in the tefillin, according to Rashi, are not in the same order as in Rabbenu Tam's. See Chapter 6.

6. I owe the description of these Moroccan customs to Chalom Danino, quoted in *Yalkut Minhagim* (collection of customs), op. cit.

7. I owe the description of these Tunisian customs to Mordechai Sitban and Abraham Bar-Tal, quoted in *Yalkut Minhagim* (collection of customs), op. cit.

8. I owe the description of these Libyan customs to Rabbi Fréz'a Zouartz, quoted in *Yalkut Minhagim* (collection of customs), op. cit.

9. Based on Avraham ben Yaakov, in *Yalkut Minhagim* (collection of customs), op. cit.

10. Based on Hannah Mizrahi, in *Yalkut Minhagim* (collection of customs), op. cit.

11. See Introduction and Chapter 1.

12. Based on Ishtaq Amédi, in *Yalkut Minhagim* (collection of customs), op. cit.

13. This entire section on secular bar mitzvahs was kindly provided to me by the CCLJ, *Centre Communautaire Laïc Juif de Bruxelles* (Brussels Secular Jewish Community Center).

# 16

# Bibliography and Acknowledgments

## Bibliography

Atlan, Henri. *Les Étincelles du hasard* (Vol. I and II), Seuil, 2003.

———. *L'Utérus artificiel*, Seuil, 2005.

Abécassis, Armand. *L'Univers hébraïque. Du monde païen à l'humanisme biblique*, Albin Michel, 2003.

———. *Les Temps du partage* (Vol. I and II), Albin Michel, 1993.

Askénazi, Léon. *La Parole et l'écrit*, Albin Michel, 2003.

Arlow, Jacob A. *A Psychoanalytic Study of a Religious Initiation Rite. Bar Mitzvah. The Psychoanalytic Study of the Child*, 1951, pp. 353–374.

Barthes, Roland. *Roland Barthes,* University of California Press, 1994.

Baudelot, Christian. *Allez les filles!*, Seuil, 1998.

———. *Et pourtant ils lisent…*, Seuil, 1999.

Bernheim, Gilles. *Le Souci des autres*, Calmann-Lévy, 2002.

Bruner, Jérôme. *Culture et modes de pensée*, Retz, 2000.

———. *L'Éducation, entrée dans la culture*, Retz, 1996.

Buber, Martin. *Le Juste et l'Injuste*, Bayard, 2003.

———. *Les Récits hassidiques* (Vol. I and II), coll. "Point Sagesse," Seuil, 1996.

———. *On Judaism*, Schocken, 1996.

———. *The Way of Man; According to the Teaching of Hasidism*, Citadel Press, 1995.

Chebel, Malek. La Féminisation du monde. *Psychoanalysis of the Thousand and One Nights*, Payot and Rivages, 1996.

Clastres, Pierre. *Chronicle of the Guayaki Indians*, Zone Books, 1998.

Davis, J. *Mazel Tov:* The Bar Mitzvah as a Multigenerational Ritual of Change and Continuity. E. Imber-Black and J. Roberts, *Rituals in Families and Family Therapy, 1988*, pp.177–208.

Derrida, Jacques and Hélène Cixous. *Veils (Cultural Memory in the Present)*, Stanford University Press, 2001.

Derrida, Jacques. *Circonfessions*, Seuil, 1990.

Didier-Weill, Alain. *Invocations*, Calmann-Lévy, 1998.

———. *Les Trois Temps de la loi*, Seuil, 1996.

———. *Lila et la lumière de Vermeer. La psychanalyse à l'école des artistes*, Denoël, 2003.

Dolto, Françoise and Juan-David Nasio. *L'Enfant du miroir*, Payot and Rivages, 1992.

Dolto, Françoise. *L'Image inconsciente du corps*, Seuil, 1969.

———. *Lorsque l'enfant paraît*, Seuil, 1978.

Draï, Raphaël. *Freud et Moïse. Psychanalyse, loi juive et pouvoir*, Economica,1997.

———. *Identité juive, identité humaine*, Armand Colin, 1999.

———. *La Sortie d'Égypte*, Fayard, 1986.

———. *La Traversée du désert. L'invention de la responsabilité*, Fayard, 1988.

Dumas, Didier. *Et l'enfant créa le père*, Hachette, 2000.

Eliade, Mircea. *Initiation, rites, sociétés secrètes*, coll. "Idées," Gallimard, 1976.

Elbaz, Raphaël Moché and ed. Pinhas Tolédano, *Kanfé Yona*, Bné Braque, 1995 (in Hebrew).

Finkielkraut, Alain. *The Imaginary Jew*, University of Nebraska Press, 1994.

———. *Une voix vient de l'autre rive*, Gallimard, 2000

———. *L'ingratitude*, Gallimard, 1999

Freud, Sigmund. *Œuvres complètes*, Presses Universitaires de France, 1992.

Gazier, Julie. *Lire pour vivre*, text from the Preface by Alexandre Jardin, Robert Laffont, 2000.

Gendreau, Joël. *L'Adolescence et ses "rites" de passage*, Presses Universitaires de Rennes, 1999.

Haddad, Gérard. *L'Enfant illégitime. Sources talmudiques de la psychanalyse suivi de Lacan et le judaïsme*, Desclée de Brouwer, 1996.

Hervieux-Wane Fabrice, *Une boussole pour la vie-Les nouveaux rites de passages*, Albin Michel, 2005

Hirsch, Shimchon Raphaël (Rabbi). *Commentaires sur la Tora* (Five Volumes), Jérusalem, 1976 (in Hebrew).

Horowitz, Yichayaou Halévy. *Mitsvat Tefillin*, Jérusalem, 1977 (in Hebrew).

Hougron, Alexandre. *Science-fiction et société*, Presses Universitaires de France, 2000.

Jankélévitch, Vladimir and Béatrice Berlovitch. *Quelque part dans l'inachevé*, Gallimard, 1978.

Jardin, Alexandre. *L'Ile des gauchers*, Gallimard, 1997.

———. *Le Petit Sauvage*, coll. "Folio," Gallimard, 2003.

Jonas, Hans. *Le concept de Dieu après Auschwitz. Une voix juive*, Payot and Rivages, 1994.

Kafka, Franz. La Pléiade, *The Complete Stories*, Schocken, 1995.

Karo, Yossef (Rabbi). *Le Choulkhan Aroukh*, Jérusalem, 2005.

Kolitz, Zvi. *Yossel Rakover s'adresse à Dieu*, Calmann-Lévy, 1998, p.27.

Kierkegaard, Soren. *Crainte et tremblement*, Aubier, 1977.

Krohn, Paysach J. *Reflections of the Magguid: Inspirational Stories from Around the Globe and Around the Corner*, Mesorah publications, 2004.

Krygier, Rivon. *La Loi juive à l'aube du XXIe Siècle*, Biblieurope, 1999.

Lacan, Jacques. *Des Noms-du-père*, Seuil, 2005.

———. *Encore. Le Séminaire* (Book XX), Seuil, 1975.

———. *Le Sinthome. Le Séminaire* (Book XXIII), Seuil, 2005.

———. *Les formations de l'inconscient. Le Séminaire* (Book V), Seuil, 1998.

Laffon, Martine. *Adam comme un conte*, Bayard, 1999.

———. *Jonas ou le refus*, Alternatives, 2000.

Lévi-Strauss, Claude. *Structural Anthropology* (Vol. II), Basic Books, 1974.

———. *Tristes tropiques*, Plon, 1955.

———. *Le regard éloigné*, Plon 1983.

Lévinas, Emmanuel. *Au-delà du verset*, Minuit, 1982.

———. *Otherwise Than Being: Or Beyond Essence*, Duquesne University Press, 1998.

———. *Quatre lectures talmudiques*, Minuit, 1968.

———. *Totality and Infinity: An Essay on Exteriority*, Duquesne University Press, 1969.

Marcouin, Francis. *À l'école de la littérature*, Éditions Ouvrières, 1992.

Meirieu, Philippe. *Des enfants et des hommes. Littérature et pédagogie. La promesse de grandir* (Vol. I), ESF, 1999.

Maisonneuve, Jacques. *Les Conduites rituelles*, coll. "Que sais-je?", Presses Universitaires de France, 1988.

Nahman de Breslav (Rabbi). *Liqouté Moharan*, Jérusalem, 1981 (in Hebrew).

Naouri, Aldo Angel Sylvie, Gutton Philippe, *Les Mères juives n'existent pas…mais alors qu'est-ce qui existe?*, Odile Jacob, 2005.

Naouri, Aldo. *L'Enfant bien portant*, Seuil, 1993.

———. *Mothers and Fathers*, Free Association Books, 2005.

———. *Une place pour le père*, coll. "Point Essais", Seuil, 1992.

Neher, André. *Exile of the Word: From the Silence of the Bible to the Silence of Auschwitz*, Jewish Publishing Society, 1980.

———. *L'Existence juive. Solitude et affrontements*, Seuil, 1962.

———. *Le Puits de l'exil. La Théorie dialectique du Maharal de Prague (1512–1609)*, Albin Michel, 1966.

Némirov, Nathan de. *Liqouté Halakhot*, (Complete Edition), Jérusalem, 1981 (in Hebrew).

Ouaknin, Jacques. *De génération en génération. Être juif*, Biblioeurope, 2005.

———. *La Bible de la table juive*, Safed, 2005.

Ricœur, Paul. *De l'interprétation. Essai sur Freud*, "Point Essais," Seuil, 1996.

———. *From Text to Action: Essays in Hermeneutics*, Northwestern University Press, 1991.

———. *Soi-même comme un autre*, Seuil, coll. "Point Essai," 1996.

Roth Philip, *Patrimony: A True Story*, Vintage, 1996.

———.*Operation Shylock*, Simon & Schuster, 1998.

———.*The Counterlife*, Vintage, 1996.

Rotnemer, Dory and Marc-Alain Ouaknin. *Tout l'humour Juif*, Assouline, 2001.

Rufo, Marcel. *Détache-moi! Se séparer pour grandir*, Anne Carrière, 2005.

Saint-Exupéry, Antoine de. *The Little Prince*, Harvest Books, 2000.

———. *The Wisdom of the Sands*, Bucaneer Books, 2005.

Scholem, Gershom. *Le Prix d'Israël. Écrits politiques*, Éditions de l'Éclat, 2003.

Sfar, Joann. *The Rabbi's Cat* (Vol. I), Pantheon Books, 2005.

Stassart, M. *Anthropologie de l'adolescence*, Cahiers du CEP, no. 7, pp. 13–37, 1996.

Steinsaltz, Evèn Israël and Adin (Rabbi). *Le Talmud*, (Complete Edition), Jérusalem, 2005 (in Hebrew).

Trigano Schmuel, *Le récit de la disparue*, Gallimard, 1977

Van Gennep, Arnold. *The Rites of Passage*, University of Chicago Press, 1961.

Vasse, Denis. *L'Ombilic et la voix. Deux enfants en analyse*, coll. "Points Essais", Seuil, 1999.

Wolf, Hélène. *Bar-Mitsva. Rite initiatique et formation de la personnalité judaïque*. In *Anthropologie de l'adolescence*, Cahiers du CEP, no. 7, 1996.

Zagdanski, Stéphane. *L'Impureté de Dieu. La Lettre et le péché dans la pensée juive*, Éditions du Félin, 1991.

Zakhartchouk, Jean-Michel. *L'Enseignant, un passeur culturel*, ESF, 1999.

Zegans, S. and Zegans L.S. *Bar Mitzvah: A Rite for a Transitional Age*, The Psychoanalytic Review, no. 66, 1979, pp. 115-132.

355

## Acknowledgments

This book is the fruit of several years of study, research, and pedagogical experiences undertaken in various places and settings. Aside from its anchoring in Jewish tradition, the writing of this book was essentially based on a crucial teaching experience: an encounter with high school students who, through a variety of projects, had had the opportunity to participate in intellectual and spiritual exchanges, including Master Classes with Philip Roth in Aix-en-Provence in 1999, the "Thinkers in the Projects" colloquiums held in 2001 and 2002 in Mantes-la-Ville, the "Generation of Peace" project, the "Brussels Imams-Rabbis for Peace" Congress in 2004, and the "Peace—An affair of state?" colloquium held in 2005 in Mantes-la-Ville. All of these projects were initiated, directed, and organized by Françoise-Anne Ménager, with the assistance of some of her colleagues at the Camille Claudel High School in Mantes-la-Ville. I was first invited to meet these students in 2001, an experience that led me to co-found the "Thinkers in the Projects" association with Françoise-Anne Ménager and Doctor Richard Rossin. The association's objective is to make the fundamental texts of our civilization accessible to the greatest number of people, and to thereby initiate people to a written culture of interpretation in an age of the spoken word, the image and immediacy.

We would like to thank all those students who accepted to explore new paths of thought and responsibility, and to acknowledge their patience and willpower. Aïcha, Candé, the two Émilies, Leïla, Loriette, Eulalie, Gaëlle, the three Nadias, Paula, Vanessa, Élodie, Estelle, Corinne, Aïssata, and Alexandra, for "the Philip Roth experience" in Aix-en-Provence.
Alexandra, Carina, Loriette, Élodie, Eulalie, the two Fatimas, Gaëlle, Hanane, Jean-Alain, Jennifer, Karima, Laetitia, Séverine, Myriam, Nadia, Paula, Piocé, Prescilillia, Sihem, and Véronique, for "Generation colloquium," Aïcha, Aïssata, Kardiatou, Rachida, Vanessa, Aurélie, Awa, Fatimata, Angélique, Djiga, the two Karimas, Steeve, Majda, Loubna, Rizlaine, Ramata, Jennifer, Hasdrubal, Yandé, Amandine, Cécile, Salamata, Johanna, Salima, Haby, Aziza, Coumba, Oulé, Dilia, and Zahra, for "Generation of Peace."

This is also the ideal place to gratefully acknowledge the Fondation Homme de Parole's efforts on behalf of peace and dialogue between the religions. My compliments to Alain Michel, its energetic, audacious president, to Cyril Dion, Jérôme Paillon, Hanane, and the entire team.

This would all have been far more difficult, or even impossible, without the constant support of the French *Rectorat* and the *Inspection académique* education authorities, and, particularly, of Françoise Girod, encouragement, and know-how of Françoise-Anne Ménager's colleagues at the Lycée Camille Claudel: Danièle Allanioux, Cyril Brocart, Sébastien Vincent and Christelle (theater workshop), Chantal Chourlay, Chantal Ebrahim, Amou Bouksara, Ghilaine Delachaise, Charlotte Bernard, Mary-Line Mora, France Gerbal, Vivianne Hersy, Vincent Simon, Jean-Yves Nicolas, Vincent Linotte, Anne Hamelin, Patricia Krimi. And let us not forget the terrifically efficient David Lalanne, the efficiency, patience and friendliness of Annie Migdalski, Viviane Blondel and André Charry, and the entire staff, all of whom are essential to the financial and human well-being of such an establishment.

I would also like to acknowledge Mr. Christian Montet, the principal of the Lycée Camille Claudel, who has provided unstinting enthusiastic support for these projects and educators, by offering them the best means of bringing these tremendously important educational and human experiences to fruition. He has warmly welcomed meetings, colloquiums, and conferences to his establishment, the impact of which have allowed me to hope for new ways of dialogue and comprehension. This is also a perfect place to express my gratitude to Mrs. Jaffre for the silent, yet efficient and generous help she provided by creating tailor-made timetables and juggling room numbers to ensure they were available in cases of unavoidable pedagogical necessity.

Speaking of hospitality, I must thank Mrs. Anette Peulvast, the deputy mayor of Mantes-la-Ville, who has shown a particular interest in these projects and allowed for students, teachers, participants, and large audiences to gather for seminars in Mantes-la-Ville's Jacques Brel Meeting Hall.

It follows that I should extend my warmest thanks to the participants in these colloquiums, all of whom responded with a passionate love of teaching that could only be equaled by the quality and depth of the words they shared with us, and the generous time commitment they made by traveling to the "Projects": Phillippe Meirieu, Alain Finkielkraut, Malek Chebel, Jean-Pierre Huster, Jean-Michel Zakartchouk, Alexandre Hougron, Fabienne Soldini, Christian Baudelot, Pierre-Yves Pétillon, Martine Laffon, Alain-Didier Weill, Sabine Melchior-Bonnet, Cheikh Ben Tounès, Rachid Benmokhtar, Mitchélé and Dominique Bertrand, Rachid Benzine, Abd al Malik, Ghaleb Ben Cheikh, Father Stan Rougier, and Luciano Rispoli.

Thank you to Yasmina Dahim, Marie-Hélène Bayle, and Valérie Amiraux for their generous participation, for sharing their love of study with the students, and for the joy of giving wings to the "Generation of Peace" project.

To Danielle Allanioux, Carina Magaelhes, Véronique Hoflack, Fatima Laaguid, and Céline Abisror, for their unwavering commitment, and their energy and efficiency. Their work was a precious contribution to the development of the "Thinkers in the Projects" association. And to Jean-Marie Touratié of the Paris education offices, who greeted the initial project with stimulating enthusiasm, and to the MAFPEN introductory course on the Jewish world organized by Monique Sander.

Thanks also to Serge Noyelles, Marie and Fred Allan, for the theater; Gérard David, for moderating; Philippe Pascal, the head of league 78, for the first colloquium; Laurent Barbut, for the Vabel printing works' printing; Pascal Bouchard of the AEF, for media coverage; Bernard Mangiante, for his La Pépinière de la paix (The Breeding-ground of Peace) film project; and Mr. Allanioux for his generous assistance.

Thank you to those friends distant and near, who enthusiastically shared in and supported this experience: Véronique Roffé, Fabienne and Christophe Villedary, Malika and Antoine Monmarché, Aubin Timsit, Nicole Hugon de Scœux, Nadine and Laurent Simon-Meslet, and Gille Pierron. Thank you all for your precious friendship over the course of these years of study. Thank you to those close friends who made the trip to support and participate in this experience: Geneviève Ménager, Marc and Gisèle Vanleynseele, Renée Cuinat, Nicolas Cuinat, Emmanuel Cuinat, and Cyril Cornet. To Sylvestre Raffo and Josette Delécaut, for their support under all circumstances.

To Hughes Delécaut, for the "shared growth."

To Irma Pascal and Anne-Marie Bourlioux, for passing on the tale of filiation without which the road to the bar mitzvah would have been closed and to Lysiane Raffo, for opening the doors.

To Raphaelle Aberjoux, for the secrets of the "mouna," and the memory of the gestures and tastes of "over there."

To Luca Raffo, my nephew, for the shared historical paths we may explore together. And to his father, Stéphane, for trusting me.

A grateful, friendly nod to Annie Terrier of the Écritures Croisées (Intersecting Writings) in Aix-en-Provence, who pulled off the exploit of inviting Philip Roth for Master Classes, and gave high school girls the opportunity to brilliantly and actively participate in these classes. To Mr. Tolédano of the Aix-en-Provence CREPS, who so generously welcomed these high school students to his institution during these Master Classes.

To Gilles Ménager, who was able to share and transmit his passion for literature, for his constant curiosity and his hunch that Philip Roth would be a determining author in my literary research and the decisive relation between man and the book. I am grateful for his patience and his devotion, without which none of this would have been possible.

To Laurianne for listening and sharing her thoughts, for her passion for pedagogical innovation, for the gift of the dancing star and the young woman she's becoming.

To Léo, for inventive and attentive Hebrew practice, for his love of great literature, his chiddushim, and his invigorating humor.
I would also like to thank both Laurianne and Léo for their patience. And
for the joy in every moment, the joy of life, and the transmission of the values
of "growing."

I would like to express my profound thanks to Philip Roth, along with my
enthusiastic admiration for his work, by repeating the very words the students
thanked him with in Aix-en-Provence: "Thank you. You have opened the
doors to literature to us." The novelist's moving response to the students
made them doubly determined to be worthy of his praise by persevering in
the study and interpretation of the texts and maintaining an interest in the
Hebraic thought Roth introduced them to.

Françoise-Anne Ménager would like to join me in thanking my students at
Bar-Ilan University, as well as the students of the Tel Aviv Midreshet Iyun,
whose director, Rabbi Roberto Arbiv has always provided such a warm welcome.
I would also like to pay a special tribute to Doctor Yaffa Wolfman, head of
the department of comparative literature, and Aliza Aldema, the department's
administrator, for the understanding and flexibility with which they responded
to my pedagogical choices and occasionally surrealist schedule.

It was a great pleasure for me to be an invited guest of a series of conferences
at the Siah Yeshiva (Givat hadagan, Efrat), headed by Rav Shagar (Shimon
Gershon Rosenberg) and Rav Yaïr Dreyfus. Thank you to my assistant
Dror Bar-Yossef, who, week after week, made our lessons more transcendent
and enjoyable, by taking charge of the *merkava* and coffee. He was supported
in doing so by Moriyah and Ouri Moché. I must also include Rolly in any
mention of their activities.

I would like to thank all those who provided me with a place to study and
form friendships: Michèle and Claude Kaminsky of the Spinoza course
(Centre Aleph seminars), Joël and Orly Abisror (Mary Kaplan study circle),
Hélène Attali (Youth Aliyah, Rabbi Williams Synagogue, rue Copernic), Marc

Weisser of the Jewish Cultural Center (Brussels), and Claude Darmon, director of the Ganénou School (Brussels). May they all find the expression of my gratitude and friendship in the pages of this book.

And may Tali (Mylène) Ehrlich (of Brussels) recognize this as a sign of my friendship and warmest thanks for her flawless hospitality, worthy of Avraham Avinou himself! And don't let me forget Dalia Wexler and Jean-Jacques Bailly.

Chabbatic studies in Jerusalem were crucially important to me, first for friendship, and secondly for the opportunity to spend some time studying the thought of Rabbi Nahman of Breslav. I would particularly like to acknowledge and thank Lior-Esther, Marlène, Marielle, Alexandra, and Ilanit.

An "Oulipian" thank you to my friend and confidant Richard Rossin, who is always available for the most unpredictable poetic and "tam-ludic" adventures, from golf to the "logotization of love."

I cannot mention Richard without including Danielle, François, David, Sandra, Anna, and Rémy.

Which leads me straight to the most dangerous Green, "Gentlemen Out Ladies Fabulous." A friendly hello to Isabelle and Jean-Hughes, and, of course, an equally friendly hello to Lazare, Roger, Marie, Olivia, Ghislaine, Sylvie, Coco, Paul, Pierre, and Antoine for Tuesday flights.

To Hélène Attali, again, for the restaurant and the cigars, as well!

My acknowledgments to Denis Assouline for his assiduous (Hasidic) comments and to Pierrette Assouline for her friendship, her passion for studying, and for impromptu Sabbaths and Bergsonian dinners.

I would like to tell Chaoul S. Moncler what a pleasure it has been to rediscover his friendship, and to thank him for his complicity over the centuries, and for his hospitality and generosity. As the Talmud says: "Whoever hasn't experienced a Pesach in Otlingue... *Lo ra'ah Pesach miyamav!*"

361

To Mitchélé (already mentioned above) and Jean-Noël for their art of hosting and their generosity, for the song and dance of colors. For their unconditional support for B. ice cream, which can be enjoyed on the terrace of a café along the riverbanks or beneath the billowing sails of the Frigate.

To Chams, Paul, Carine, Favio, Joëlle, and Paollo, for their understanding of the lilting accents of distant lands, and, of course, for the poppies on the challah bread. To Ion, Nicole, Radu, Dan, and Lelia. To Laura and David, for their creativity especially when "I would prefer not to!" and for the barbecue by the pool. Let us not forget Aurélia, Anne de Broca and Alain (for Juliette and Victor), Fabienne and Stéphane (for Jonah and the reference to Faust), Claudine (for a shared passion for dreams), Jean Daviot (for light play and Uncle Elias's legacy), Nathalie Seroussi (for the dream of Picasso and the birds of serenity).

To Mikaël, Armand, Rachel, Jérôme, Steeve, Patrick, Jean-Claude, Suzanne, Mariette, André, and all the others I haven't forgotten, for their friendship, their faithful presence, and their questions, which open the door to the future.

To Franck Lalou, for his unflagging attentive friendship and shared creativity.

To Danièle and Marc, for a shared interest in country houses and Freud's private life. The most important thing is that the ocean is blue and the seagulls are wild. …It's a question of hearing! Thank you to the Taï-Chi Master, for the Ganédénisation!

To Aldo Naouri, and Jeanne, for keeping a vigilant critical eye on my Lacanian flights of fancy, and for their invigorating chiddushim. To Georges Pragier, whose excessively silent presence provides an important depth to the words of study (though he doesn't know it). To Gérard Garouste, about whom I will say more below. To Alain Didier-Weill and Dominique Bertrand for the "bearded and bald" dialogue. To Sylvain for the "quantum canticle."
As always, I must extend specific, warm thanks to Itshaq Schein, "Grand Master of the chiddush," who has taken study to the most demanding, highest levels

year in and year out, with his constantly renewed attention to the sounds of Hebrew. Itshaq's work produces sparks of meaning which drive thought to its utmost potential, despite the fact that he can get a little annoyed with Lacan from time to time. I would like to thank him for his trust and his friendship. I will continue by acknowledging my "video-ctors" and "audio-passio" friends: Daniel Lellouche, Serge Saada, Julien Mineur, Gilles Boustani, and Ariel Wizman, and all those who accepted to be the first audience for this experience. Martine Chemana, Laurianne Robert, Vanessa Löwy, Laurence Aïach, Eva Junes, Rachida Arab, Béatrice Aaronson, Cynthia Fleury, thank you all for your talent. Thank you, also, for the File Zilla course.

The bar mitzvah is also a cat's desire!
A very friendly hello to Joann Sfar, whose humor, and profoundly inspired imagination cast a fresh "tam-ludic" (he, too) light on this celebration. He provides an entry into the world of "growing" that retains the freshness of childhood without any angelism. Thank you, also, for the "klezmerization of happines," but that's another story...

363

Thank you to Gérard Garouste. His work approaches thought with a solemn humor and a depth whose frequently subterranean paths always spring up as an invigorating Source. I am very honored to have maintained a dialogue with him since the Haggadah and would like to thank him for the opening and closing illustrations for each of the fifteen chapters in this book, each of which is worthy of infinite Talmudic and Kabbalistic commentary. May he recognize the expression of my profound admiration and friendship in these words. I must also include Elisabeth, for her generosity.

Thank you to Radu Mihaïlanu, who, in his own way, is very present in the pages of this book. May his film go, live, and become, and may he recognize herein the sign of a creative friendship and dialogue which will continue to participate in bringing various peoples closer together.

After painting and film, we find the world of photography. To mention photography, however, one must start by stating that this volume is the fruit of a close collaboration, both on a personal and professional level, with the highly talented Laziz Hamani, one of the greatest photographers of our generation. His intuitive sense of composition, of color, of tonalities, of the play of light, and of the art of shadows he holds the key to, contribute to making this book more than a simple pedagogical introduction to the symbols of the bar mitzvah, but an actual guided tour to the frequently misunderstood world of this ceremony. I must express my deepest gratitude, admiration and friendship to him.

Some of Laziz's photos were taken at the synagogue on rue Copernic, while others were taken "live" during a bar mitzvah which took place at the synagogue on rue de la Roquette. My warmest thanks go to the Tolédano family—Marcel, Golda, and young Yohan—for being so hospitable and allowing us to photograph their wonderful celebration. I would also like to acknowledge Rabbi Safran and Rabbi Soudry as a friendly reminder of the time we spent in their synagogue.

I must also acknowledge Saber and Fabien of the Arôm floral arrangement shop on avenue Ledru-Rollin (Paris 12e) who, aside from giving me the opportunity to please my friends by giving them beautiful flowers for the Sabbath—I have a weakness for the "Espérance" rose, though "Blue-jean" isn't too bad either—allowed me to discover that the ceremonial cutting of hair, which I discuss at length at the beginning of the book, is alive and well, for they have delivered flowers on such occasions. Thank you for your aromatic words.

A friendly hello to Aurélien Alizadeh of the Parsifal bookstore, an authentic book lover, whose constant hospitality makes reading books tinted with the Diwan and the sounds of Bach particularly pleasant.

Naturally, I would like to take this opportunity to acknowledge those shopkeepers in the Pletzel neighborhood (in the Marais) who contributed to the writing of this book, and particularly to Laziz's photos: the Bibliophane bookstore, the Diasporama gallery, the Marciano bakery, and the Benchétrit grocery shop.

A book is a lot like a movie. The shoot is just the first stage of a very long working process involving reading, editing, photo selection, layout, iconographic research, copyrights, rereading, correcting, cutting, and various mutations and transformations. I would like to acknowledge all those who exercised their tact and creativity to bridge the often difficult, complex gap between the camera and the illustrated page, and the text file and the printed page: Christine Claudon, Céline Devillers, Charles Fritscher, Valérie Tougard, Stéphanie Guarneri, Cécile Bouvet, Aurélie Négret, and Nestor Bautista deserve my sincerest thanks for all the attention they devoted to this book, and for sharing my passion for books in general.

I would like to congratulate Sarah Chiche for her exceptional work. She stuck with the composition of this book with dedication and efficiency from the first line to the last, ensuring that the timing, the text and images, and the book's format were in keeping with the goals we had set for this volume. Sarah also gives me the opportunity to repeat a saying from the Zohar: "God loves the tears of women..."
Let me also send my best to Mathieu for his friendliness and smiling faces.

A friendly thank you to Esther Kremer, whose devoted work and passion for the Hebrew language and for Jewish thought and tradition gave wings to the words and ideas of the bar mitzvah and allowed them to cross the Atlantic.

None of this would have been possible without those who oversaw this volume's creation. Let me take this opportunity to reiterate my deepest and warmest feelings of friendship for Martine and Prosper Assouline— as well as for their son Alexandre—who honored me with their trust. Their know-how, their uncanny patience and exquisite taste have provided this book with its unique tone and power.
May these few lines also bear witness to our common passion for books and to our shared ethic of transmission and welcome.

And let us not forget the Mysteries of the Manchego...

*Acharone, acharone chaviv,* to a greater extent than with my previous books, this volume owes a great deal to the teachings and advice of my father, Grand Rabbi Jacques Ouaknin, an eminent specialist in the teaching of and initiation to the bar mitzvah, among other subjects. As far back as I can remember, I can see him recording the parashah for his students. I even occasionally had students recite the parashah when I was a mere boy of 8 or 10. His talent as a *Baal Koreh* allowed me to travel and develop an equal appreciation for Sephardic and Ashkenazi reading, and even Sfard-Polish. (As I write these words, I cannot help but be moved at the thought of Mr. Nussbaum of Lille who, more than thirty-five years ago, initiated me to the *Pirkei Avot* as a present for my own bar mitzvah). To my mother Éliane-Sophie Ouaknin, whose presence was felt through attentive, joyous, dynamic, and uninterrupted encouragement, and the passion for study and teaching she has consistently demonstrated by remaining faithful to her Friday classes which allow women of various ages to be bat mitzvahed. May they both recognize herein the pleasure and joy I have always experienced by acknowledging them with affection, gratitude and admiration.

## Photographic Credits

All the photos in this book were taken by Laziz Hamani except p. 21: © Antoine Lefébure; p. 29: © Miró Estate/Adagp; p. 43: © All rights reserved; p. 47: © David Rubinger/Corbi; p. 49: © Gallimard; p. 59: © Lloyd Yearwood; p. 77: © Erich Lessing/Art Resource, NY; p. 82: © photo CNAC/MNAM Dist. RMN © Philippe Migeat; p. 89: © BPK, Berlin, Dist RMN © Jorg P. Anders; p. 97: © Alain Mahuzier; p. 100: © Musée d'Art et d'Histoire du Judaisme, Paris; p. 101: © Musée d'Art et d'Histoire du Judaisme, Paris; p. 103: © Caroline Rose; p. 109: © Collection Christophe L.; p. 159: © Dargaud; p. 165: © RMN/Gérard Blot; p. 205: © Walch, Paris; p. 207: © Museum of the Grand Rabbinate, Jerusalem; p. 209: © All rights reserved; p. 213: © London, British Library; p. 217: © RMN; p. 226: © Coll. Victor Klagshald, Photo Walch, Paris; p. 242: © All rights reserved; p. 248: © Rose Eichenbaum/Corbis; p. 265: © Photo CNAC/MNAM Dist. RMN © Philippe Migeat; p. 293: © All rights reserved; p. 297: © akg-images; p. 302: © All rights reserved; p. 311: © RMN © Gérard Blot; p. 320: © Mark Peterson/Corbis; p. 336: © Ted Spiegel/Corbis; p. 342: © Israel government press office; p. 345: © All rights reserved.

## Text Credits

Pp. 8: Rudyard Kipling, If…, © AP Watt Ltd for the National Trust for Places of Historic Interest or Natural Beauty; pp. 11, 203, 323, 324, 326: Gilles Bernheim, *Le Souci des autres*, © Calmann-Lévy, 2002; pp. 19–20: Pierre Clastres, *Chronicle of the Guayaki Indians*, © Zone Books, 1998; pp. 24, 25, 45, Marcel Rufo, *Détache moi. Se séparer pour grandir*, © Anne Carrière, 2005.; pp. 33–35: Philip Roth, *Operation Shylock*, © Simon & Schuster, 1993; pp. 88, 170, 298: Emmanuel Lévinas, *Difficult Freedom*, © Albin Michel, 2000; pp.131, 136, 137: Jacques Derrida and Hélène Cixous, *Veils*, Geoffrey Bennington © Stanford University Press, 2001; pp. 162–164: Armand Abécassis, Les Temps du partage, © Albin Michel, 1993; pp. 159 Joann Sfar, *The Rabbi's Cat*, Pantheon Books, 2005; pp. 221: Georges Bataille, *Theory of Religion*, © Zone Books, 1992; pp. 268, 269: Anatoli and Avital Sharansky, Un aussi long voyage, © Lieu commun, 1986;

Unattributed images and texts are drawn from unidentified sources. Every effort has been made to identify the copyright holders; errors and omissions brought to the publisher's attention will be corrected in future editions.